Working in Mysterious Ways

WORKING IN MYSTERIOUS WAYS
My Life Through the Rosary

Resource Publications
An Imprint of Wipf and Stock Publishers
199 W. 8th Ave., Suite 3
Eugene, OR 97401

www.wipfandstock.com

PAPERBACK ISBN: 978-1-6667-1092-2
HARDCOVER ISBN: 978-1-6667-1093-9
EBOOK ISBN: 978-1-6667-1094-6

JUNE 14, 2021

Working in Mysterious Wa

My Life Through the Rosary

Kathleen A. Heininge

RESOURCE *Publications* · Eugene, Oregon

For Ken

CONTENTS

ACKNOWLEDGMENTS

VIRGINIA WOOLF ONCE SAID, "Each has his past shut in him like the leaves of a book known to him by heart; and his friends could only read the title." My friends have read far more than the title, and I am grateful for their help in opening the book of my life to a wider audience.

Helping with the inception of this project were the members of my writing group, Abigail Favale Rine and Cor Beals, who encouraged me to continue. Melanie Springer Mock, my writing guru, has been an inspiration to me in countless ways: colleague, author extraordinaire, and partner in writing and in snark, she never fails to give sage guidance. The colleagues with whom I spent so many years teaching and celebrating writing will always be a light in my life, especially Gary Tandy and William Jolliff.

Fr. Mike Walker has reviewed many of the chapters to make sure I have not fallen into heresy. Any slips I have made are not his fault, but at least I can go to him for confession.

Constantly adjusting and correcting my accounts of events were most of the people listed in this book, but Michelle Tressler in particular has a memory at least as formidable as mine, and we have laughed all over again at many of the stories told here.

My family may or may not thank me for the tales shared, but I am eternally grateful for who they are and who they have made me to be. They know enough stories to make up the next volume.

Finally, Ken, my partner in all things inspirational and aspirational, has provided unceasing support. Whether he is bringing me tea, listening to the chapters, or blurrily responding to the ideas that come while I lie awake in the middle of the night, he has never complained when dinner is late (or when he is left to prepare it on his own) after I lost track of time. He is more forgiving than the dog.

INTRODUCTION

THE STUDENT COMING TO meet with me was unusually tall, unusually strong, and unusually angry. The only appointment time he could manage was 7:00 p.m., long after everyone else in the building had gone home, leaving me alone in my office on the third floor. It occurred to me such a meeting was potentially unwise, but I could hear his steps clomping up the stairs as I pondered, too late, how to meet him somewhere more public. He loomed at my door, thrusting his graded paper at me, and announced, "This is bullshit." Rocking back and forth from one foot to the other, he spluttered, unable to think of anything else to say. I asked him to come in and sit down so we could talk; he declined. I asked if he had read my comments on the paper; he said he had only read the grade, and repeated his assessment of it. I asked if we could go through the comments together so he could better understand why he had earned the grade on the paper, and thus I unleashed the torrents of his anger.

No, he did not have time to go over the comments. No, he did not have time to revise the paper. No, he did not have time to spend on this class. No, he did not have time to be a student. No, he did not have time to even breathe. He was engaged to be married, but could not afford a wedding. He had gotten his girlfriend pregnant, and they had moved in with her parents way out in the country after the baby was born, only it was more like the parents had moved in with him, since they were both deadbeats and drug addicts, and now he was supporting his girlfriend, her parents, and their baby, in a home with no electricity, no hot water, and a long commute for him. He was working full-time and trying to finish school so he could get a better job. He ended his plaint by declaring he didn't even know why he was continuing at this Christian school; he was certain he would be thrown out if the administration knew he had gotten his girlfriend pregnant, and he wasn't even sure he believed in God anymore, since the only prayer he could even think of these days was, "Fuck you, God."

Pausing here, panting, he gazed at me defiantly, clearly expecting me to be shocked enough to throw him out. "It sounds to me," I said, "that you just became a real Christian."

He collapsed into the chair, at last. I explained my thinking. "You are angry at God. God can take it. The key here is that you are still speaking to God, and if you had no belief at all, you wouldn't bother. But more to the point," I asked, "do you think God is unaware of your thoughts? Of your heart? Of your frustration? How honest would you be in your faith if you were to repeat words you don't mean, that are unconnected to your soul? A real Christian trusts God with the truth, even when that truth is ugly."

I was teaching English literature at a relatively small liberal arts college, founded by Quakers but largely taken over by evangelicals. I am Catholic. The fit sometimes required shims and shavings, wrenches and hammering, but little actual dismantling of structures. One of the best parts about being in a Christian institution is the ability to incorporate my faith and beliefs into my teaching, parts of myself that were unwelcome in other, secular classrooms. As I discovered when teaching at state colleges, it is difficult to teach James Joyce without discussing his tortured relationship to his faith and to God. Christina Rossetti makes no sense without an understanding of her commitment to God. Even if religion is reduced to its cultural capital, a shared body of knowledge from which to draw, it is impossible to teach T. S. Eliot's "The Journey of the Magi" alongside "The Magi" by W. B. Yeats without explaining who the magi were. And yet when I tried it at a state college, I was accused of trying to evangelize by even mentioning Christianity. So teaching at a Christian school was, to some extent, a relief.

But I was in a place where I heard over and over again "Christians and Catholics," as if they are two separate entities. I was interviewed once by a young woman whose assignment for a course in comparative religions asked her to speak to someone from "another faith tradition" than her own; she picked me, which already amused me, but I was game. Her first question was, "Do you know anything about the way your faith tradition developed?" I said I did. She asked me if I could briefly summarize it, and I said, "No, not briefly," and laughed. She looked puzzled, so I said, "Well, to be really brief, we started it and y'all left." She took a moment to understand, and then clarified, "So you really ARE Christian?" Sigh.

Over the years, I "explained" about Catholicism many times, sometimes in the classroom and sometimes in my office and sometimes over lunch. While I was often asked about our "idolatry," our desire to bypass God and Jesus in favor of Mary, our problems with child-molesting priests, our sexism, and so on, the conversations were generally respectful and illuminating. At the very least, I strove to demonstrate that labels and assumptions are not helpful, so when I was asked (oh so frequently), "How can you be a Catholic and a feminist?" or "How can you be a Catholic and a Democrat?" or "How can you stay at this school as a Catholic?" I had many answers, honed over the years. These conversations forced me to stay dynamic in my faith, which can only be a good thing, even in the face of challenges.

At this same institution, I headed the Women's Studies program, which gave me the opportunity to connect with many young women, quite a few of whom were struggling in their own faith. They sought to reconcile their growing sense of the unfairness of patriarchal structures, especially those within their churches, with their faith; a complaint I heard echoed dozens if not hundreds of times is that these women could not find themselves in the Bible, or in the church. Why would I stay, they often asked about both me and themselves, when I was clearly omitted?

Of course it was not only the women who felt themselves left out of the narrative, especially when that narrative seemed to be reduced to a moral code full of "Thou Shalt Not"s rather than a deep consideration of our relationship to God. The young man who came to my office full of ire believed any transgression left him permanently out of God's favor, and so he was being punished. When he talked about his son, however, his face softened, and there was a slight loosening of his tension, though he remained frustrated that God allowed the pregnancy when they tried so hard to prevent it. I asked him if he believed God regretted and despised this child, and he recoiled to think of it. It was then I suggested he turn to the Rosary. As I explained it to him and to so many other apprehensive students, the Rosary takes us through the story of Jesus and the church primarily through Mary's eyes and her experience of her son. It is impossible to remain mired in our own troubles, convinced no one else has ever endured what we endure, when we contemplate Mary's life. An angel? A mysterious pregnancy? A manger? Why would anyone believe such a

ludicrous story? And then to lose her son to a rigged "trial" and a crucifixion? To consider her position is to give perspective to our own.

For those unfamiliar with the Rosary, there are fifty beads on a
looped chain, divided into groups of ten, and then another chain with
more beads and a cross that dangle from that loop. Each bead represents
another prayer, and helps to keep track of where you are in the prayer
cycle. For each group of ten beads, you say a prayer, the Hail Mary, ten
times, and that is called a decade. Each decade is associated with a different episode in the life of Jesus, Mary, and the church, and there are five
decades in the circle of beads. There are four sets of mysteries to each
five decades: The Joyful Mysteries, The Sorrowful Mysteries, The Glori-
ous Mysteries, and the Luminous Mysteries. In other words, if one were
to pray all the mysteries, one would pray the Hail Mary 200 times. The
other beads are other prayers, but the general idea is that as one prays,
one contemplates the story in a different way in order to gain a "fruit," a
blessing or a learning, from that story. It is impossible, then, to pray the
Rosary and not to find oneself, especially as a woman, fully engaged in
and connected to the life of Jesus. Because I learned this process very
early, when I was seven, I have never had that experience of feeling lost or
disconnected from God; I have always felt I was as necessary to the story
of church as Mary was necessary to the story of Jesus. Teaching others to
find themselves as integral to the story as well has been a powerful part
of my career.

The prayer itself is not nearly as heretical as many evangelicals
have been taught to believe. "Hail Mary, full of grace, the Lord is with
thee. Blessed art thou among women, and blessed is the fruit of thy womb,
Jesus. Holy Mary, Mother of God, pray for us sinners now and at the hour
of our death. Amen." It is a call to Mary, who is as close to the Lord as is
possible for a human being to be, who is blessed among women, whose
womb has been blessed. We ask her to pray for us. Many students who
thought it was some kind of neo-Pagan invocation are startled to find it
so innocuous; the words are taken directly from the Bible, quoting the
Angel Gabriel and Elizabeth.

That being said, I was not trying to convert a bunch of evangelicals to Catholicism (though that did happen quite a few times). I always
told students that my big conversion push only came once a year, when
I taught Bram Stoker's *Dracula*: the Eucharistic host helps the heroes to
conquer the vampire, but it only really works if there is true belief that the

host is more than a symbol, that it actually IS the body of Christ. Without such belief, the vampire would win. Consequently, I pointed out, students would be better off if they went ahead and converted now, before the vampire apocalypse, at which point it would certainly be too late.

Lest this makes me sound as if I have it all together and have genuinely led my life since I was seven years old by the strictures and fruits of the Rosary, quite the opposite is true. The Rosary has been, for me, more like a lighthouse: Caroline Stephen, a Quaker mystic, said that faith was not like a bright light guiding one on a clear path to God, but was more like a lighthouse, intermittently flashing upon us to show us where we had missed the path. For me, the Rosary has worked this way: it reminds me of the way the story functions in my life, and the fruits from each mystery will have a different impact on me at different times of my life. The stories themselves will always bring to mind events from my past, or concerns of the present, and I will see my own successes and failures (sometimes simultaneously) in those connections.

Having taught over the last thirty or so years, I have had occasion to tell many of those stories, stories about cancer and death, about family and travel, about infidelity and miracles, about children and jobs; I have been asked many times when I was going to write them down. Here, then, I have connected some of those stories to the mysteries of the Rosary, because I cannot disconnect them in my own head from the years of praying about them, over them, and through them.

1

THE FIRST JOYFUL MYSTERY: THE ANNUNCIATION

The Angel Gabriel tells Mary she will have a child.

Rape

I ONCE HAD A sweatshirt that read, "is there a hyphen in anal retentive?" which made me laugh and laugh and laugh. Maybe a bit hysterically. As an English professor with control issues, I thought this was the height of hilarity; as if the hyphen anxiety were not enough, the refusal to capitalize the beginning of the sentence tickled my obsession for correctness even more. Our son, Aaron, asked me what "anal retentive" meant, and I explained with examples: Someone who has every book in the house organized first by genre, then by size, then by author's last name, might be considered anal retentive. When all the CDs in the house are organized first by genre and then by artists' names, that might be anal retentive. When the closets and drawers are organized by color, when the cupboards are organized by food types, when the spices are organized first by sweet and savory and then alphabetically, and when one responds irrationally to those who might put things away in the wrong place . . . well, you get the point. He asked, puzzled, "But how else are you supposed to find stuff?" and I laughed, noting he only agreed with me because he is also somewhat anal retentive.

While I come by my control issues honestly, they are at odds with the First Joyful Mystery of the Rosary, the Annunciation. When the Angel Gabriel comes to Mary to announce she is going to bear a child, despite her virginity, she initially responds "with wonder." "Wonder" seems like a no-brainer there, perhaps even a bit of understatement. But the Angel assures her all will be well, that God has a plan, and she responds, "Behold the handmaid of the Lord. Be it done to me according to your word."

This is the first of the Mysteries of the Rosary, and begins the story of Jesus as told through Mary's perspective. It is among my favorites, not because the story is sweet and tells us Mary is having a baby, and not because it begins the gooey Nativity story. I am not attracted to the story because it speaks to my womanly desire to give birth, or even to a sense of security because God has everything in hand, with a clear plan, if we will only trust in that plan. Every time I reflect on this story, which is often, I am amazed by Mary's willingness. Her words are, to me, among the most amazing words in the Bible, and reflect an unfathomable ability to relinquish control.

We are told the mystery is meant to confirm in us a sense of humility; for me, it elicits a sense of inadequacy. I ponder how a person can come to be so willing. I often dwell on the next nine months for Mary: When everyone is castigating her for what seems an obvious lie, while she endures the whispers and the doubt, while she is riding a donkey to Bethlehem despite presumably swollen ankles and a bladder being stomped on by the Son of God, I would like to think Gabriel popped in a time or two just to say, "Hey, you're doing great! This is how it's supposed to be, I promise! God is watching and, although the birth won't be all that comfy, you're good to go!" I need to imagine such interactions because I am pretty sure I would need some assurance, some confirmation that my suffering is really the plan. I am pretty sure I could imagine a better way to go than having a young unmarried woman carrying the Son of God. And I am pretty sure I would be entirely incapable of Mary's response. Thus my feelings of inadequacy.

While I realize part of praying the Rosary is to feel ourselves as part of Jesus' story, and to connect with both the humanity and divinity behind these Biblical people, part of the mystery relates to my own humanity, to my personal lack of sainthood. I begin to feel guilty for being so incapable of Mary's response, but then I feel ridiculous for feeling guilty, since my own humanity is part of the mystery. While I realize that although the story is hardly about me (how self-centered can I get?), it is also ALL about me, and praying it reflects the way I interact with God. The difference is that Mary apparently has little compunction about agreeing. She "wonders," and speaks up so far as to say she is a virgin, but then immediately capitulates.

I, however, have control issues, and must learn to capitulate over and over again.

And then again.

My control issues are the scars of experience. Scars are not all bad, however; they remind us of where we have been, and they serve to protect the deep damage done to us. I have tried many times, and in many ways, to reopen one of those scars in hopes it will heal in a less ugly way, and here is yet another attempt.

I grew up in a fairly idyllic small town in California. Summers were perfect. Nearly all the mothers were at home, and nearly all the children and dogs were outside from the moment breakfast was finished to the moment we were called for dinner, and then we were back outside again until dark. We played Mother-May-I and Simon Says and Red Light, Green Light. We told scary stories while lying on the haystack. We rode our bikes ferociously to the top of the hill and then freely to the bottom, with the playing card clipped to the spokes with a clothespin so we sounded like we had ten-speeds. We played in each others' yards. We almost never went into each others' houses, because there was nothing to do inside. We played baseball and football and frisbee, tag and hide-and-seek. We taught each other how to avoid using the rose bushes or the apple trees to stop our bicycles, and how to suck the juice out of the honeysuckles. We dug a hole (who knows why?) that was about four feet deep and ten feet wide, which became a swimming hole or dirt fort, depending on the weather. We used half of a rain barrel to set up a teeter totter, or turned it upside down and filled it with water to sail boats in, and we used the cardboard box from the new freezer as a fort. It was great.

There were many children in the neighborhood, including three who lived across the street from us. Their mother was one of the two single mothers in the neighborhood, and she had to work, leaving the children unattended for most of the day, but the eldest was Steve who, at seventeen, was surely able to watch thirteen-year-old Grace and eleven-year-old Clay. Being five, I was somewhat discouraged from playing with them, since they were so much older than most of the rest of us. Besides, everyone knew they were inadequately supervised, and therefore undesirable as playmates.

I don't remember what took me down their driveway one afternoon, whether we were all playing, or whether I was lured. I do remember that when Grace and Clay grabbed me, one clutching either arm, I knew I should not have gone down that driveway. It was longer than most everyone else's, the only two-story house on our block set back from the road, and there was a small shed to the right of the front door. The door to the shed itself faced the front door of the house, so it was not visible from the street, and it was to this shed that they fairly dragged me, telling me they had something important to show me. Inside, their big brother Steve was sitting. I remember it was dark, and I remember starting to cry. Then all was a blur: Grace holding me with my arms pinned behind me, Clay holding a large rock over my head, and Steve telling me I would be fine; he was just going to go pee-pee inside of me.

For many years, the rest of the afternoon was a blank, and I was grateful to have it so. The next clear memory is that same night, crying in my bed, plucking at the chenille on the pink bedspread, hurting and afraid. My mother, bending over me, begged me to tell her what was wrong. I resisted telling her, remembering their threat to "bash everyone's heads in with rocks" if I told. I felt a tremendous weight of responsibility for the lives of my family members. And so when I told them what had happened, I felt overwhelming guilt in having jeopardized them all.

There was more blurry stuff: my father's fury, the police, the ice cold clinical examination at the hospital, and then nothing. I have been told the evidence was inconclusive. My mother says I was terribly upset, but when we went to the district attorney's office, I seemed fine, telling them we were "just playing around," though I don't remember this; I do know the abiding and overwhelming memory was my betrayal of my family. I jeopardized them by speaking up. I may have thought I was protecting them with my refusal to admit what had happened. Steve and his family moved soon after, but in our family, the subject was over. Years later, I brought it up with my mother, and she said she was sorry they made such a big deal out of it; she thought they had overreacted.

I was certain the event had no effect on me, and was a little bit proud to have had something so dramatic occur without any telltale signs. I have, however, had nightmares for most of my life, blazingly real dreams where I am chased and beaten and stabbed and shot and raped and made to walk over broken glass to save my parents from murderers, and although I was pretty sure there was a connection, I didn't think it was necessary to dredge up the rest of the memory; how could it help?

But as I grow older, I realize there are other consequences. Whether consciously or not, I determined never again to let someone have that kind of control over me. I find it difficult to relinquish things: food, books, possessions, plans, being in charge, doing things the "right" way. I aspire to be easy-going, and sometimes I give that illusion, but I feel great anxiety when my husband drives me to work and takes a route different from the one I take. I am unreasonably frustrated when a meeting is scheduled unexpectedly in my day. I am, again, aggravated when things are not put back properly, and can determine at a glance when something is missing or is where it ought not to be. Asserting control in my world matters to me, and when I am able to (with effort) let something go, and truly be at ease in doing so, I feel a great sense of achievement.

One element in my life I have never been able to control is my weight. I have struggled with it for most of my life; I recall the first time someone laughed at my "bubble butt," and the words burrowed deep down in my brain to formulate my self-image forever. I recognize the connection to control and eating, and I know food controls me in a way I have never let anything else control me. I also know it provides a kind of insulation from being hurt; even though my brain knows molesting a child is not an act of sexual desire as much as it is an act of power, I still, somewhere deep down, fear being desirable. It is too dangerous.

Some time ago I decided to try fasting. I had a variety of reasons to try it, some spiritual, some physical, but I wanted to see how long I could go without food. On the second night, after more than forty hours without food, I was lying in bed, nearly asleep, when suddenly, for no apparent reason, the entire memory of Steve and the shed came flooding back to me. I had not been thinking about it, and it is not something I tend to dwell on, but all at once I was five years old again. I could smell, hot on a summer's day, the must and dust that comes in a seldom-used shed. I could see where we all stood, with me facing the door. Steve sat inside the door, on a carton or bucket of some kind, and I had a hard time seeing him because of the light behind him. Grace kept pushing me, and Clay stood with the large gray rock, just off to the right of me. Steve had his pants down, and his penis was exposed, swollen and shiny, purple and terrifying. He was wagging it around to show me how unthreatening it was, but I knew better. As he began to shove it into me, I heard the voice of his mother, having returned home from work. She was calling to Clay, and they all froze, Grace's hand already over my mouth to keep me from calling out. Steve laughed and quickly pulled his pants back up, and they all hissed at me that if I ever told another soul they would smash the heads of my family in front of me and then they would kill me. They let me go.

The memory, submerged for nearly forty-five years, shocked me. It was so vivid and fresh. I lay in bed, shuddering and crying, but unwilling to awaken my husband. I wanted to remember on my own first, and I was afraid to lose the vision again after all that time. Surprisingly, along with the memory came compassion for Grace and Clay. I wondered what happened to them to make them participate in such behavior, and what became of them afterwards. I wondered how such dysfunction occurs in a family, and what kind of love had to be missing for anyone to lash out at a five-year-old. I found myself even thinking of their mother, a single woman trying to create a better life for her children in a nice small town, someone who had named her children for God, to be grace-filled and to be molded into something better. I prayed for them all, for the first time in my life.

As much as I would love this to be the magic moment to change my life, such is not my story. I have not suddenly been able to control my weight. I have not been able to let go of the control I need to have in my life. Instead, I have come to understand the Mystery of the Annunciation in a different way. God asks sacrifices of us that may seem unreasonable, impossible, heartless, cruel. We are asked to endure circumstances that appear inconsistent with a benevolent God's will, and not only to endure but to embrace those things.

The rape of a five-year-old girl is certainly not part of God's plan, for my life or for the life of those children who conspired against me.

That which Mary embraces is not God's will, but God's word, and the word is that "The Lord is with thee." The Lord was with me in that shed, not to prevent the moment or to protect me but to stand with me. Humanity, in its glory and its ugliness, will assert itself, will inflict itself, upon us all. Holiness comes when we accept humanity in ourselves and in others, and believe that regardless, the Lord is with us. While it still hurts me to say this, because of the injury done to me, the Lord was with Steve and Clay and Grace as well, if they could only have seen it; my prayer is that at some point in the intervening years, they have come to see God at work in their lives.

For each of us, then, maybe we will be asked to carry a child within us who will become the Son of God. Maybe we will be asked to face evil. Maybe we will be asked to face glory. We will fail and we will succeed, maybe even in the same moment. We just have to do what is before us, what is asked of us, and know capitulation is our lot, but we are never alone. That, for me, is the mystery. It is, however, a mystery which needs reiteration and reminding, over and over, and with each reminder, I try to get closer to being able to say with Mary, "Be it done to me according to your word."

2

THE SECOND JOYFUL MYSTERY: THE VISITATION

Mary, pregnant with Jesus, and her cousin Elizabeth, pregnant with John, meet.

Ireland

FAMILY IS COMPLICATED. I was raised far from any extended family and barely knew my grandparents. Both grandfathers were out of the picture, one dead before I ever met him and one estranged before he died. I met each of my grandmothers fewer than a handful of times before they both died as well. Aunts, uncles and cousins were shadows still more distant, everyone living in the Midwest while we lived in California, and I was always a bit jealous of people who had large, rambling, connected, intimate families.

When I decided to go to Ireland, I had no idea the recognition of family would ring true for me in my deepest being.

My friend Lisa and I had scrupulously saved for three years to go backpacking through Europe, and Ireland was high on my list. I was twenty the first time I visited, returning to the birthplace of my father's parents. My grandmother, the eldest of twelve, was the only one of her siblings who came to the United States, and she had left behind a lot of family, none of whom we had ever met. I called her to ask whether there were still family in Ireland we could visit. She laughed, and said there was plenty, but, she admonished, "If you can't stand the smell of pig shit, you had better stay home."

I was shocked for a couple of reasons, not least of which was having a grownup swear in my hearing, but also because she was seemingly unaware that my father was, despite being an insurance agent, an aspiring farmer in his spare time. We had an acre of land, and at alternate times, had raised a couple of cows, sheep, chickens, and indeed, a pig. I was familiar with more than just the smell of pigs, having mucked out my share of their excrement.

My grandmother didn't know me any better than I knew her.

She told me about the town where some of the family had settled. Though she had been raised in County Mayo, on the rocky west coast of Ireland, some of her siblings ended up in Westmeath, in the Midlands. Although we were Carrigans, they were all Corrigans, the name having been changed by the scribes at Ellis Island who were too inundated by foreign accents to spell names correctly. She told me about my Great (and great) Aunt Margaret, her younger sister, and said I should go visit her. They didn't have a telephone, however, so I should send a letter and then just show up in town. People, she assured me, would take care of me once I got there.

At twenty years old, with no traveling experience, I was naively unconcerned by such vague advice, relying on people who knew better than I. I duly sent the letter, and received a warm reply saying I would be welcome, and instructing me to take the bus to Castlepollard, and go to the pub called Carroll's. This was all I knew.

Taking the bus from Dublin was an adventure in itself in the days of old rattling green school buses, with windows that temperamentally ratcheted up and down (sometimes randomly), and seats with more springs than padding. The roads were narrow and winding, and the heater was always on too high, so the condensation of the rain on the outside and the steaming breath of the passengers combined to make sweltering and nauseating conditions inside the bus. After nearly two hours, we were shaky and grateful to clamber down off the bus, seventy-five-pound backpacks in tow, in front of Carroll's pub.

The pub, a long narrow room, was dark inside, a solid miasma of smoke hanging from the ceiling to the level of my head. The bar extends about halfway down the room, on the lefthand side, and the room opens up into the parlor beyond, where no one was sitting. Several men were seated at the bar, hunkered protectively over their drinks, and an older man and woman stood startlingly close together at the railing on the right side of the room, leaving a very narrow passage. Everyone turned to stare: two strangers, two backpacks, young women, in the pub in the afternoon. Definitely American. Definitely noteworthy.

I asked if they knew how to get to the Corrigan's farm, and there was a moment of silence as they regarded me, balancing my knowledge of a local with my apparent ignorance of everything else. The man behind the bar said one of them would be in any time now, and we should wait, as it was too far to walk with our bags. Having no other choice, we sat at the table nearest the door, uncertain about taking what was probably someone else's chartered territory and sensing that entering the empty space of the parlor would be some kind of violation. We ordered a Guinness each, which shocked the barman. "Are you sure you wouldn't rather have a Shandy?" he asked, proffering the nasty drink made of half lemon-lime soda and half weak beer. In a glass, not a pint. (Insert shudder.) We declined, assuring him we wanted a pint of Guinness. Much later, I learned how unladylike doing so was considered, but we were, again, ignorant. And thirsty.

As we lingered over our drinks, a man walked into the pub. I gaped. I had no idea who he might be, not having been privy to the list of the dozens and dozens of relative I might have in the town, but I knew he had to be related to me: the resemblance to my own father was jarring. He had the same walk, the same physique, the same hair, the same twinkling eyes, the same laughter-lined face, the same mannerisms. He smoked in exactly the same way my father did, with the cigarette miraculously hanging to his lower lip as he talked, the ashes entrancingly bobbing up and down, defying the laws of physics. Oblivious to us, he walked in and began to joke with those at the bar, until the barman motioned to me—I was still staring with astonishment at this unexpected manifestation—and said, "I believe she's one of yours."

This is how I met my Uncle Joe, a man I had never heard of before. The youngest of my grandmother's siblings, he was born long after she had left for the United States, and so he was not really on my grandmother's radar. She hadn't thought to mention to me I had a great-uncle living on the farm abutting Aunt Margaret's. She had certainly met him a number of times on her visits back to Ireland, but she never told me to prepare myself for family who looked so much like her own sons. Nor was he aware of my existence, but he accepted it with perfect aplomb—it probably helped that I, unbeknownst to me then, also looked very much like my cousins—and drove my friend and me out to the farm to meet his sister.

Aunt Margaret and Uncle Mike had nine children of their own, and although those children are my father's first cousins, they are closer in age to me, so we just call each other "cousin" to save on having to figure it all out. There are a lot of cousins in this county. A lot. So many. Michael John runs the pig farm on the other side of Aunt Margaret's home, so Aunt Margaret's fields are sandwiched between his and Uncle Joe's fields, on Lake Derravaragh, a magical place where the Children of Lir spent the first 300 years of their accursed swan lives. On this first visit, however, Michael John still lived at home, and did much of the farming with his father.

Aunt Margaret asked Michael John to entertain us one afternoon, so he loaded us into his truck and took us with him. We thought we were just going to go sightseeing, but he had "one quick errand" to run first. So he handed us some branches, parked the truck in a small passageway with hedges on either side of us, and strode off, instructing us to wait for him. After some time, when my friend and I began to speculate on what the "one quick errand" might be, he came running up the hill with a herd of cows in front of him, slapping and yelling at them to keep them coming. Toward us. The two girls with little sticks. When he got near enough, he yelled at us to just hit them if they tried to go anywhere except into the back of the truck, and to not let them get into the hedges.

We did our job admirably, if a bit hysterically, smacking the cows on their haunches with the twigs we were given (which seemed ever smaller as the cows got nearer). As the cows clambered into the truck—the truck with wooden slats on the sides—they were, shall we say, perturbed. When cows get perturbed, they tend to let loose from certain orifices. Wooden slats on the side of trucks are entirely inadequate for containing such loosened, splattering elements, and two young ladies with stems standing on the side of said truck are likely to get sprayed with odiferous slime. As we did.

When Aunt Margaret saw us, slathered in greens, yellows and browns, she was horrified, and chastised Michael John about his inhospitable treatment of the two Americans. We, however, were laughing too hard to be angry, and Michael John and I became fast friends as well as cousins.

For all the amusement of that first visit, the hospitality of family still stuns me. Because there was no way to reach me while I was on the road, so long before cell phones, the family did not have the chance to warn me about the poor timing of our visit. Peter, my eighteen-year-old cousin, had been in a nasty motorcycle accident, and was in a coma still. I was mortified when I arrived, feeling we were intruding, but everyone was amazingly gracious and kind to us. Apologetic to be unable to take us around to see the sights, they still welcomed us into their homes and lives.

When we were leaving, Uncle Mike drove us back to the bus stop, ruefully responding to our enthusiastic assurances of our impending return with, "That's what they all say, and we never hear from anyone again." Anne, their daughter, said much the same thing when we left her in Dublin. Regardless, this was the first of many visits to Ireland. I love that they refer to my visits as "coming home," as in, "When were you last home?" and when I come into the pub now, most people barely look up, bleary-eyed, from their drinks.

In the years since, Carroll's was bought by Anne and her husband, and it is now Comiskey's, serving the best pint of Guinness in town. Uncle Mike, Aunt Margaret's husband, died before my second visit there, and Uncle Joe died some years ago. Michael John, as I mentioned, moved out and has the farm next door, but cared for Aunt Margaret's property as well for many years. Peter and I had cancer at the same time, often commiserating over the phone, complaining about the people who had to lower their voices to express their sympathy when they asked, "How *are* you?" Sadly, he did not win his battle, dying several years ago. Tony, another son, has Parkinson's. The sisters are spread far and wide, but we manage to see each other as often as possible. There are new generations of children, and some of those children are having children. They are all cousins. There are scandals and tragedies, joys and celebrations, rifts and mendings. We have had parties and innumerable hours spent at Comiskey's, some of them after hours, laughing and telling stories over pints. Many of my grandest nights, those nights we can only call "epic," have been spent in Ireland with family.

I lived in Dublin for three months while I finished my doctoral dissertation, spending long days in dusty and thrilling libraries while living in town, and spending weekends with Aunt Margaret, where she and I would watch snooker on the television, and eat her homemade brown bread, a treat all the world should have been able to experience. I have a tin of tea I cannot bring myself to drink because once it is depleted, I will lose the smell taking me back to the peat stove in her kitchen; I only open the tin to sniff when my homesickness is too intense.

Tea is, of course, the answer to everything: tea with breakfast, tea after the breakfast dishes are done, tea at lunch, tea whenever anyone comes by, tea after dinner, tea before the pub, tea when we return from the pub, tea whenever anything of import needs to be discussed, tea when someone needs solace. Late at night, often at 3:00 a.m., when I came back from the pub, Aunt Margaret would have the tea things set out for me, my nightgown warming on the stove, and a hot water bottle in the bed.

Aunt Margaret died at 93 years of age. The last time I saw her, she was in a nursing home after she had had a stroke, and I was told she was confused, but she knew my husband and me right away. We were told she thought she was back in her school days, until we realized that when she said she had to go to school, she was talking about a class she was taking in making rosaries; she didn't want to miss it. We were still less convinced about her dementia after we failed to come by one afternoon in favor of doing some sightseeing, and she greeted us the next day: "Ah, it's grand of you to come. Where were you yesterday?" I will miss her forever.

Diasporic people speak of cultural belonging, of a genetic inheritance of place. The recognition of connection goes beyond the visual, beyond the flesh, enmeshed in our very DNA. Such recognition comes as a kind of click in one's soul, as if everything is right with the world. My father, who died never having visited Ireland or having known any of his aunts and uncles or cousins, could not escape his roots, and chose to live in a place as similar to Ireland as any other I have been. The fog, the cool air, the rolling hills, the green, the misty rain, are nearly the same in Northern California as they are in Ireland. He never knew how closely he aligned himself to his cousin Michael John's life.

Such elemental recognition, the sense of homecoming and rightness and connectedness, is the essence of the Second Joyful Mystery. Mary and Elizabeth, cousins, are both pregnant, and the child in Mary's womb leaps for joy at the recognition of his unborn cousin, a cousin who will be consequential to his life. Elizabeth exclaims, "Blessed are you among women, and blessed is the fruit of your womb." Mary replies, "My soul proclaims the greatness of the Lord, and my spirit finds joy in God my Savior." Both Jesus and John will experience much tribulation and much joy in their lives, and so will their families, as they love each other the way family loves each other, even when that family is distant. The connection of family is inescapable, conceived with us in the womb, buried in our

DNA, whether we are all raised together or not. My heart leaps for joy and my soul proclaims the greatness of the Lord, and I am deeply blessed to know and love these people.

3

The Third Joyful Mystery: The Nativity

Mary gives birth to Jesus in a manger.

Children

I HAVE NEVER BEEN pregnant. I have never felt the flutter of a life growing inside of me, or the gobsmacking wonder of creating a human being. I have certainly been near those who have, and have watched in amazement as a person wreaks havoc on a woman's body in order to come into being. I have certainly pondered pregnancy and childbirth every time I pray the Mystery of the Nativity, and been envious of the relationship between a mother and child who are so inextricably tied. All of the trite things ever said about childbirth are trite simply because they are so true, so when we speak the words, "I cannot believe an actual human being comes about like that," those words remain the truest way to speak about the mystery of children.

With a mess of a body, I had little hope of giving birth, despite my father's continued assurances (never very comforting in my teen years) that my hips were made for child bearing. While I was grieved for many years over what I perceived as a lack in myself, I thought I had circumvented any maternal urges by marrying a man who already had two children, Amanda and Aaron. Although their mother was still alive, I believed the love and abilities I had to offer would make me a good second mother to them, and I looked forward to helping raise them.

I was young and wide-eyed.

It all began so well. Two children, a seven-year-old girl and a five-year-old boy, came into my life. We shared custody with their mother, switching houses every Sunday evening. I had made only two stipulations about helping to raise them: I would not take them to the dentist because I did not want to inflict my phobia upon them (and because it looks bad to take your children to the dentist with a margarita in hand to calm your own nerves), and I would not teach them to drive (for similar reasons). Otherwise, I agreed to clean up vomit, take them to schools and doctors, cook and clean, read to them, play, and otherwise attempt to recreate my own childhood for them.

We had wonderful moments.

The battle in the rainy front yard with the cooked lasagne noodles was memorable in its silliness, slapping cold wet slime on each other.

Setting off the Piccolo Pete fireworks in the kitchen to wake the children up so we could do fireworks when their father got home from working swing shift was, perhaps, not our best idea, but it was pretty funny, so much louder and smokier than we had anticipated; it also failed to arouse either enthusiasm or children at 3 a.m.

Singing along with Dr. Demento in the truck, building forts under the willow tree, making up the dog's Bye-Bye Breakfast on camping trips with whatever leftovers there may have been, family parties where we all stood on the porch and did the Queen's wave at each other, chanting, "Elbow, elbow, wrist, wrist, touch the pearls and blow a kiss" as we mimicked being on a parade float: these are all happy memories.

When Seamus Waymus O'Maymus Gustav (our fluffy white and gray cat) was run over intentionally by a passing driver, that was less fun, but we did get two more kittens the next day.

Aaron running down the hallway projectile vomiting in our new house, on the spotless light gray carpeting, was less fun, but funny in retrospect. He tried so hard to avoid making a mess, and instead made a much bigger one. A surprising number of vomit experiences are funny in retrospect: Aaron after eating the whole chocolate Easter bunny before breakfast one morning, our nephew after too many root beer floats, and so on.

We went every year to the Christmas tree farm in my home town, choosing and chopping our own trees, and sitting around the apple wood fire afterwards, partaking of apple pie and apple cider; it is a tradition the children have continued in their adult years.

It felt like we were doing things right, despite the challenges of sharing custody with someone who had a very different style of parenting.

I am certain, however, my desire for my own children and my nostalgia for my childhood got in the way of my ability to be a good step-parent. The relationship of step-parent is not, and never can be, the same as that with a biological parent, and I failed to understand that with my heart, even while I understood it with my head. I thought enough love could transcend anything. I longed to create the perfect family, to give them the security they may have lost in the uncertainty of divorce. My expectations all too often led to frustration for all of us, and to disappointment.

The Halloween party, for example, is the classic example of differing expectations. For some time early in our marriage, we lived in a tiny, 625-square foot one-bedroom, one-cruiseship-sized-bathroom house, while we saved to buy a home. I was working the graveyard shift as a 911 dispatcher, while my husband worked swings as a police officer for another department. The kids were in school, but to complicate the schedule, one was in year-round school and the other had a regular schedule with summers off. What this effectively meant is that there was someone asleep in the house nearly 100% of the time, a detail greatly appreciated by the cats who loved to snuggle. So when we moved to a larger, three-story 1922 Craftsman house, with a basement, we felt like it was a palace. We decided, that first year, to have a haunted house Halloween party, and the planning began.

We took the wooden truck box from my husband's Ford and put it in the basement, decorating it to look like a coffin. Then we took the innards from the vacuum cleaner bag, filled with dust and the hair from our pets, and molded it to look like a dead body; we arranged it on the dirt floor that constituted part of the basement, behind an access door. In the middle of the "decomposed body," we put fresh raw chicken livers, to look like a human heart. We hooked up skeletons and spiders to fly at people when the door was opened. Spider webs and writhing rats abounded.

The food, of course, had to reflect the theme. I spent days making round iced sugar cookies to look like eyeballs, with red licorice thinly sliced for the veins, Lifesavers as the irises, and black cinnamon dots for the pupils. I made a witch cake, turning a Bundt cake upside down and sticking a Barbie doll into it. She had a chocolate-covered sugar cone hat, and gummy worms wiggling all around her. We had "snot punch," with sherbet floating around in it, and melty dips with innovative names like "Frankenstein Guts." All was set.

We wanted to usher the children down to the haunted basement in small groups, so their screams would beget other screaming and build the suspense. As I brought them down the stairs, lit with a dim flashlight, I took them into the room where sheeted ghosts flew at them. Grimly, slowly, I opened the coffin, where Ken popped up, glow-in-the-dark mask positioned, and with a beef liver hanging out the pocket of his shirt for increased gore. They screamed. Then we opened the door to the "dead body" under the house, and had sticky bats and clackety skeletons fly at them. They screamed. They caught a look at the glutinous liver "heart," and they screamed. It was wonderful.

We left our kids for last; this was as much a surprise for them as it had been for all the other children. As I led them downstairs, prompting the appropriate screams, all went well—until we opened the door to the dirt under the house, when my own screams joined theirs in earnest. Oscarina Squidgins, one of our cats, had found her way under the house and was happily chomping away on the chicken livers in the dust, tail swishing protectively, creating a most gruesome effect. Everyone was delighted.

At the end of the evening, all of us satiated and exhausted, we began to clean up, putting away the leftovers, gathering the remains of livers and vacuum dust. As we worked, we compared notes on people's reactions, when our son, eight at the time, came in, holding a grocery bag expectantly. We were initially puzzled when he announced he was ready to go trick-or-treating. It was nearly 10:00 p.m., entirely too late to go out. We explained the party was in place of schlepping around for candy, pointing to the abundance of candy leftover from the party as well as cookies and punch and other munchies. As only a treat-deprived eight-year-old can do, he threw a fit, beyond disappointed. No cajoling, no explaining, no pleading, and finally, no yelling, could convince him we had not just ruined his Halloween and, logically, his life. We were angry at his failure to recognize and acknowledge the amount of effort we put into the party, but our efforts could not assuage his desire to have it all. What we had planned as a special evening became one fraught with hard feelings all around.

The pattern, I see now, was established; maybe it had been earlier, but this is when I first see it as intransigent. The harder we—I—tried to "create" ideal situations, the more frustrated I became with what I saw as a lack of gratitude. Vacations became struggles between doing what I thought they should want to do and what they wanted to do, as they preferred playing video games to going on a Jamaican plantation tour, or to participating in a holiday dinner, or to engaging in the world around them. Or, again, that's how I saw it.

I didn't do *everything* wrong. My desire to instill in them a faith in their own instincts paid off. We urged them to come to us if any situation or person ever creeped them out, no matter what or who it was, and we would take care of it. I remember the abhorrence I felt as a child when certain people, often at church, made my skin crawl, but I still had to politely endure their embraces and painful, probing comments and questions because they were friends with my parents. I wanted them to learn our skin crawls for a reason, and they needed to believe their own responses. So when our daughter came to us and told us she was uncomfortable with the hugs and tickles given to her by my best friend's husband, much as our immediate reaction was to be amused—he was SUCH a nice guy—we talked to him and asked him to stop. Some time later, when we learned he was indeed molesting children and pretty much anyone else, we were relieved, to say the least, to have supported her instincts. This remains among my biggest triumphs.

Another source of pride for me is when we pretended to go to foreign countries, long before we could afford real travel. I had scored a used set of Time-Life cookbooks, published sometime in the mid-1960s, at a garage sale, and from these we would choose a country to visit. Together, we would examine the books, filled with pictures of local food and traditional dress, and armed with that research, we would go to the local thrift stores and do our best to recreate the garb. Then we would do research online to discover other details about the country: weather, decorations, music, language, whatever we could find.

Then the cooking would begin. Living in the California Bay Area at the time, we had access to nearly unlimited numbers of ethnic stores, and we took advantage of them. When we went to Italy, we decorated with red and green, played Italian music and dressed to approximate peasants, while we ate all kinds of relatively obscure Italian food. Spaghetti was wholly inadequate for our purposes. When we went to Russia, we printed our name cards in the Cyrillic alphabet. Germany was, perhaps, the most memorable. With our lederhosen and dirndls, we set out to eat our sauerbraten, our spätzle, and our beer cheese, acquired from the local specialty deli.

We had a key rule in our house, meant to encourage the kids to willingly try strange foods: if they made the negative comment or the nasty face before they tasted what was to eat, having only seen it or heard the name, they had to eat it all. If they tasted whatever it was with an open mind, and genuinely didn't like it, then fair enough, they didn't have to eat it. This meant one miserable night for each of them when they were sure we weren't really going to enforce this rule, and they resisted, and we had to wait out a tirade or two until they ate the food at which they had sneered, but once the rule was established, it worked out very well. It was an effort to counter other extended family members' tendency to be ridiculously picky eaters, and it led to adventurous eaters as well as greater satisfaction for those preparing the meals.

On this occasion, however, there must have been something wrong with the beer cheese. We knew it was supposed to be pungent, but it put the "ugh" in pungent. Still, we were adventurous. Aaron was the first to try it. Apparently the rule was so well-ingrained by then that he forgot the second half of it: if you didn't like it once you had tasted it, you didn't have to eat it. He froze. He turned pale. He couldn't chew. He couldn't inhale. He couldn't exhale. He couldn't open his mouth to speak. He couldn't swallow. His eyes grew tremendous. We told him he could spit it out, and it was so strong, he didn't even spit it out on his plate, choosing instead to run to the bathroom and spit it out in the commode. We laughed as we heard him rinsing his mouth out, and chose to believe him; none of the rest of us tried it out. He was laughing, but guardedly, when he returned.

So, being us, as a joke the next day, we put some of the beer cheese in a plastic sandwich bag and tucked it into his lunch. As a joke. Except I had no idea the cheese was so strong it would actually seep through the zip-locked bag and ruin all the rest of the food in his lunch with the smell. I still feel badly about that one.

Still, we laugh about it. It is a good memory. More or less.

For as hard as I tried, however, parenthood did not go as I planned. (This probably sounds incredibly naive to pretty much every parent ever, but there it is.) The children came to resent me, and to resist my efforts to love them. The home grew to be increasingly miserable, with Amanda struggling with an eating disorder and Aaron suffering from serious depression. I became, somehow, the enemy. We went to family counseling, and the therapist said something that rang deeply true for me, and that seemed a revelation to the rest of my family: Step-parenting is the worst job in the world. No matter what I do, I'm screwed. If I try my hardest to be a better mother than their biological mother, they will resent me for trying too hard. If I don't try at all, and become a worse mother than their biological mother, they will resent me for not trying hard enough. If I work hard to be exactly the same kind of mother as their biological mother, they will resent me for trying to be the same. My own ideals about how to raise children become irrelevant and largely ignored. I can't win. On the one hand, this understanding released from me some of my frustration; on the other hand, it also gave me permission to stop trying so hard, and to start taking care of myself, perhaps to the detriment of our relationship.

By the time the kids were teenagers, our home life was anything but peaceful, and I felt superfluous and unappreciated. I returned to school, to get a PhD in English, in hopes of returning to teaching. I felt I needed to do something for myself, and hoped one day they would understand that, though even that decision had repercussions I did not anticipate. At this point, the children were in high school, thinking about college. When they saw the amount of work I had every week, work that kept me reading tomes of literature, taking voluminous notes, and agonizing over writing papers, all while I sat at soccer games or while I stirred the spaghetti sauce or folded laundry, they opted to skip college. Assurances that grad school is nothing like undergraduate college met with disbelief, and I could not change their minds. My work load was too daunting.

There were always, of course, other factors to our relationship, among them the souring relationship between their mother and us. But my own deepening resentments did not help, I am certain. The pain of overhearing a conversation between the kids and the daughter of my best friend still stings: she was raving about how much she adored me, and how lucky they were to have me for a mom, and our son scoffed that he despised me, and that he wished I would just stay out of his life, or die.

Again, I realize such scenes are endured by biological parents as well, but Aaron's feelings did not, seemingly, change with his mood. We eventually reached the point where his anger was so great that I refused to be in the home when he and the guns were both there. (My husband was a police officer; guns were a part of our home.) At the worst of it, their mother moved out of state, and they moved in with us full-time, for the first time, at about the time I finished my doctorate and was on the job market. They resented us because we no longer had to pay child support. While the financial arrangement between us and their mother was something we had never discussed in front of them, for fear they would feel like commodities, their mother had seemingly not felt the same. She announced she could no longer afford to live in California because of her decreased income, and she let the kids believe we were at fault for her having to move. Their bitterness became most evident one day, when I fell down the stairs carrying a load of firewood, and lay at the bottom of the stairs, moaning in pain, covered with firewood, and unable to get up. Our son's bedroom was several steps away, and though he was home, and I cried out for help, he ignored me. I knew then how firmly he had turned against me.

Depressed by our home life, by the difficulty of getting a job, and by yet another painful injury from which I was struggling to recover (the fall resulted in a dislocated knee cap, so I was on crutches—another in a long line of injuries from accidents), I seriously considered suicide for the first time in my life. I lay in the bath one night soaking my knee, feeling like a failure and unable to muster up the wherewithal to go through another long stint on crutches and in pain. Ken was at work, and the children were at their mother's. I felt my life had been one long struggle, and every decision I had ever made (yes, depression allows that kind of absurd exaggeration) was bad. I had wasted precious time and money to get a doctorate, I had ruined the lives of my children and husband, and I couldn't even take care of my body, as it was injured yet again. I pondered all the leftover pain pills I had in the house from assorted injuries, and, crying, considered how to take enough to kill myself without making me pass out or wretch.

At that moment, Sven, our beloved orange tabby cat, jumped onto the side of the tub, something he had never done before for fear he would land in the water. He gazed at me, watching me cry, and gently laid his paw on my face, in the trail of my tears, and left it there. I stared at him, and he did not look away; nor did he remove his paw. I felt deeply that I was, in fact, loved, even if only by my cat, and that he was my angel sent to counter my sense of futility. When I got out of the bath, he continued to follow me around the house for the rest of the evening, as if watching to make sure I didn't do something stupid. This was the lowest point in my parenting, and indeed a pretty low point in my life.

Since then, improvement has come incrementally. The children are older, and our daughter has her own daughter. For all these years I have longed for the moment when they would tell me I was a good parent after all, and that moment has not occurred. (Worse yet, in her senility before she died, my mother-in-law ranted one night about what a terrible mother I was, accusing me of all kinds of nefarious deeds I never did; it was painful even as I knew she was literally out of her mind.) I am trying to let go of the hope my love will be recognized, but I do note when Amanda insists on many of the same rules we had in our house, and with some of the same traditions, so I couldn't have been all bad. While our few communications are treasured, we do not have the closeness for which I always longed, the closeness I felt with my parents, a fact that grieves me. We are not their first line of defense from the world.

When I pray the Mystery of the Nativity, then, it is with complicated emotions. I feel envy for Mary, even knowing how difficult it must have been to lose her son to such violence after having given birth to him under trying circumstances. But the fruit of the spirit behind the Nativity is not related to the exultation of having children, of watching them grow in love, of taking pride in their maturation: it is meant to be "poverty of spirit," and this is something to which I can relate, given my own parenting. I feel poor, both because I was unable to have children of my own, and because the children I do have remain distant. As my pastor points out, poverty of the spirit is self-emptying and draining love, and my love for Amanda and Aaron is deep; if it were not, their distance would not be so painful. Our lives together have been complicated by great fun and great difficulty—but what family cannot say the same?

I cannot help but think, then, less about Mary and more about Joseph, the ultimate step-parent. While the cultural context was quite different from our world today, without the same kinds of hangups about biological parenting, I still wonder what Joseph must have felt as he helped to raise Jesus. When Jesus may have seemed, by our standards, a bit flippant to his mother, such as at the wedding at Cana, or in the temple after having been missing for several days, I realize being the biological parent does not make one immune to the pain children can inflict on their parents (as if I ever really thought that).

But Joseph? Nearly everything I can think to say about what it must have been like for him would be borderline sacrilegious, but I cannot help but think them anyway. God is the Father of the child who lives with you? How do you compete with that? How do you avoid being nearly a footnote in that child's life? We hear so little about Joseph and his influence upon Jesus; what expectations did he have for his family? Was he disappointed he was not the one to father his first child with his wife?

Was he ever resentful? Did he ever feel his authority would never be hon-ored in his own home? Was Jesus grateful to him?

Ultimately, I cannot regret my life as it has been. I know I have been given great gifts. If I had achieved all of my expectations in having chil-dren, would I treasure the gifts they have given me as much as I treasure what my step-children have given me? Would I take them for granted, as being such a part of me I would not see them for who they are meant to be? In the impoverishment of my own spirit and the thwarting of my desires, I learned to be grateful for every moment I do have with my children, and for every dear memory I hold. In the end, I am beholden to them more than they are beholden to me.

4

The Fourth Joyful Mystery:
The Presentation of Jesus in the Temple

Jesus is recognized by Simeon and Anna in the Temple.

Medjugorje

SISTER MARY MICHAEL WAS the first nun I ever knew well, and so my concept of nuns is not the usual one. Far from prim, dour, severe, pious, and cold, she was one of the funniest women I ever knew, filled with a strong love of God, justice, and humanity. She signed herself SMM; we pronounced it "Simumum," sort of like "cinnamon." She loomed over us all in her dove gray and white habit, which she wore long after most nuns had discarded the tradition. Once part of the Dominican tradition, she and several other women left their order and moved to our small town to found the Hermitage of Christ the King, and although the other nuns were cloistered, she was the contact to the world, working enthusiastically with the poor and disenfranchised in our area. Early on, she figured out my father was also a true servant, and she took amiable and confident advantage of him, so we spent a considerable amount of time at the Hermitage. Thus I was "presented" to her, and she recognized things in me I had not yet seen.

I wonder, as I pray the mystery of the Presentation where two old and faithful servants of God understood his significance at once, whether

Jesus knew about his fate from the beginning, or whether the perspective of others who recognized in him a greatness never before seen may have helped him see what that fate might be. Consequently, I wonder about the role SMM had in shaping who I was to become, and how much would have happened anyway.

The Hermitage property was fairly large, in a rural area just outside of town, and I remember the rambling house with different levels and mysterious rooms. The public was only allowed in the antechamber, and we communicated with the rest of the house through a screen and an intercom, until SMM could attend to us. Later, as the Hermitage dwindled to just SMM and Sister Mary, the cloister was largely lifted, and we came to know the rest of the house as well; I still remember my surprise to find beyond the screen ordinary rooms, with books and couches and lamps, and even bathrooms.

As I grew up, the nature of my time with SMM changed, but at every step, she saw something in me I couldn't see for myself. When I was very young, I went with my father to help work around the property, pulling weeds around the pond and feeding the ducks, or hauling junk discarded in the blackberry brambles; she teased us and talked endlessly, always directing what we should do next.

When I was in high school, I would go out to the Hermitage for special events, such as the living Nativity scene after Christmas. SMM instilled in me the sense that the true Christmas season begins with the birth of Christ, not with the shopping season before Christmas. Now, we do not take our Christmas decorations down as soon as Christmas is over, because the real celebration begins on December 25 and ends with the Baptism of the Lord. SMM's living Nativity scene came at Epiphany, the Twelfth Day of Christmas, when the shepherds and wise men arrive at the manger; we would gather at the Hermitage and I would play the guitar as a very diverse crowd would sing carols around the lively, unpredictable and smelly animals she had borrowed from somewhere.

SMM also got me my first full-time job. I had worked briefly in high school for my English teacher, who had attempted to run a print shop in town, until the day I showed up for work and the presses had vanished. My dismay was great—printing presses and their paraphernalia were not easily pocketed and whisked away—because not only was the shop closed and my job gone, but he owed me $76.00 in back pay. (He still does.) But SMM knew of a print shop where she had her newsletter published in the next town, and knowing I now had some experience, she put in a good word for me, getting me the job operating the presses.

This was the beginning of our practical joke era. The parking lot was behind the print shop, and one had to go through a maze of paper cases, stacks of orders, and machinery to get to the front of the shop; she was one of the few customers who came that way rather than through the front door, and she always made a great entrance, her habit swaying among the boxes, her laugh preceding her.

She started it. One day, on my way home, I noticed people honking and waving at me, smiling. Puzzled, I did not yet know to be suspicious, but when I got home, I found a large sign, on fluorescent orange paper, in her handwriting, saying: "Honk to congratulate me! I lost 35 pounds; only 65 more to go!" I carefully prepared my revenge, lying in wait until her next visit, when I placed a large sign on the back of her already unwieldy station wagon: "Honk to congratulate me! I just became a grandmother!" And so it was on. I think the Limburger cheese on her engine block was the last one we did, and we finally called a truce after that.

SMM never preached to me, but always drew me into her work, sometimes in subtle and sometimes less than subtle ways. She had no compunction about "using" people, as we used to tease her, as long as doing so furthered the work she was doing. Her skill at including everyone she encountered was remarkable, as she always made us part of her mission; she assumed we had something to contribute, regardless of age or ability or wealth. Never one to believe in "charity," she helped people by including them in helping themselves.

It is not as much of a leap as one might think, then, to see how I became interested in the convent as a choice for myself. I admired her deeply. I was drawn to the same spirit of service, to the life she led, to the time spent in prayer, and to the way she actively demonstrated the gospel to the world. I liked the idea of living, praying, and working in a community of equally committed women. While I was attracted to the idea of a cloister sheltering me from the ugliness of the world, SMM's example showed me how delusional such thinking was.

I began to go to the convent for weekend retreats when I could; there were small cabins up past the pond, and I would bring my guitar and sing to the ducks, and sometimes for the services they held at the Hermitage. I would read and write and pray and sing, and life was perfect. And we would talk, sometimes in the library and sometimes at the pond. She never charged me for these weekends, accepting only whatever I could afford to give, which was very little at the time but seemed extravagant to me. She began to direct my reading, giving me Thomas Merton and Henry Nouwen. I entered discernment to become a Dominican nun, which is a process through which a woman studies, prays and works toward trying to decide whether the convent is the right place for her, but SMM was unconvinced that I would be "nunnified," as we called it, telling me I did not have the call. At the time, I resented her judgement, but she saw something in me I did not.

I moved away, and we did not correspond frequently, though I still got her newsletter and saw her when I went home for holidays. I remained in discernment, but I was struggling, torn between wanting to be a nun and wanting to be in a relationship, fearful to admit part of the desire to join a convent was directed by my despair over failed romances.

When she called one day and asked if I wanted to go with her to Medjugorje, in what was then Yugoslavia, I was surprised. For the last nine years, she explained, the Virgin Mary had been appearing to six children, and the place had become a site of pilgrimage. She was leading a group of twenty and wanted to know if I would go. I laughed and said I'd love to, but there was no way I could come up with that kind of money. I was working five jobs and going to school full time, trying to recover from health and financial setbacks. She told me someone had donated money and my trip would be covered, if I wanted to go. Knowing nothing about Medjugorje, and highly skeptical about the supernatural accounts I was hearing, I agreed to go; it was, after all, a free trip. I assumed she invited me as an able-bodied person who could help out when elderly people needed assistance with luggage, or whatever. I just knew I was going to Yugoslavia. I even planned, secretly, to help get everyone there, and then go off on my own to see the country for a bit. I had pretty low expectations.

Perhaps that thing SMM sensed in me at the time was a rather appalling lack of mysticism. I was comfortable in my belief of God as distant being, one who interacted with my life on a plane that vaguely touched mine. I had experienced blessings, and trials; I was, after all, still considering dedicating my life to God as a nun. And yet I had not quite applied, for instance, the Biblical stories to anything I might ever experience, thus maintaining my distance. What was true for people back then was not necessarily true for me, for now. The idea, then, that Mary would be appearing, in my lifetime, seemed unlikely at best.

Despite my faint heart, we went to Medjugorje. I knew several people on the trip, including Pete and Virginia, a couple who had been friends with my parents for years. In fact, they were the people who had agreed to raise the four of us children should anything happen to my parents. I knew them as my parents's friends, which meant I didn't know them well at all, but they were hardly the feeble people I had expected. Most of the group were quite capable, so I was still further confused as to why SMM had invited me, but we were having fun, and I did not look the gift horse in the mouth.

We flew into Dubrovnik, where we stayed at a lovely cliffside hotel across from the old town. I still remember standing on the balcony, having just taken a shower to rid myself of the grime of so many hours of travel in international planes when smoking was still allowed; the warm evening breeze from the Adriatic barely rippled my fresh nightgown, creating one of the finer moments in my life. We swam in the sea, buoyant in the heavy salt water, and we went to Mostar, where I bought earrings on the 500-year-old bridge only a short time before soldiers blew it up. It was June of 1990, just before the coming war would bring an end to Yugoslavia; in fact, we were there for the elections that lit the fuse, but we were largely unaware of the repercussions soon to come. We went on to the tiny town of Medjugorje, where we were staying with a young family whom SMM knew. A beautiful and peaceful place, in 1990, Medjugorje remained a small town despite the crowds of people.

Our routine while there was simple. Adopting the requests Mother Mary made to the six children, we fasted on Wednesdays and Fridays, eating nothing more than bread and water on those days. The church was the center of activity, and we met there to pray the Rosary in the evenings, and went to Mass daily. The celebrations were vibrant and multilingual, with translations available, and we sang continuously. I was inspired and refreshed, but a little childishly disappointed when all the miraculous things I had heard of had not happened to me. There were special moments, getting to know the other people on the trip, wandering through the gardens of roses in the rich red soil, and singing Cat Stevens songs with Jakov Colo, one of the children to whom Mary had been appearing. But I felt something was lacking.

Then I made my confession. I went to an Italian priest who had limited English, secretly thinking the best cop-out ever to revealing the ugly truth about myself would be to confess to someone who couldn't understand me, but, without going into particulars, I will just say the sacrament was truly a renewal of spirit.

From there, I went to the church for the Rosary. Every evening, as we prayed, the birds would flock to one of the towers of the church, purportedly because that is where Mary showed herself to the children, but my skeptic heart assumed someone was feeding the birds there to attract them every evening. I had also heard rumors of the church being suffused with the scent of roses as the Rosary was prayed every night, but I had never smelled them. That evening, however, the smell of roses was so powerful it was almost cloying; I couldn't help but look around me to see where the scent was coming from, but I saw nothing, nothing except flocks of birds circling the tower, never alighting.

Mass was often crowded to overflowing, so chairs were set up outside, with speakers so we could hear. (Having been to the overly-developed town of Knock in Ireland, another place Mary is said to have appeared, I imagine by now huge screens probably, lamentably, disrupt the surrounding view in Medjugorje, but they were not there yet.) As Medjugorje translates to "between mountains," we were tucked into the valley, and the feeling of protection was powerful. That night, I was watching the hills, and the sun turned a kind of pale green, looking almost one-dimensional like a communion wafer, and began to dance over the tops of the hills, back and forth, like the bouncing ball in a karaoke machine. I watched for several minutes, curiously, with a sense of peace that at last I was witnessing that which I had heard about. It did not seem strange at all.

There were many unusual experiences after that: the metal in my rosary changing from silver to gold; finding my way, easily and quickly, even fearlessly, down from the hill in the dark with unerring steps on the rocky, uneven path (truly a miracle for clumsy me); sitting comfortably on a marble floor for three hours listening to one of the priests, Fr. Jozo Zovko, speaking in Croatian, able somehow to understand him. This same priest laid hands upon me, and although many people around me were being "slain in the spirit" (a term with which I had been unfamiliar), I was beyond dubious that such a thing would happen to me, or even that it was really happening to them. I figured there was a lot of hysteria going on, perhaps even faintness from sitting on marble floors for three hours. And yet, when he barely touched me, down I went, with a wholly unexpected shock. It took days for my body to recover; I'm not sure my spirit ever has.

Near the end of the trip, Pete and Virginia (who were convinced along with SMM that I should not become a nun) suggested I consider praying for a husband. I was nearly 30 years old but had never considered doing so. I had certainly prayed for particular relationships I wanted to work out, and cried when God refused to answer my prayers, but had never thought about praying for a husband blindly. It was an intriguing idea, but I still thought I was going to become a nun, so I smiled and nodded.

That evening, during Mass, I again sat outside, watching the sun dance across the mountains, when I had the overwhelming sense of light being poured into the top of my head, a veritable waterfall of a peaceful and preposterously illuminating light. I felt—rather than heard—a voice telling me, "You aren't going to become a nun." The tone was almost re-proving, like it was the most obvious thing in the world, and it was silly for me to think of it. There was even a bit of an eye-roll to the pronounce-ment. "Your mission in life is to marry, and to teach your children to pray." Again, so obvious. So clear. No question. Duh.

Other sources of doubt suddenly clarified for me, so brightly I couldn't recall why I had struggled with them before. The Trinity, for ex-ample, ceased to haunt me with its inexplicable nature: it simply is, and I could let that be. Predestination versus free will? Not really all that com-plicated. Even the question of the virgin birth suddenly seemed simple. Why would we question whether the God who could create everything, I mean everything, from the machinations of an ant colony to the predict-ability of the stars, who thought up the very process by which children are born, could have one woman's egg sprout into a child? It seems like such a small thing compared to everything else ever done.

My experiences on this trip remain with me. When I am inclined to doubt—and my doubt has far more to do with the Church than it does with God, though God and I have our moments too—I cannot un-know what I learned in that moment of revelation. My faith went beyond belief to knowing, and resting secure in God's knowing. I began to understood just how great God's faithfulness really is.

I returned from that trip on June 25, 1990. I remember the date because on the following day, I began to pray a novena, asking for a hus-band. The prayer took on the formal tones of the novena, but also my own prayer style, which is quite chatty: "Look, apparently I completely suck at this picking out a guy thing. I think I know what I want, but that hasn't worked for me. So *you* send me someone. Whatever. Just make it work, please. I'm tired of doing it my way." On the ninth day of the novena ("novena" comes from the Latin for "nine"), July 4, I met Ken, the man who would become my husband.

The Fourth Joyful Mystery is the Presentation of the Lord in the temple, where Jesus and Mary submit to the laws that do not bind them, and where Simeon and Anna recognize in Jesus the Messiah. Simeon's prophecy, that Jesus will be the downfall and the rise of many in Israel, and that Mary's own soul will be pierced with a sword, is certainty. The spiritual fruit of this mystery is purity in mind and body, and that purity I felt in Medjugorje and afterwards. But beyond the purity, for me, is the sense of recognition and fulfillment of the message and purpose of Christ, in my life as in Simeon's. I knew, with a prophetic certainty, what I was to do from thence, and it was fulfilled. In some ways, my struggle was over; in others, it was just beginning.

Some time after my return from Medjugorje, SMM called me again. She was bringing Jakov to the United States, along with the family with whom we had stayed, and she wanted to know if I would go with them to Marine World. She felt strongly that a young boy (he was sixteen at the time, if I remember correctly) who had been regularly meeting with the Virgin Mary had precious little time to be a child, and she wanted to let him have a relatively anonymous day doing touristy California things. Of course I agreed, and we had a splendid day, laughing and being wholly ridiculous at Marine World, eating horrendous and delicious food, going on all the rides, consequently feeling nauseous, and simply being tourists. At no point did I ask him about what it was like to speak with Mary, a fact of which I am partially proud as it gave him a chance to be normal, and partially regretful, as I still would love to have that conversation.

Amusingly, only later did it occur to me we may not have appeared as normal as we felt, since we were, after all, a group of five people of varying ages who spoke only Croatian, one obviously American young woman, and a quite large nun in full habit. But it seemed perfectly normal to us.

A year and a half later, Ken and I were married. SMM was there, sitting near the back of the church, in her full habit as usual. As my father and I began our walk down the aisle, she whispered (wow, she was a terribly loud whisperer!), "Ha! I always knew I'd see you take the veil one day!" thus ensuring I would laugh all the way to join my husband.

She died several years ago, having declined into severe Alzheimer's for the last few years of her life. I did not see her during that time, and it breaks my heart to know such a light could have gone out so sadly; I prefer to think of her as the force she was as I knew her, and to be grateful for her presence in my life. She lived out the example for me of being able to submit to laws (she was faithful to her calling despite a very wealthy family who continually tried to bribe her to leave the convent), while always demonstrating how those laws could bend (showing me a place where the sun dances over the hills; bringing a visionary to Marine World; laughing, always laughing). And she played the role of both Simeon and Anna who recognized something extraordinary in the child before them, something maybe even that child had yet to recognize.

5

The Fifth Joyful Mystery: The Finding of Jesus in the Temple

Jesus disappears for three days and his parents find him in the Temple.

Ken

While I was scrupulously seeking the perfect man, I had a long list of "nevers," those features too unacceptable to live with. I had dated a number of different men in my life, and tried out a couple of long term relationships, and thought I was close to getting married twice before those relationships blew up spectacularly.

The aspiring cop I had dated, the first man I thought I loved, was all too eager to demonstrate his authority and power, to those around us and then, ultimately, to me; being two years older than I, he presumed to have all the answers and liked to order me around. He was so enamored with himself that he liked to share his luster with many different women, I found out later, and he drew first blood on my heart, standing me up for prom. Besides, I was completely opposed to guns: there would never be one in my house, and cops have guns. So cops were out.

Another man I dated for six years was divorced, with a small child he was raising, and the issues with overcompensating for shared custody were too complicated and ugly for me to want to return to the debacle of divorced dads; why screaming obscenities at Little League games is supposed to demonstrate support is beyond me, but it seems a shared feature among the part-time fathers I had known. His issues had more to do with insecurity, or at least that's how he explained his infidelity to me. He broke off our engagement on my birthday.

One guy I went out with was amazing on paper. Good looking, a great dancer, a tennis pro, exotically Bulgarian, he invited me to his apartment in San Francisco, overlooking the Embarcadero (before the Loma Prieta Earthquake permanently changed the landscape just a few months later); he said he would cook me dinner and then we would go out. I asked what I should wear, not knowing where we were going after dinner, and when he said, "As little as possible," I told him up front there would be no sex. He agreed, apologizing for the insinuation. When I showed up, warily, he gave me a tour of the photos of himself with many famous politicians and celebrities, and told me all about his very expensive BMW, stereo system, wine collection, wardrobe, blah blah blah. I was trying to give him the benefit of the doubt, knowing insecurity when I see it, until all at once he threw himself on top of me on the couch. Startled, I began to laugh. Not a chuckle, but a belly laugh, one that had me curling up in tears as he backed away in bewilderment. I couldn't get a breath to tell him why his presumption was so funny, but it didn't matter, because my hysteria was an effective way to end the date and the relationship.

I went on one almost-date with a man I had met at a party, and this remains my worst dating story ever. We were sitting at a steak house, where we had waited some time for our reservations to be honored, and had finally placed our order. As the waiter left, my date (I am so grateful to be unable to remember his name) looked me in the eye and said, "You know what I like?" His tone was so exaggerated in its suggestiveness I assumed he was being ironic, because—well, it was our first date, and he couldn't possibly be about to say something lewd. So I said, "I don't know. What?" And he said, casually, as if this were a normal observation, "I like it when a woman sits on my face and gets it all wet. And then I let it dry there, and later I peel it off and eat it like potato chips." I stared at him for a moment, trying desperately to convince myself I did not really hear what he said (a sensation I have had a startling number of times in my life), and then I reached for my purse, without a word, and went to the front desk to call a cab. I hid in the bathroom until the cab came. My father used to insist I bring "mad money" on a date, enough money to escape a bad situation should one arise; when he was right, he was right.

Another brief engagement was to a man who seemed really great at first, sweeping me off my feet, buying me jewelry, speaking of marriage far too soon, praising my beauty and my talents, going to Mass with me, until he abruptly—in one night—changed into an unrecognizable abuser who belittled me and screamed at me: I was worthless and always in the wrong, stupid, ugly, and a bitch. I was a nymphomaniac because I let him kiss me on the second date. The only reason, he insisted, for me to have five jobs is because I clearly thought I was too important to let any of them go. I still remember the night as one of the most frustrating and enraging I have had; I was completely blind-sided and bewildered by his attack, stupidly trying to apply logic to an argument that defied logic. Not long after the implosion of that relationship, I went to Medjugorje, pretty done with men. No wonder the convent was so attractive.

Therefore, when at age twenty-nine I prayed my Novena for a husband, I still, in a pretty spacious corner of my mind, held my list of men I was *not* interested in: no cops; no divorced men, especially with children; no men with guns; no whack jobs. There would also be no motorcycles in my life; as if it were not enough that my father was an insurance agent and had already instilled in me a full awareness of all the perils of motorcycles, I was the first on scene when a boy I had grown up with was hit on his motorcycle by a little old man who didn't see him, and it was I who had to hold his leg as it dangled in far too many angles while we waited for the ambulance, so motorcycles were out.

That was my non-negotiable list. Before I had gone to Yugoslavia, friends had attempted to set me up with some guy they knew, but he was too many of those "nevers": divorced, children, cop, *motorcycle* cop ('cuz God has a sense of humor), and certainly guns. What are the chances he was not a whack job? I declined. Many times.

On the Fourth of July, some of those friends were having a summer barbecue to which I was invited. It sounded like fun, so I got my potato salad together and went. I knew most of the people there, and all was fine, until this guy showed up, in a Mickey Mouse gray sweat shirt, with some woman. At once the muttering began, which is how both my future husband and I found out this party was apparently part of the great Secret Set-Up. They figured if no one told either Ken or me about the set-up, our meeting would be nice and casual, and we would hit it off. It hadn't occurred to them that in not telling us, one of us might bring a date. Disgusted, they now began to badmouth Ken, saying he would date just about anyone after the divorce, oblivious to the impression such comments might be having on the one with whom they were trying to set him up.

Ken and I spoke for several minutes, here and there, throughout the day. At one point he left, taking his date home for whatever reason, but he returned; he was playing football in the street with another group when I had to leave. I waved and said good-bye, but he didn't respond, so I assumed he was a snob. He claims he waved and said good-bye, but I didn't respond, so he assumed I was a snob. Not a very auspicious beginning.

Several weeks later, the barbecue people called me again. Ken's roommate, a guy I had briefly gone out with to dismal effect (he spent the entire date telling me what a waste of time academics, religion, literature, music and football all were, pretty much depleting all my topics of interest) had a new girlfriend and they wanted to have me over for dinner. Ken had dumped his girlfriend, and they were eager to have me give him another shot. They still insisted he was a great guy, despite the woman he had been dating. With some reluctance, I agreed to go. (I do recognize all the elements of pathos in this story, and I'm not sure why I agreed; nor am I sure why he didn't call me himself, but there you go.)

Okay, there was a lot of reluctance. One of my best friends was Fr. Michael, the priest at the church where I was working as musical and liturgical director, and that Saturday afternoon, I had come to the church to make sure the arrangements were in place for that evening's Mass, a Mass for which I usually played the guitar and sang. Things were quiet, so I popped in to the confessional to say hello, and he asked about my plans for the evening. When I told him, in the dreariest tone possible, about my impending date, he laughed at me, reminding me it might just be fun. I guffawed, moaning, "Sometimes you are up for meeting new people, and sometimes you just cannot face meeting yet another guy who is too dumb to find the hole in his sweater." It is possible my outlook could have been more positive.

I vividly recall the date. Dinner was the five of us, because Ken, in true cop fashion, ended up having to work late, showing up in time for dessert. Still, everything was going fine, until Ken got there, and then suddenly everyone else turned into 12-year-olds; I feared at any moment I was going to have to pass a note asking someone to ask whether Ken likes me, but they would all giggle too hard to pass it on. Whenever Ken and I began to talk, they got really quiet, whispering to each other, "They're taaaaaalking!" They dramatically tiptoed out of the room for dishes or coffee (it was a tiny apartment), quite obviously trying to get us to talk more. But when we did talk, they interrupted with useful questions like, "So, Kathy, what do yoooooou like to do on a first date?" and the snickering would ensue.

Finally, Ken asked me if I would like to go somewhere else and get a drink or something, and talk without benefit of an audience. I was so relieved to avoid the others, I immediately agreed. He went to get his things, and while I stood by the door, his roommate taunted, "Gee, Kathy, Ken just bought a new bed. Maybe, if you hit it off tonight, you can both try it out!" I was appalled and embarrassed, and didn't know what to say to these people who had just given me quite a nice dinner. Instead, Ken stuck his head back into the room and said to his roommate, "You're a pig." Surprised, I thought to myself, "Ooh! I kinda like this guy."

We went to a Mexican restaurant and got margaritas, and we talked for hours. We closed the place, and then stood outside in front of his house for several more hours, talking. At the end, he gave me his business card and asked if he could see me again. I agreed. Then, peering at the card in the dark, I asked him how to pronounce his last name (Hi-ning, like "wining and dining" and "whining").

It was not long before we went out again, this time on a Wednesday evening, and this time out to dinner, but again as a double date with the barbecue people. He impressed me that night because he was unfailingly polite, generous, gracious, funny, and considerate. He did not try to order my meal for me, or to tell me what I wanted, or critique what I did order; he apologized for having been a little bit late, but although he was late because his ex-wife had been late picking up the kids, he refused to badmouth her. He did not try to attack or grope me, but he did hold my hand at one point, and he danced very well. He made me laugh. He was cute. He did not make rude comments, or invite me back to try out his new bed. At the end of the night, when I closed the door behind him, I remember leaning against the door, reviewing the evening, and thinking, "Well, *that's* strange. I had a really good time! He wasn't offensive or stupid or any of the things I've gotten so used to. Hmmm." He didn't even appear to be a whack job.

Believe it or not, I was still not thinking about the Novena; enough time had passed between the Fourth of July—the end of the Novena—and our dinner that I had pretty much forgotten any possible connection. Besides, the idea of saying a Novena for a husband still felt a bit too superstitious me to credit it.

Ken and I went out the next night, Thursday, and then Friday he came to my apartment when I hosted a party for the church choir I directed. They loved him. I mean, loved him. He was the perfect host, ensuring everyone was taken care of (including me) without assuming a position he had not yet earned. He helped to serve, to cook, to clean up, and circulated to get to know everyone. People kept pulling me aside to ask how I had kept our relationship under wraps for so long, unable to believe we had only been dating for three days.

Saturday night we went out again. It was then I learned he had had a vasectomy, and wanted no more children. I was crushed; even knowing my body was incapable of bearing children, I had always imagined myself as a mother. We talked for a long time, and decided it was best to discontinue the relationship. I cried myself to sleep, but told myself it was better to end it now before my heart was completely lost.

Going to church the next morning, the choir members continued to rave about how great a couple we were, and it was all I could do not to cry. I was feeling rather surly as I told them all we had broken up, if you could even call it that after such a short time; they knew better than to pursue the discussion when I was in that mood.

Monday, I went to my job at the veterinary hospital, where my co-workers and clients, all day long, kept asking me what was wrong; I apparently looked like I had just lost my best friend. I alleged I was fine, but was getting increasingly snappish at all the solicitude over some guy I had only gone out with a handful of times. By late morning, I was disgusted with myself and couldn't focus on my work. I called the local florist and send a bouquet of roses to him at work, at the police department, saying, "I can't do this anymore. Can we talk?" Then I waited. And waited. There was no phone call.

I went home from work, terribly upset, feeling snubbed. A friend was coming over to watch the first Monday Night Football game of the season, and his first comment coming in the door was, "Geez, who died?" After I kicked him, I explained, and he was amazed. "I've never seen you like this!" he laughed. I insisted my heart was not so easily broken by some loser I'd only seen for three days who couldn't be bothered to phone me after I sent him flowers. Still, he noted the proximity of the phone to the couch where we sat, and my awareness of its remarkable silence.

At 11:18 p.m.—I had been contemplating the numbers on my clock radio as they flapped the night away, telling myself to just be happy the 49ers had won—Ken called. I briefly considered pretending he had woken me up, but didn't think I could pull it off. He told me he had gone to work that day, unreasonably depressed, and at the last minute decided to take the day off and go water skiing with a group of friends. Only when they dropped him back off at the department, where he stopped in to get his stuff, had he received the message from the front office, jeering, "Hey Keeeeen! Someone sent you flowwwwwwers! They are in the front office!"

Suffice it to say, he came over. We talked. While I still wanted kids, I hoped step-children would be enough, and I didn't want to lose him. A week later, we discussed marriage. Eight weeks and two days after our first date, we bought the ring.

The temptation to end there, with this lovely little romance story, is overwhelming. But that would also be dishonest. Not all went so well. Because he had been divorced, in order to marry in the Catholic Church, he had to have the marriage annulled, a bizarrely unpleasant thing to endure. The process involves digging up everything that happened with his first wife, both prior to and during their marriage, in order to demonstrate the marriage was not valid in the eyes of the Church. This includes finding witnesses, taking statements, and dredging up much pain and anger. And it takes a long time.

In the meantime, I was falling more and more in love with him. He kept doing such amazing things.

I had two cats when we met, Carmen Miranda and Edgar Allan Po' Kitty. Carmen, a tortoise shell with a face resembling an orange and black checkerboard, was my first kitty, and we adored each other. She did not adore the people (especially men) I brought home, although she didn't actively spray them. Mostly, she made herself scarce; on occasion, she scratched, if they got too close to me. Ken, however, was another story. The moment he came into my apartment, she snuggled up to him, even climbing on his shoulders and draping herself around his neck, which she only had ever done with me. She liked to play cards this way; she would perch on one of our necks and then occasionally reach to point at a card; we always played that one. Though she was a terrible card player, she made up for it with her taste in men.

Early on in my relationship with Ken, I came home from work one day to find my cats traumatized to hoarseness, and my bathroom a mess of shredded bath mat, cat poop, and broken perfume bottles. There was also a note from the apartment manager saying there had been a gas leak somewhere in the complex, so they had to enter the apartment to do some work; the cats had been too curious and noisy, so the workers locked them in the bathroom for the day (with no water or kitty litter, I might add). I was livid, and called the manager in a rage. Far from appeasing me, he told me they would need to continue the work over the next five days, and they would have to continue to lock my cats away to do it.

In despair, I called my new boyfriend, crying. He told me to pack them up and bring them to his house for the week. I demurred, hesitant to inflict my very pushy, spoiled, and traumatized cats on him, but he insisted. So I gathered all their stuff and drove over to his place. When I got there, it was dark and raining, but he met me to collect the cat carriers and usher his new roommates into his house while I parked the car. I grabbed the rest of the stuff, and found him in the kitchen on the floor with both kittens, showing them the cat food and fresh litter he had already gone out to buy for them. My heart melted. He even had a night-light for them, as he worried they would be uncomfortable in a strange place. I'm not exactly a "Love me, love my cat" kinda gal, but he certainly won me over with his concern.

Soon after this, Ken and I moved in together. We were saving to throw a wedding and buy a house, and we moved into a cute little rental where we had plenty of room for the kids. I was ridiculously happy. These decisions—the engagement and the moving in together—were all made before my family had had a chance to meet him. They only lived an hour and a half away, but our schedules did not allow room for a visit. Consequently, when I told my parents about our engagement over the phone, there was a long silence. They had endured with me all my unhappy relationships and knew my record in choosing men was not exactly stellar.

I told them, "I nearly got married before, remember? And I asked you then how you could know it was the right decision, and you told me you just know. Mom, you told me you were at the movies with Dad, maybe your second date, and you thought then you would spend the rest of your life with him. You just knew. I thought you were full of crap and you just didn't want to tell me. But that's how I feel about Ken. I just know." More silence, and then Dad, on the extension, said, "I have the biggest smile ever."

Then I told them we had moved in together. The fallout was enormous. It was one of the most painful conversations I have ever had. I was told I was slapping God in the face, I was evil, and I was a disappointment to them. I was certain the first was untrue, as God had sent Ken to me;

I was less certain about the second; I was devastated by the last. Never mind that my siblings were living with their partners, and had not faced the same accusations, but I tried to explain how I had been through so much in my life, and Ken was the first person who was actually helping me to lift my burden. My mother told me I was the strongest person she knew, and she blamed me for being ridiculous. I suggested she was missing the point: Ken was the first person who didn't *expect* me to be the strongest person he knew, and the relief was tremendous. Someone was finally there to help me.

We eventually went to see them. They were polite. Viciously, unmitigatingly polite. Ken thought it went well. I laughed bitterly and told him if things didn't improve, that would be our last visit home. These were not my parents. Our family is raucous and hilarious and obnoxious and fun and rude and teasing. We are emphatically not polite. Even when we are supposed to be polite, on those rare occasions when we pull it off, we are only faking it, storing up things to laugh at later. There was not one funny moment in our entire day spent with them. It was torture.

The annulment took a year and a half, and then we were married. In that time, my parents came around (my siblings loved Ken from the start), and my parents learned to love him as well—so much so I feared that if we ever split up, his invitation to Christmas would be assured, mine less so.

After so much heartache, loneliness, despair, and hilarity, I had found the man I could love deeply and forever.

Why do I include this story under the Fifth Joyful Mystery? The story of Jesus having been missing for three days, and being found at last in the Temple, holding forth to people of great learning, has always puzzled me. Jesus does not seem to be shown in the best light; he seems flippant with his parents, who had to have been frantic with worry over him, when he rebukes them: "Why did you search for me? Did you not know that I must be about my Father's business?" How were they supposed to know that? How could they do anything but go frantic with worry? For me, the story is about Mary's anxiety, her terror at having lost what has been entrusted to her. The spiritual fruit of this mystery is supposed to be "obedience," although I have trouble seeing that connection. Obedience to whom? While Jesus was being obedient to his call in life, he was not being obedient to his parents when he disappeared (though he was obedient to them when he returned with them, awaiting his time). Rather, to me the lesson is one of patience and acceptance, perhaps obedience to God's plan: despite Mary's great fear, Jesus was safe, waiting and trusting she would know where he was, and would show up at the proper time.

In a similar way, Ken was living his life, I mine, and although I searched high and low, fearful I would never find a man I could truly love, when I relaxed and trusted in God, Ken and I met. The obedience I see here is the same as in the Annunciation: trusting in the Word of God and surrendering to that. We were both, unknowingly, going about the business God meant for us to engage in, preparing ourselves for each other, until such time as we found each other and were ready to be found.

To be clear, I do not believe there is one perfect person reserved for us by God, and if our paths don't happen to cross, we are alone forever. What I do believe is Ken and I met when we were ready for each other, and I cannot separate that from the Novena. I don't know, for example, what might have happened had I prayed a Novena ten years earlier, long before we could have met. Occasionally, we ponder what our lives would have looked like had we met sooner. Would we have even liked each other at an earlier stage in our lives? Would we have ended up together had we not each had the experiences which formed who we are? Would we have appreciated each other the same way had we not had other relationships to compare? Would we have had children of our own, and would that have made any difference? Ultimately, we know we met when we were supposed to, finding each other going about God's business.

So many of the Joyful Mysteries are about recognition and trust: trusting the angel really came from God, trusting the infants who knew each other from their wombs, recognizing Jesus as truly the Son of God; the fruits of each mystery encourage us to live lives that will allow God to work in us, if we can only let go of our own sense of control in favor of trust. Only when I let go of my highly-manipulate list of "nevers" was I open to the possibility that God may have had a better plan for me than I did.

6

The First Luminous Mystery: The Baptism of the Lord

John baptizes Jesus in the river.

Water

WHEN WE GO FOR a hike with our dog, Roscoe, the first thing he does when he leaps from the car is sniff for water. Part Border Collie and part Australian Shepherd, he is pretty sure he is the boss of everyone anyway, so he guides us unfailingly to whatever the source of that babbling sound might be, leaping in and splashing happily once he has found it, while remaining cautious, careful to avoid slipping in over his head.

He is our own personal divining rod.

Following one of my many linguistic rabbit holes one night, I found myself lying awake pondering the word: Divination. The term "divining rod," used to describe the tool for dowsing or finding a water source, is derived from "divination," the magical or occult practice of foretelling the future, and often alludes to a kind of witchcraft. I can see how the concept evolves, since using a forked stick to locate water must seem like at least a trick, if not proof of supernatural interference in the logical world. Far more intriguing, however, is the slippage between "divination" and "divine," so that "divination" is occult—and therefore bad —and "divine" is holy. However that slippage occurred, the lineage of the word is clear:

the discovery of water is the discovery of the divine. Roscoe knows. And so do I.

Whether soaking, cruising, fishing, snorkeling, paddling, floating, splashing, sprinkling, drinking, I crave the magic of water. I like it in a tub, a pond, a pool, a shower, a puddle, a glass, a river, a sea, an ocean, a lagoon, or a squirt gun. My ideal vacation is one involving water. I have been in the Adriatic Sea, floating under the stars outside the old city of Dubrovnik. I have been in the Caribbean, helping carry our daughter through the water after she injured herself and couldn't get her foot wet. I have swum in the Mediterranean, the Pacific and Atlantic Oceans, the Aegean, the Gulf of Mexico, and the waters of French Polynesia. I have sailed through the Norwegian Fjords, the Panama Canal, the North Sea, the Gulf of St. Lawrence, and the Mekong Delta. I have luxuriated in the Blue Lagoon, the geothermal waters near Reykjavik, Iceland. Where there is a body of water, I long to be in it. Nothing is as tranquil and empowering as being soothed and surrounded by water. Weightless, buoyed, I am pain-free when floating.

I have no problem understanding why water is used to baptize, to purify, to sanctify, to remind us of divinity. As a "cradle Catholic," baptized when I was an infant, I have had cause to be reminded of baptismal waters over and over again throughout my life.

And yet, for someone who loves being in the water so much, I am not a strong swimmer. I have come close to drowning several times, mostly because I find myself literally getting in over my head in alluring but treacherous water: I can't always get out of it by myself. I have been saved by multiple people when I overreached: the time I went off the high dive at the public pool (on a dare, of course, because I was feeling invincible after a whole two swimming lessons) and spluttered until the local lifeguard hooked me out; the time I tried to water ski and believed my friend's evil older brother who told me no matter what, don't let go of the rope; the time I snorkeled much too far out in Grand Cayman, able to see my family waving to me on the shore but unable to get out of the current holding me in one spot; the time I hurtled over the handlebars of the wave runner in Mexico and found myself unable to lift myself back on, having dislocated my knee cap on the way over.

Even as I write this, the metaphor for my life seems so obvious as to be almost lurid. Why do I not learn my lesson and stay out of the water? (Why do I not take some decent swimming lessons?)

On my first trip to Europe, when I was 20, my friend Lisa and I took a ferry across the sea from Rosslare, Ireland, to Le Havre, France. Being neophyte travelers, we had failed to book a room or even a seat for the trip, so were left to our own devices, wandering in search of a perch as a violent storm kicked up, with waves knocking us about as if a particularly demonic child were playing with us in a bathtub. It was November, and we had no right to expect anything less. Those with pre-booked rooms locked themselves away immediately. Others had seats, which they were not leaving for fear of being tossed across the room. The rest of us wandered around, but we quickly realized the overheated rooms were not helping seasick patrons get over their seasickness; though barf bags were placed in all the strategic locations, there were simply not enough of them, and the smell was becoming overpowering.

Six of us, more afraid of the contagious effects of the odor than of the raging storm, went out. I know (now) it was foolish, but we behaved as though we were on a private amusement park ride. Playing with the water and gravity, we slid up and down the decks, pretending we were surfing. Screaming with laughter, we let the waves blast us over and over again, not caring about how wet we were; at a certain point, one cannot get any wetter, so why avoid it? We had to keep wiping the crusted salt out of our eyes so we could see, and only when we realized the salt on our eyebrows had frozen did we think maybe it was too cold to be doing this. As soon as we opened the door to the ferry, however, the combined heat and smell washed over us more powerfully than the water had, and we decided the cold was worth it, returning to our games.

Of course I had cause to regret my actions. The train ride from Le Havre to France, still in our wet clothes, left me cold down to and through my bones in a way I had never experienced before; I could not stop shaking enough to hold a cup of cocoa, and I could not feel the heat of that cocoa as it sloshed onto my hands. I could hear my mother's voice saying, "You'll catch pneumonia," and she was right, I did. But having cause to regret my actions doesn't actually mean I *do* regret my actions. The ferry ride remains one of my favorite water memories just in its rashness and fun. It was my first encounter with the true power and majesty of water, and I was both elated and intimidated, baptized in a whole new way.

After I met Ken, though, my relationship to water took a whole new turn, because we began to travel, encountering new bodies of water.

I was working as a 911 dispatcher and still working as Director of Music and Liturgy at my church, so time off was virtually unheard of. I was exhausted all the time, and growing increasingly depressed about the lack of downtime. I was also still trying to finish my MA. Ken and I, still new in our relationship, had very little time together. One night, when I came home from a long shift, ready for my weekend, Ken greeted me with far more enthusiasm and perk than seemed warranted. My eyes were already closed as I went upstairs to go to sleep, and so I tripped over the suitcase on the floor by my side of the bed. Befuddled, I wondered why it was there, and tried to step over it, deciding to ignore it. Ken laughed and asked me to pick out a bathing suit, but I knew I misheard him because the weather was not at all warm enough for that; besides, I was going to bed, not for a swim. He, however, announced we were going somewhere, though he declined to tell me where. I protested, as I was still working at the church as well and needed to be there the following morning. I won't go through the entire conversation; I was entirely too foggy to process what he was saying, but he explained he had secretly arranged for all my duties to be suspended for four days; all of my bosses had somehow agreed to let me have time off. Four days. I could not even imagine four whole days with no work. So I woke up just enough to throw a bathing suit in the luggage, Ken having packed everything else, and we headed to the airport, with me still clueless about where we were going.

Cabo. He took me to Cabo San Lucas for four days. I slept on the plane and was somewhat revived when we disembarked into a soft cushion of heat that eased me into a sigh, saying to me, "Here. Just here." Surrounded almost immediately by vendors joyously referring to us as "Mi amigo," we bought a couple of icy beers and were on our way to the resort.

I had never stayed in any place like that before. The white of the building was blinding, and the white of the lobby was cool and delightful, and the white of the walkways in the grounds, only interrupted by the blue of the sea and the blue of the pools and the green of the vegetation and the pink of the bougainvillea, was alluring. We sat in our room, looking out over the water, our feet up on the edge of the balcony, having another beer and chatting up our resident gecko. I could have stayed right there for the four days but it was not to be. There was, after all, a pool.

This was my first experience of a swim-up bar at a pool. If I were not so prone to sun burns, skin cancer and a small bladder, I would never leave a swim-up bar. To rest on a tile seat, elbows planted on the bar and lower half of the body still in the water, while lovely people bring you margaritas and nachos, is all anyone could ask out of life. But we also had Jon Secada singing "Just Another Day" and an iguana begging us for tortilla chips. We were in the off-season, so there were very few other people at the pool, rendering us free to leave our repast on the bar while we gently floated backwards, swimming a lap or two, dunking our heads in the water, and returning to our seats.

When the wrinkles in our hands became so deep they were catching on our swimsuits, we conceded to leave the pool for short periods of time, in order to go on a sunset catamaran cruise through The Arch (El Arco) of Cabo San Lucas, in order to wander the then-undeveloped streets, in order to gorge on the shrimp feast at Pancho's, but these were brief excursions serving only to interrupt the time spent in the water.

I was hooked. Water was the curative I sought.

Another late spring, on our anniversary, we couldn't get out of town. I was again recovering from some broken leg or other ridiculous injury. I know I was recently out of a cast and still unsteady in walking. Ken plopped me into the living room and forbade me to move without permission, while he skedaddled away busily and secretively. There was a great deal of commotion, and I had trouble deciphering what the noises might be. When he was finally ready, he brought me my bathing suit and asked me to put it on. I pouted (again) about how cold it still was, but he assured me I had no cause to worry.

When he brought me to the back yard, I was amazed. He had purchased a plastic kiddie pool and set it up, filling it with warm water. A small stand and an ice chest were perched next to it, and Ken gave me a box to open up. Inside was a baseball cap reading "Raul's Pool Service" (our favorite bartender in Cabo was named Raul) which he promptly put on. Inside the ice chest was a plate of peeled shrimp and a pitcher of margaritas. Knowing I needed curing, he made me my very own swim-up bar in our backyard, and not only did I get to bask in the warm water, sipping on my margarita and nibbling on cold shrimp, but then he painted my toe nails for me while I luxuriated.

Falling in love with cruising, then, seems inevitable. We honeymooned on a cruise through the Mexican Riviera, where Ken taught me to snorkel; I still panic in the initial moments of snorkeling, certain I will inhale water rather than air through that untrustworthy tube, and can only really relax if Ken and I are holding hands; then it is one of my favorite things to do. We also raced out into the waves in Mazatlan, fully clothed, losing my sunglasses, for the sheer desire to be in the water. It was an auspicious beginning to our marriage.

We know some people find the idea of being surrounded by seemingly limitless water to be intimidating and terrifying, and we know those who get seasick even thinking of a bathtub; we are not those people. Discovering the bounty of stars in the middle of the Atlantic, with no light pollution to hide them, was a revelation, and the sense of nothing but water and the mysteries hidden within it for as far as we could see is freeing and exhilarating. Watching dolphins and whales play alongside our ship makes us long to play with them. A really good storm, one that makes the bow of the boat slam as it is lifted and then reenters the water, makes us giggle with glee, and we have been known to get on our knees on the bed in the middle of the night, watching the waves hit our window, riding as if we were on bucking broncos. (Breakfast crowds tend to be pretty scant after such nights.) Cruising has given us some of our favorite water memories.

One cruise took us to Nassau, in the Bahamas, in November. We had booked a dolphin excursion with a local company, one not sanctioned by the ship, so had some trepidation; part of the adventure is not knowing for sure just how dicey some local, unvetted companies might be, but often the pay-off is worth it. Six of us were still waiting on the dockside for our contact when about 250 people from the ship passed us by, boisterously loading onto a catamaran with a huge sign: *The Dolphin Experience*. My heart sank; I had heard mixed reviews about "swimming with the dolphins," about how you maaaaaybe got to swipe your hand on one as it swam past all 248 other people in the water, and the sight of congregations of people pushing onto the boat seemed to bear out that possibility. They sailed off, though, and we still waited.

Our contact arrived, a young woman with a clipboard who spoke little English; she pasted stickers with different colors on our jackets, and beckoned us to follow her. We were then turned over to a couple of young boys who were operating a small uncovered boat, though surely they were too young to be doing so without adult supervision. They ushered us on and we sped out of the harbor. While everyone else huddled at the back of the boat, Ken and I sat up front, figuring if we were going to be in the water anyway, why not enjoy the ride? We were soaked (see how I never learn my lessons?) when we arrived at a small island about forty-five minutes outside of Nassau.

To our surprise, the others on our excursion were not there to swim with dolphins. One other couple was supposed to join us, but decided the water was too cold, so they changed their minds. Clearly, they had never been soaked by the Irish Sea in November; this water was cool but by no means cold. Their change of plans left me, Ken, two handlers, and two dolphins in a large enclosure, for an hour. To play. To swim. To fall in love. Dixon was the less aloof of the two dolphins, and charmed me to a ridiculous level. He danced, sang, flirted, danced some more, nuzzled, kissed, danced some more, blew water on me, and showed me all his dolphin tricks. I got to pet him and hold him, and I am sure he was as smitten with me as I was with him. In fact, I told Ken I thought I should toss my address into the water so he could find me again in Oregon; Ken thought that would technically be considered littering and discouraged me from doing so. I'm pretty sure Dixon is heartbroken. As am I. It was one of several moments in my life when my facial muscles hurt from smiling so hard.

To celebrate Ken's retirement, we cruised through French Polynesia. Every day of our cruise, we told ourselves we ought to do something other than snorkel, but every day, we thought, "Nah. Why?" and donned our gear and went into the most blissfully warm and clear water I'd ever imagined. I had a lemon shark swim up and nudge my leg; though our guide had assured us they were harmless, I still puckered a bit. We did a helmet dive in Moorea, standing on the sea floor and interacting with the fish, feeding them from our mesh sacks of bread. Because Ken and I were the last ones in the water, we got to be the last ones out. I was still standing at the moment all the fish in the ocean at once realized I was the only one left still holding bread; they all turned to me, hesitated for a moment, and then "attacked." Hundreds if not thousands of brightly colored fish were lightly sucking at every part of my body in hopes I tasted like bread. I was literally being smothered with fish, and I was laughing so hard I fell down, and Ken had to help me up. The guide became alarmed until I gave him the thumbs up that I was only delighted.

In Bora Bora, we got to feed the stingrays, and the guide showed me how to invite one to come up to me. I fed her as she rested on my chest, her head just under my chin, and her velvety wings flapping around my body as if to hug me. The guide took my hand and brushed it down her body, where I could feel the babies she was carrying; it was an enchanted moment. And then, snorkeling around on our own, we got to see an octopus in full hunt mode, as it floated gently over an outcropping of coral, letting its legs drape around it, until it puffed up to make a kind of balloon around the rock, expanding to encompass it, changing colors so it seemed to be part of the coral, and then withdrawing, sucking all the fish into itself until it was sated, moving on to another coral rock. It was amazing to watch, as we floated above it in the perfect water, and a soft warm rain pelted our backs.

When I finished with my cancer treatments, Ken and I became members at the local pool, where swimming helped heal my soul and my body. Still weak, with wounds that made weight-lifting difficult, I found the soothing stretches required to swim from one end of the pool to the other helped me reconnect with my traitorous body, letting my arms find movement that eased the scarred areas and feeling the water reclaim my flesh. We continued that until our schedules no longer allowed, and I know my ideal home would have a swimming pool.

Water is divine. There is no other way to speak of it. Baptism cleanses, purifies, renews. It reminds us of our connection to an essential substance.

John, who recognized Jesus when they were both still in their mother's wombs, who is a distant cousin, baptizes Jesus, though he knows he is unworthy to do so. The water represents a renewal, a rejuvenation, the beginning of Christ's ministry on earth, and Jesus opens himself up to the ritual committing himself to God, but in doing so, he also commits to us. It is a sign of great humility. Jesus was, after all, already the Son of God. Why did he need to be baptized? For us, baptism is a proclamation of our covenant as children of God, and we are washed clean of our sin. Jesus was sinless, and while his covenant to God is obvious, undergoing baptism seals his covenant with us. The water unites us.

The fruit of the mystery of the Baptism of the Lord is gratitude for faith, and there is no moment I am in the water when I am not aware of that gratitude, when I don't feel the wonder of such a great gift. When I swim to the edge of an infinity pool, gazing out at the waters beyond Mazatlan while I paddle gently, I am aware of the divinity of the water that surrounds me. When I step out into a rain storm that clears the air of smoke from forest fires, I am aware of the divinity of the water. When I feel the splash of water from a waterfall; when I take a long draught of cold water on a hot day; when I feel the blessing of the water rite during Mass; when Roscoe dances through the sprinklers, barking and waving his flag of a tail, I am aware of the divinity of the water surrounding me. Even when it threatens to kill me, water is divine.

7

THE SECOND LUMINOUS MYSTERY:
THE WEDDING AT CANA

Jesus performs his first miracle by turning water into wine.

Weddings

THE FIRST MIRACLE JESUS performed was turning the water into wine at a wedding, when the wine was running low. I am often baffled over the choice: was wine that essential? Would the wedding not have gone on without it? Would the guests have rioted? Would they have starved? Loaves and fishes I get; wine, not so much, despite my being a big fan of wine. If you're going to do your first big miracle, why pick that one? Why not one to fulfill a genuine need, one that would make the difference between life and death?

I keep returning to Jesus' love of a party. Most of his greatest teaching moments come amidst food, wine and celebration, right up to the end of his life. In this case, he chooses to highlight his first miracle, even though "it is not yet his time," at a wedding, confirming marriage as a blessed sacrament. So I find myself thinking about weddings and parties as I pray this Mystery.

When Ken and I got married, nearly thirty years ago now, we wanted (like everyone else) to do it right. My experience providing the music for weddings for so many years taught me a long list of things to do and things not to do.

The wedding where the groom had failed to try on his tuxedo pants before the morning of the wedding taught me to make everyone try on everything long before the anticipated day: he had been given pants in a child's size, so ended up being married in a tuxedo with jeans. Watching the photographer trying to manipulate every pose so only the groom's top would be seen (and the bride's scowl was not) was memorable.

The wedding where the groom's mother, in protest at his marrying a woman of whom she disapproved, showed up late to the church, making her entry several feet behind the bride, shuffling up to the front pew in her statement-making black cotton house-dress and fluffy black slippers—all while I uncertainly continued to sing "Ave Maria"—taught me about what a family could do to a ceremony.

The wedding where the power went out just as the ceremony began, leaving us without not only the microphone but also the organ that was my only accompaniment, taught me to always have a back-up plan in case the unthinkable happens. A capella doesn't work for all musical choices.

The wedding where the couple earnestly longed to have Barry Manilow's "Looks Like We Made It" sung taught me how important it is to sit down and really hear the lyrics of a song, even if the song had been the one you first danced to: "Looks like we made it, left each other on our way to another love" may not be quite the desired inspiration for a lifetime together.

The wedding where the adorable little girl who was supposed to scatter rose petals up the aisle, but who chose instead to dance, somersault, say hello to everyone she knew and many she didn't, and then throw a screaming fit as she arrived at the altar because there were no more rose petals in her basket, taught me to avoid including people in the wedding who were going to upstage me as the bride.

The many many weddings where the couple does not think through having their favorite song serenaded to them as they stand gazing adoringly into each other's eyes, while all their family and friends watch them, taught me that if one must have such a moment, the song needs to be very short. Otherwise, it's virtually impossible to make it through without uncomfortable snickering if not outright laughter, often from the couple but nearly always from the audience.

By the time Ken and I were getting married, I knew what not to do.

The best-laid plans, you know.

It really wasn't bad. It could have been worse.

We had 325 people invited. Both of us included our siblings in the wedding party, as well as several friends and my about-to-be-stepchildren, Amanda and Aaron. (At seven and nine years old, they were less likely to spring into cartwheels down the aisle.) Fr. Michael, one of my dearest friends, married us, having taken us through our marriage preparation courses where there was far more laughter than was customary. (We used to laugh that there was no better way to kill a party than to have a priest, a cop, and an English teacher show up.) I had written the music for the Mass, and the choir I directed sang, with nearly every member we had ever had in attendance. A friend did the photography, another friend did the catering, my brother designed the invitations, another friend printed the invitations, and another friend tended bar. I made both the flower arrangements and my bridal hat, using the same pattern of lace from my dress. I knew to bring comfy shoes. We had it all figured out.

Yet another friend was driving me to church in his spruced-up vintage 1957 Chevy Bel-Air. It was beautiful. As my family and I were loading into the car, I noticed my brother's cummerbund. "It's the wrong color" I said, bleakly. The tuxedo rental store was a good forty-five minutes away. Everyone held his or her breath. My father asked what we should do. I said, "Go get married. I don't give a shit." In maybe the first time my father ever approved of my language, he laughed and said, "Perfect words. Just perfect. Let's go."

So we all piled into the car. And it wouldn't start.

There was some more language, but this time it wasn't mine, as my friend ripped off his suit jacket and began tinkering with the engine. I am not ordinarily a serene type of person, and I hate being late more than nearly anything else, but for some reason I was pretty calm, which alarmed my family, but I knew that whatever else happened, I was going to married by the end of this day, if it had to be in a garage. "It'll be fine," I kept saying. And it was, and we got to the church on time.

The ceremony went off without a hitch, though it's a dangerous thing to have one of your best friends giving the homily; he knows me just a little bit too well, and there were many jokes, but it was lovely.

The reception was wonderful. I have never understood the point of having all your nearest and dearest come to a huge party, a party you have spent months planning, a party some of them have traveled a long way to attend, so you could leave early before the party was over. So we didn't. We stayed until the end. I was dead on my feet, even in my comfy shoes, and had eaten virtually nothing; my dress was smeared with make-up from being hugged, with champagne that was spilled on me during hugs, and with footprints from people who were hugging. I had no idea where my purse was. My mother wanted to know how much I had had to drink, and I laughed because I had lost track of my champagne flute ages ago. I was purely exhausted.

As we were getting ready to go, two things occurred to us we had omitted in our plans. The first is that, having been driven together from the church to the reception, we had no plan for getting back to the church for Ken's truck. The second was we had no plans for how we were going to transport all the gifts from the reception to our home. Oops.

I don't recall how we got the gifts home, but I remember someone drove us back to the church for the truck. Late at night, still in our wedding finery, we went to knock on the rectory door. Fr. Michael came to the door in t-shirt and shorts, a highball in hand, surprised to see us. "It's your wedding night. What are you doing here?"

We laughingly told him the marriage preparation only took us through the wedding, but had not discussed the wedding night, so we were hoping for some instruction. He shooed us away.

It was great.

Seventeen years later, my parents celebrated their 50th wedding anniversary. My mother not being a terribly social person, we knew she didn't want a big party, and we kept asking her how they wanted us to commemorate the day. She finally told us she wanted us all to go dinner at the Top of the Mark, an upscale restaurant in San Francisco. Before she started dating my father, long before "dating" meant being exclusive or intimate, my mother was supposed to go on a date with some other guy to have dinner at the Top of the Mark, but Dad asked her out for the same night, and she stood the other guy up. We were horrified. Stood him up? Like, never told him you weren't coming? Like, left him at this restaurant waiting for you for hours? Like, he could still be there? Mom was chagrined, but not that much. She had liked Dad better, so she went out with him. But, lo these many years later, she had still never been to the Top of the Mark.

Game on.

Plus we wanted to see what the guy looked like, having waited there for fifty-some-odd years.

We made all the arrangements for a spectacular evening in The City, with just the family.

My older brother, Jim, is a Bohemian kind of guy, having lived his life racing bicycles, working as a freelance chef, and refusing to "work for the man." Three years before this, he had provided my parents with their first biological grandchild, Harmony. His girlfriend, Gretchen, who is much younger than he, was having some pretty significant issues with postpartum depression, and their relationship was volatile. My parents, having been initially horrified by him having a child out of wedlock, adored Harmony more than one would have thought was humanly possible. Every conversation inevitably turned to her antics, her adorableness, her brilliance. The question of her legitimacy seemingly became irrelevant.

Jim arranged for our transportation from my parents' house to San Francisco, a drive of a little more than an hour. He had a friend who ran a kind of limo company, and we hired her to take us all. She was eight-and-a-half months pregnant, so some of us questioned the wisdom of her driving us all that far, but she insisted she would be fine.

I am the second-born, about a year and a half younger than Jim. While I was, at the time, the only sibling who was married, Ken and I were hovering on the edge of divorce after I found out he had been cheating on me. I was feeling pretty bitter and cynical about the whole marriage thing.

Next in line is Mary, who has worked for years at a garden supply company. She had been living with a man eighteen years her elder (but emotionally, twenty years her junior) for a number of years. Their relationship was also volatile, and she was most often finding more company in vodka and cats than in him.

The baby of the family, Rosie, works in convention management (I have never been able to tie her down to an adequate job description so we'll just leave it at that), and has been living with her partner, Pat (as in Patricia), for many years, but had yet to come out to our parents.

So there we all were, gathered, dressed up, and ready to go.

The drive to the city was filled with the customary level of hilarity. When we got to the restaurant, we were ushered into the bar, looking out over The City, trying to behave like decent human beings and largely failing. We made the circuit of the room, looking for the guy Mom had stood up, but she couldn't remember his name, so that impeded the search. But we didn't see any moldering old men, cobweb-encrusted, mournfully watching out for her, so we had to assume he had given up at some point.

Then again, he wasn't really expecting the marauding group we were, so he may have been hiding.

We were seated in a more private (but not private enough) area, which we promptly took over. We get a bit boisterous. Everything is, when you come down to it, quite funny. Until it isn't. (Mom always used to warn us, as she gauged the level of hilarity in our voices, "Someone is going to end up crying," and she was always right.)

Dinner was lovely. Dad, ever hopeful and helpful, kept pointing out guys, asking Rosie, "What about him? He's good looking!" The rest of us just laughed and suggested all the guys Dad was suggesting were a bit young for her, muttering to each other, "Plus, they're guys."

But then we had to have speeches. Geez, whose idea was that?

We spoke about the enduring love of Mom and Dad, solid after so many years. We talked about the way they never (almost never) fought, at least not in front of us. We admired the way they clearly adored each other, holding hands and smooching and making googly eyes at each other still. We wondered at their faith in God and in each other, and the way they provided such a strong example of what a marriage ought to be, a true partnership of support and love and laughter. We blamed them for the fact that we were such slow starters in the relationship department, because none of us was willing to accept less than what they modeled for us. We reminisced about the hardships they had overcome, and about what horrible children we could be.

As we talked, my parents beamed at the head of the table, smiling at each other when they were able to take their eyes off Harmony (who was, admittedly, very cute in her finery as she pranced around the room and stole the hearts of all the patrons). It meant they were also entirely oblivious to the subtext of what was going on.

I don't remember who started it, but it may have been Mary who first pushed herself away from the table, wiping her eyes, excusing herself. I know I followed her, concerned, to the bathroom where she sobbed about how she had wasted all these years with her boyfriend who was clearly not marriage material. She would never have a 50th anniversary with him, and though they had discussed marriage off and on over the years, they had never both been of the same mindset at the same time; it was unlikely to happen now. She felt she would never experience the kind of happiness and connection our parents had.

I think I mostly held it together, but was on the edge when we returned to the table to hear more adulation of my parents. I was still raw and heartbroken over Ken's infidelity, still trying to decide whether to stay with him or not, and when the conversation turned to the unbreakable holy bonds of matrimony, I choked. Rather pointedly, my father made some comment about how the sacrament of marriage ensured long healthy relationships, and though I knew he was aiming such comments at my unmarried and seemingly uncommitted siblings, the barb found its way to my bruised heart, not as protected by the sacramental nature of marriage as I had assumed, and I too made my way to the bathroom, crying about what a crock marriage really was.

When I had mostly composed myself and was heading back to the table, I passed our chauffeur, whom we had invited to join us at dinner; she was making her sobbing path to the bathroom. I turned and followed her back. She told me she already had a twenty-one-year-old son, so she had already raised a child. But newly divorced, she went with friends to see a band one night and had sex with one of the band members; now she found herself knocked up and single, without a plan. She saw in my parents the fulfillment of everything she once thought she would have but now felt was impossible for her.

I don't know what my parents thought I was doing for so long in the bathroom. It's not like one of my many maladies was irritable bowel syndrome. They may not even have noticed because, well, Harmony. But before the driver and I had even left, Gretchen came in, crying. It was a tough night for mascara.

Gretchen and Jim had not been together for long before she had found herself pregnant. Jim offered to marry her then, but she wanted wine at her wedding and knew she couldn't drink while she was pregnant, so she agreed to marry him after the baby was born. Her depression was so great by then, though, and they were fighting so much, marriage was off the table. They were still together, but just barely, and she was having a hard time watching my parents in their happiness while she felt like her own was so elusive.

I did make it back to the table, finally. I don't think Rosie actually ended up running from the table in tears, but I remember her bitter asides to me that it must be nice to be legally able to marry the love of your life so you could one day celebrate such a milestone. (This was before gay marriage was legalized.)

So there we were, in just about every possible iteration of relationship: happy, sad, faithful, unfaithful, married, unmarried, hetero- and homosexual. We were mismatched in age, with or without children, with or without faith.

And yet as I think back on that night, what I recall most vividly is the great love we shared. Despite all our differences, we remained deeply aware of each other's situations and pain, and we reached out to heal together. Except for Mom and Dad, who were entirely oblivious to the whole drama playing out in front of them. (Also except for Harmony, but she was three, and was busy distracting them.) Even their oblivion, however, is a testament to our love, because as each of us fell apart in our own ways, we also worked hard to protect them from our heartache as they celebrated their heartbliss.

Because we are family.

A union is a frightful and wonderful thing, a miracle in itself.

At Cana, both Mother Mary and Jesus understood the power of weddings, and recognized the need to celebrate them. A marriage is sacramental because it is meant to be the closest we can get to modeling God's love—including vast amounts of forgiveness—for us on earth. So the Mother of Jesus, recognizing a need in the wedding celebration (running out of wine is much more significant than the wrong color cummerbund), knows her son can help the celebration along. Her knowledge (suspicion?) by itself is extraordinary. If this is his first miracle, what does she expect him to do? How does she know he can do anything at all? Is this a maternal desire to have her son, whom she knows is the Son of God, display his power? Have they been holding onto this secret all along? Has he been doing cool stuff for them in private before this? Could he change the color of cummerbunds? Mary chooses this moment, a moment of union and celebration, when Jesus can serve the needs and desires of the people, to encourage him to fix the situation. It is a public, visible example of what he can do, and despite rebuking his mother that it is not yet his time, he does change the water into wine. The party goes on, and the wedding is celebrated. And the ground is set for future miracles, nearly always centered in hospitality and relationship.

8

THE THIRD LUMINOUS MYSTERY:
THE PROCLAMATION OF THE KINGDOM

Jesus speaks of the Kingdom.

Place

When we were children, my two sisters and I shared a bedroom. Territory was firmly defended: sides of the room, drawers in the dresser, segments of the tiny closet, access to the windows, ingress and egress. On good days, we lived harmoniously together, sometimes even sitting on each other's beds, sometimes sharing Nancy Drew books so we could balance them on our heads to practice ladylike gliding across the floor; on bad days, hurling of encroaching toys and clothes and shoes—and even Nancy Drew books—would ensue. Once, in a rage over some forgotten slight, I stomped on what I thought was a crayon, hoping to smash its waxy color into the hard tile floor to make my point, only to discover it was the caterpillar I was trying to nurture into a butterfly, having escaped its peanut butter jar.

As we grew, the limitations of our space only rankled more.

My father, in an attempt to provide us with some sense of space and privacy, allotted us each a spot in the shed. It was a fairly large shed, roughly the size of a four-car garage. When we first moved into the house, we were delighted to discover mysterious remnants the previous owners had left behind there, including forgotten eggs laid by forgotten hens which we promptly threw onto the concrete floor (there's a smell not easily forgotten, even after all these years); including abandoned bottles of strychnine, with labels we couldn't read but with fascinating pictures of a skull and crossbones so alluring we immediately drank the contents (leading to further unforgettable consequences).

Dad got the bulk of the shed space for his work bench, tools, pot-bellied stove, riding mower, etc. (Years later, when we had all moved out, he tried to reclaim the space as his by insisting it be called "the shop" and not "the shed," but that was a comically failed attempt at—I guess—gentrification. We are not a family easily budged from tradition.) Jim, my older brother, got the back corner, and built a wall for himself made of bicycle parts and random bits he could tinker with. It was his own kind of workshop and smelled strongly of the oil he would squeeze from the copper pink oil can onto a bicycle chain. Mary and Rosie, so much better at sharing than I ever was, opted to combine their space and made a kind of Susie Homemaker's dream: a pretend kitchen with banged up pots and chipped crockery, and a real (but not working) old kitchen stove. My spot became my library. I had a ratty old rocking chair, covered with an old blanket, and shelves made out of overturned wooden crates and loaded with books, any books. Anyone who knows us now would see patterns set for each of us which would never change.

We were more open to sharing our shed spaces than we were our bedroom spaces, maybe because we didn't *have* to share the shed space and so were afforded complete ownership, including access and decorative choices. No compromising was required of us. These places were, by all important measures, our kingdoms. We were in charge, and so these kingdoms asserted something about who we were and what we valued.

I remember finding a box of books among the castoff items in the shed, and delving into them, I was sure they were some kind of contraband, or why else would they be in the shed? So I devoured them, secretly. My favorite was Henry Wadsworth Longfellow: reading the poetry was purely spellbinding, and even as I couldn't guess at the meanings of the words, I could love the sounds. I had no idea what a Hiawatha was, and puzzled over whether Endymion was pronounced "En-dee" or "En-dye," searching for clues in the rest of the poem. (At least Lord Byron tells us Don Juan rhymes with "true one" rather than "John.") I knew for sure that any poem that begins, "Listen, my children, and you shall hear," is directed at me, a child. I was thus welcomed into private kingdoms in both the words and the stories of the poems, finding a kind of holiness in the pure sound of language. Dr. Seuss knows what I'm talking about. So, in fact, did my father, who regularly went about reciting, "In Xanadu did Kubla Kan a stately pleasure-dome decree," the beginning of a dream poem even Coleridge, the author, didn't understand.

The shed was our safe haven. On any rainy day, especially, when the house felt like it had shrunk, our mother would urge us to go the shed so she could clean or make dinner or, indeed, watch her "programs" in peace, and we would all troop down the yard to our places. On the truly magical days, Dad would build a fire in the pot-bellied cast iron stove, using the fragrant apple wood from our Gravenstein apple trees, and make us hot chocolate in the blue tin saucepan. We would then retreat to our respective corners in bliss. On a really perfect day, the dog would pick me to hang out with, settling on my feet as I read.

There were other parts of the property that might serve as escape. I read *The Call of the Wild* while sitting in an apple tree, spying on those below me, eating the unripe apples until I was sick. I believed I had made friends with a hive of honeybees outside my bedroom window until one of them perfidiously stung me. For a time, we had a large weeping willow in the middle of the property, under which we would play, until the septic system sprang a leak in that very spot, making it highly pungent and slimy. But none of these spots could we claim as ours alone, not like our spots in the shed.

On the day I turned sixteen, we were well on the way to adding on two bedrooms and another bath to the house. One bedroom would go to my brother, whose room up until then was really a sun porch off the kitchen; in order to access the back door, we had to tromp through his room, and since no one ever used the front door unless it was one of my dad's clients or some complete ignoramus of a stranger, there was a lot of tromping.

The other bedroom would be mine.

The addition still had only plywood flooring, and we had just blown in the texturing on the walls; the smell had not yet dissipated. I had spent the day frantically painting my room a baby blue with white trim. The electricity was not yet hooked up, and there were no curtains or doors. I didn't care. I dragged my bed in, hooked up an extension cord for a lamp and my clock-radio, and I was set to go. It was the best birthday present ever. (Well, I also got my own guitar that year, so there was a lot of joyful weeping. I was a blubbering mess, covered with paint and sweat and grime, when my brother brought home the guy I had a crush on, thinking he would set us up. First impressions count. I never spoke to him again.) (Okay, now I have to defend my brother. It was also the year he gave me my first Jackson Browne album for my birthday present, beginning my lifelong obsession with Jackson Browne's music, so it really was a pretty great birthday.)

I loved my new bedroom; it was truly a kingdom, with walls and at least a doorway with a sheet hung over it to serve as my moat. I could go shut myself in, away from everyone else, and people could only enter with my permission. Because I had been working odd jobs since I was eleven, I had my own money, and so I put in my very own phone line, with my baby-blue Princess phone. I could lie on my bed and talk until I fell asleep. I had a used phonograph player, where I would listen to the Bee Gees, Neil Diamond, and Chopin, endlessly. It took a while before my parents figured out that sending me to my room or, even better, grounding me was no punishment at all. I had books, music, phone, and bed. What more could a girl want?

The desire for my own kingdom has haunted me throughout my life. After I moved out, I had a succession of roommates, to varying success. Stuart routinely stole books from my room and when I called him on it, became furious and hurled the books at my head, still swearing they belonged to him. (I took this as an admission of guilt; who would ever throw his or her own book?) John and Cheryl, having assigned each of us an inviolate shelf in the refrigerator, frequently stole things from my shelf when I could ill afford to lose my small rations; they even invited me to partake in Cheryl's birthday cake, and then charged me for my share of it. Cathie alone was the perfect roommate; we cooked together, trampolined together, even worked together.

Dennis—oh, Dennis. Dennis could get his own chapter. Dennis was a psychologist who placed an ad at my college seeking a roommate in his brand new house. He took "thrifty" to whole new levels. He did not own a vacuum cleaner, so would scrape up the blue residue of the new carpet and try to make pillows with it. His furniture consisted of a few pieces of wood sawn together with uncovered foam rubber on it; he had carefully and inexplicably written in red felt pen which was the top of the foam rubber pad and which was the bottom. He stored plastic bags in the pantry, hundreds and hundreds of plastic bags, nothing more. He recycled Scotch tape on the refrigerator, and had no dishes other than used yogurt cups. He refused to pay for garbage service so would gather what he had and take it to the nearby hotel's trash bins.

To be clear, Dennis was not poor. We were in a brand new house in a new subdivision in a nice neighborhood. He had a television in every room in the house, including the bathrooms, and had them all on, all the time, each on a different channel; the cacophony was unbearable. Nor was he a scrupulous recycler, taking nearly new, perfectly usable items to the hotel bins.

One day, he determined I was late coming home from my classes and decided to feed my cats, so he put a partially cooked whole chicken in the middle of the kitchen floor, oozing grease across the tile. When I got home, the cats were still warily circling it, knowing something was not right, and he was mewing at them that this would be their dinner. Fortunately, living in the brand new house with Dennis was how I learned about my allergy to formaldehyde, which is used to treat wood in newer houses; when I began regularly vomiting blood, I had a good reason to break the lease.

I decided it was time for my own space, and got a cheap apartment in an undesirable location. I loved it. My clearest memory was the first time I made myself some tuna salad, and put the remainder in the refrigerator; I was genuinely shocked to find it still there, in the very same place, when I returned home from work later that day. Nothing like this had ever happened to me. I stood at the door, smiling to myself, knowing I was going to like having my own kingdom.

With a little more money in my pocket and a lot more crime in the neighborhood, I moved to a better apartment, and then an even better one. Every time, there was great joy in making the space my own. My first home with Ken was perfectly hideous, in retrospect, and we loved it. The orange shag carpet, the blue linoleum, the avocado green appliances (when the fridge died, our landlord sought high and low for another green one but sadly had to settle on white, to our delight) all made quite a picture. The landlord, who lived next door, raised bees and his wife made baklava with the honey, sharing it with us; what's not to like?

Then we moved to a very small house, 625 square feet, which had been previously occupied by a friend of ours, a bachelor who loved to hunt. We spent a sizeable amount of time scraping dried, congealed, greasy blood from the backsplash behind the stove, from the bottom of the freezer, from the walls of the refrigerator, from the floors. But that house, too, we made our own. I still miss the bright purple bougainvillea that spilled over the west side of the house, so when the sun was just right, it looked like we had stained glass windows.

With each space, I felt my kingdom grow more expansive, not just because it was larger, but because I felt more secure in it. When we bought our first home, a 1922 Craftsman, we were in bliss. We had many, many parties there, for holidays and birthdays, graduations and funerals, divorces, and any kind of momentous occasion. We loved to decorate it and to share it, to fill it with people we cherished. We painted, refinished floors, replaced windows and plumbing, but always kept its quirkiness.

When I accepted my job at a university, Ken was still five years from retiring. Amanda was about to be married, and Aaron entered the Air Force for a six year stint. I moved to Oregon more or less by myself; Ken commuted back and forth to California, but the house was "mine." Having spent all our lives in California, with all our family and friends still there, we had a hard time envisioning an actual life in Oregon, so we told ourselves I would just be there to work, and would return "home" during school breaks. It took less than a year to feel at home in Oregon, and to desire less and less time in California. There were so many things to do in Oregon, more places to explore, and greater accessibility to those places. There was less traffic, less pollution, and less stress. No one ever flipped us off in Oregon, or tried to run us off the road. It was such a delightful change.

While the house was "mine" most of the time, Ken still came every few days, and I had to share, a mixed blessing. But my office! At work, my space was my very own, and I was back to having everything where I would leave it. It was by far the coziest space on campus, with sage green walls and white wall-to-wall bookcases, and books. I was surrounded by books, all organized according to the plan in my head. I had two dilapidated red leather wingback chairs from St. Vincent de Paul and a rocking chair, a small refrigerator and a tea kettle. There were theater posters covering the walls, maps of Ireland, fairies everywhere, artwork from students, and paraphernalia gifted to me by those who knew my love for Jackson Browne, Virginia Woolf, and Johnny Depp. I even had a life-sized cardboard cutout of Captain Jack Sparrow, donated by a student. In my closet, I had stashes of Earl Grey and Good Earth tea, oatmeal, and protein bars. In my desk, I had the requisite gradebooks and sheaves of paper, but I also had my supply of rosaries, my aromatherapy oils, and my snarky "Bullshit" button that I could press whenever I needed a private moment. I had small totems: my St. Brigid's cross, my wooden turtle from Guatemala for luck, my Greek evil eye, my stone from Iona; I never had the nerve to bring in my Sheila-na-gig, so I left that at my home office.

I had probably been in my office for three years when one day I realized I had basically recreated my space in the shed. Rocking chairs, books, blankets, slippers, tea, even, on occasion, my dog at my feet: all I was missing was the wood-burning stove. It felt like destiny. No wonder I loved it so much.

So these have been my kingdoms, all of which I have loved. For the last year, for a variety of reasons, I have had to let most of these spaces go. Ken's parents both died within a short time of each other, and we had to say goodbye to their home, where we celebrated many events, almost always with the "happy birthday machine," created when we taped balloons to the ceiling fan and turned it on. (Less than a month after their house sold, we heard from a neighbor about a fire in the house, begun when the new owners tried to rewire the electricity to start a marijuana grow. We don't even have the soul's ease of knowing another family is making memories in the house.)

At nearly the same time, we lost the tenant in our Craftsman and decided to sell that house, after having found it trashed. Seeing it in such terrible condition and then selling it was far more emotional than I had anticipated; memories of a life spent, of children raised in that space were overwhelming.

My mother is still alive and living in the same house where I was raised, but my brother lives there now as well, and it is nothing like the home I remember, leaving me with a different kind of sadness.

Finally, because of budget cuts due to the COVID-19 pandemic, I have retired early from my job, and have lost my office. Cleaning it out meant, for me, abdicating my kingdom.

The fruit of this Third Luminous Mystery is supposed to be a desire for holiness as we ponder the ways God's kingdom is proclaimed. What is a kingdom, after all? Is it only a place where you get to be the boss, to exert control over your surroundings, to make all the rules? Is it a place where you get to dictate who gets in and who stays out? Is it a place of welcome and hospitality and entertaining? Or is it a place of refuge and retreat and calling, "Olly Olly Oxen Free"? Is it a place to be held lightly or clung to fiercely, defended against all intruders?

For me, all these things have been true about my kingdoms, but I also think of God's kingdom, and our longing for it, as desire for wholeness, for belonging. I have been attached, probably too attached, to my spaces and my things, for most of my life. As I write, I am still effectively quarantined to my space, to our home in Oregon, with my husband and our two cats and our dog, Roscoe (who thinks quarantine is the best thing that ever happened in the whole history of the universe, so much better than a snow day or two). We have found great consolation in that space, and have had the time to complete many projects we never had time for before, but we have also found ourselves needing less and less, divesting ourselves of many nonessential things that have previously occupied our kingdom. I have my own office, where I am again surrounded by books, with a rocking chair, and good light, though I have to go all the way to the kitchen for my tea. My dog is almost always at my feet, and these days, my feet are almost always in slippers. But in combining my office at work with my office at home, I had to get rid of nearly a thousand books. For the first time in my life, I am growing more at ease with letting things go, and with resting in a sense of holiness and wholeness that has always eluded me. As Longfellow reminds us, in "Song":

> Stay, stay at home, my heart, and rest;
> Home-keeping hearts are happiest,
> For those that wander and they know not where
> Are full of trouble and full of care;
> To stay at home is best.

Being grounded/quarantined, after all, is not the torture it might be, as long as I still have books, where the kingdom of God is proclaimed in so many ways.

9

THE FOURTH LUMINOUS MYSTERY:
THE TRANSFIGURATION

Jesus is surrounded by a white light on the mountaintop.

Death

ONE NIGHT, I DREAMED I was with Jesus, Peter, James and John at the Transfiguration. This was not my usual run-of-the-mill gruesome nightmare which typically occupies my sleeping hours, but a very vivid and real dream, in which I lived out a story I had never really spent much time considering. The five of us walked up a stony path to the top of the mountain; I was winded, as I would be in real life, and the others were pretty chipper in their hike, only one of many reasons I wondered even in my dream how I ended up hanging out with these fit guys. We were all talking and laughing, and it felt very natural. I did not magically become a "Biblical" person—in my jejune mind, someone wearing flowing but mildly dirty robes, funky sandals, and speaking in a language that would be stilted even in the original, someone with perhaps a hint of a halo glowing just above, with no sign of snideness about them at all—but I was myself.

When we reached a clearing at the top of the mountain, we were astonished by the view spreading below us, and while I was still trying to catch my breath, an amazing white light suddenly suffused everything. It was not a white I had ever seen before, and Jesus was even whiter than everything else, glowing from within, but not at all supernatural. I responded as I'm sure I would in real life, saying inane, inadequate and inappropriate things like, "Holy shit! What is happening?? This is sooooo awesome!" Peter, James, John and I stood a little bit back, intimidated (okay, terrified), but trusting in Jesus, because he didn't seem at all alarmed (even, I must note, by my language). I suspected, in my dream, he knew all along this stupendous thing was going to happen, and I was a little peeved he hadn't warned us. He acted so natural all the way up the hill. I know he was talking to someone, but I was still confused, unable to see through the glare of the light, until I heard a stunning voice from the sky announcing, "This is my Son, in whom I am well pleased. Listen to him."

Had you asked me, outside of the dream, to recount what exactly God had said during the Transfiguration, I am not sure I could have, but there it was, in my dream. The voice was loud, soothing, permeating, ubiquitous, but not booming or terrifying (in case you wondered what God sounds like). We exchanged looks of amazement with each other, still not entirely sure whether we should be frightened, and we murmured about how cool it all was, Jesus still acting like it was no big deal.

When the light had dissipated, as we stood there with our senses obliterated, then the real moment happened, the moment which strained my credulity: Jesus told us to tell no one. I laughed, thinking he was kidding. (Jesus is quite the kidder in my imagination.) He repeated it. As it dawned on me that he was serious, and that this was yet another of my hallmark times I laughed just a moment before I realized I shouldn't have, I told him there was no way I could keep a story like this secret, and didn't see the point of it anyway; people would *love* this story! It would make even more people turn to him! The PR glitz would be spectacular! He insisted. I argued.

Such has been the pattern of my life.

When I woke up, I continued to be amazed. My big epiphany, after my very realistic dream, was that the things taking place in the Bible, as unreal and improbable as they seem in their very storybook familiarity, happened to real people. People like me. People who would have responded by saying things equally inane and inadequate, maybe even inappropriate, with words which clearly didn't get recorded. There is no way those guys didn't argue with Jesus about having to keep the story a secret. If they had succeeded in keeping the secret, we would not know of the event now; if I had succeeded, I would not be telling you about my dream.

In thinking deeply about the reality of biblical events, events recounted often enough for me to internalize the story without even realizing it, I came to understand anything can happen, to anyone. We could be walking along with Jesus, laughing and joking, a little breathless because wow, he is a much better walker than I am, and suddenly, there may be some astonishing light and we could hear the voice of God.

Or, your dad could die.

My father was a vibrant, active, funny man, certainly not an old man approaching death. He had given us health scares over the years: his kidneys failed him when I was about eight, too young to understand the severity of the problem. Being Irish and being outdoors a lot, he had skin cancer in all its manifestations over the years, and we would laugh uproariously when anyone asked if he had any visible scars. His most visible scar had occurred before I knew him, when he was mixing nitroglycerine as a boy and lit his chest on fire; the resulting skin grafts gave him an interesting and textured chest we used to run our fingers across when we were children, sometimes driving our Hot Wheels through the contours of his scars. It was fascinating and provocative and quite normal to us; I was actually repulsed the first time I saw a strange man's smooth chest sans scars. It was kind of disgusting and really boring.

When Dad got melanoma on his head, he had to have surgery rather than the usual in-office zapping he underwent regularly; the resulting crater in his head was impressive, but he generally wore a hat. When, however, he banged his head into an apple tree while mowing the grass, the thin membrane of skin covering his skull separated and refused to heal. He had to have his scalp reconstructed in order to cover the part of his skull which had begun to deteriorate from exposure. As the doctors were considering a plan of action, we came up with all kinds of helpful suggestions. He had little viable skin with which to graft such a large part of his scalp, so we suggested they take it from his rear end, so we could legitimately call him "Butthead." Or we thought a metal plate to cover his skull would be an option, and then we could decorate his head with magnets to celebrate various holidays, or to help him remember things, so much better than Post-It notes. Regrettably, the doctors did not take our suggestions, patching a quilt of skin from around his body. His surgery was a success, although the scarring was somewhat gruesome, and for a while it looked like he had a hot cross bun sewed to his head. But we had plans for his Halloween costume, for sure.

Shortly after he finished the treatments for his head, and shortly after my mother had finished her treatments for lung cancer, we were all exultant when at last, neither he nor my mother had any upcoming medical procedures or even doctor's appointments for a while. They decided to come visit Ken and me in Oregon, in time for Oktoberfest at Mt. Angel. It was autumn, and the tomatoes were perfect from the garden, fragrant and plump as I brought armfuls in; apples were crisp, and I made apple pies. But Dad was experiencing some chest pain, and the doctors said it was GERD, warning him to stay away from acidic foods, so he abstained from much of what he loved to eat and nearly everything I was making. We were concerned about him; he had so much trouble sleeping he would sit up in an easy chair all night, trying to nap, but he refused to go see a doctor, preferring to wait until he got home. He did call his doctor from our house, which perhaps should have been a clue to us that something was terribly amiss, since he ordinarily forestalled doctors whenever at all possible.

At the end of their visit, I tried to get Dad to let me drive them back to California—my mother didn't learn to drive until she was fifty-five years old, and was still not comfortable for such long distances—but he refused that as well. I tried to insist, but that was not always a workable option with my father, and I failed. He did call his doctor again, and she suggested he hook himself up to a blood pressure cuff and monitor that while he drove; he did so, and got home safely.

According to my mother, when they arrived at home, he lugged in the suitcases, dropped them in the kitchen, and went to the phone to call his doctor—another clue. The doctor had him come in right away, and she set him up for some tests the next morning. Within hours of his arrival at home, he had been admitted to the hospital, waiting for a triple heart bypass.

My family is not noted for its compassionate bedside manner. The more terrifying something is, the funnier we get about it. Certainly we are irreverent, but more than that, we see the absurdity in everything, and medical disasters abound in absurdity. We are also subject to a kind of ridiculous optimism: we just can't believe things are going to be more than a blip of horror in our existence. We have survived much. But the unspeakable, the unimaginable, the irreversible, had not happened to us. We might cry for a bit, knowing our fear, but we would rarely discuss the fear until it was over, when everyone was safe, when we would cry for joy. (I sobbed with relief when my mother didn't need to have chemo for her lung cancer, for example.)

Mostly, we make jokes. When my sister Rosie was having a hysterectomy because of fibroid tumors, we waited in the lobby en masse (we do like to bring an entourage), where a lovely woman was playing on a harp; but when she began to play a soothing version of "Stairway to Heaven," we nearly wet ourselves laughing about the possibility of waking up from surgery to hear that song being played on a harp, of all things!

So there we were, communing in my father's hospital room. It was late September, and the weather was still warm, with the leaves beginning to fall, and the evenings were beginning to get crisper. Inside, we were a bit crowded. Dad was not a happy camper. Because he had smoked since he was fourteen years old, he had to stay longer in the hospital, weaning himself from the cigarettes, so his system could try to recover just a little from all the abuse before the operation could occur. Cranky cranky cranky. Perhaps adding to his crankiness was the amount of time my mother and sisters had to go outside for smoke breaks without him, returning smelling like that oxymoronic combination of smoke and fresh air. We brought him food (fresh garden tomatoes, which he now knew he could eat) and Word Search books and stupid stuff, like the stuffed animal that played "La Bamba" every time someone touched it. We watched television, but mostly we sat around and teased him and each other.

At no point did it occur to us he might actually die. His best friend had already survived a couple of much worse bypass surgeries, and he was fine, more or less. The doctors were not worried, though they didn't like the condition of his lungs and veins. We behaved as though it were a party. A stressful party, but a party nonetheless. I wouldn't say we were relaxed, because of course we worried about how his recovery might go, and how his life might change after this, and how we were all going to keep him off the cigarettes from then on, but we didn't think he was going to die. Not from this.

The surgery itself went fine. The doctors didn't expect him to wake up for at least 24 hours, but at the end of his surgery day, he sat up and opened his beautiful blue eyes and laughed at us all as we exhaled huge sighs of relief and hugged him tentatively, trying to avoid all the tubes and bandages.

Ken and I were staying with my mother, and at 2:30 in the morning, she woke us up to say the hospital had called; Dad was back in surgery.

She knew very little about why, but we were all making a beeline for the hospital from our various places. The six of us spent all night in the waiting room, for the first time genuinely terrified the worst could actually happen. To us. To him. To us.

We cried. We prayed. We all brought rosaries, even those of us who no longer went to church. We didn't laugh very much at all (also for the first time). We hugged each other. We sat in silence. Finally, the weary doctor came in and announced they had saved him. His nurse—an amazing woman for whom I still pray—had noticed his tubes filling with blood, and within minutes they had him in the operating room, opened up, pumping impossible quantities of blood out of his chest. The wall of his aorta had exploded (I guess I mean ruptured, but they said "exploded") in a place other than the surgical site, due to the increased pressure of his blood and the poor state of his veins. There were heroics, but they got him through. He would, however, be unconscious for some time.

We had dodged the disaster yet again. I now realize underneath my fear was a sense of being invincible. Nothing in life would justify that feeling, except I had not had to endure losing a parent or sibling. I had lost my sister-in-law only the year before, to melanoma, which was very difficult, but she had not been an essential part of my life from the moment I was born as my father had been. She was not core to my being. The level of unthinkability was not the same. So I was not terribly surprised my father had pulled through, though I was tremendously relieved.

We went home. We slept. We cried tears of joy. We spent much time over the next days at the hospital. He kept crashing, and they had to shock his heart back into its proper rhythm a number of times, but each time worked, confirming us in our optimism. He was unconscious for five days, and very confused when he woke up, but we resumed our usual level of teasing him.

The first few days were difficult, as he had no idea how much time had passed or what had happened. We teased Mom that she should wear a lower-cut blouse to wake him up, and at one point, when she leaned over him, he looked over at her, winked, and put his hand down her top, bobbling her breasts; we howled, not least of all because she actually let him.

We reported on the progress of the 49ers, finally playing some good football for the first time in several years. We commented on his new zipper scars and on his tubes, on his bruises and on his fashionable hospital gown. We sat with him, took Communion with him when the priest visited, watched football with him on the worst little portable screen ever (that my brother kept hogging), and gave each other worried looks.

I got a new haircut one afternoon, and when I came in, he told me I looked like a "perambulating haystack," to the delight of my family and the nurses, who were impressed with his ability to come up with such vocabulary in his condition.

We tried to get him to blow into his Devil Device (as he called it) so he could get his lungs working properly. When he couldn't seem to turn his head all the way to the right, I sat on his right side to try to get him to look at me, and he announced to the nurse that she should "tell that bitch to shut up." Since my father rarely cursed, I was pretty amused. Mostly.

He thought he was in prison for something, and he apologized to his brother (who was still in Ohio) for some unknown sin committed in his childhood.

Sleep eluded him, until finally, after several days, he had fallen into a restless sleep, from which he was awoken by a male nurse who had ignored the sign forbidding waking him up; in his confusion and frustration, my father threw the pacemaker at the nurse, hitting him above the eye in a wound requiring stitches. This was not our father, but having endured the personality changes that came with my mother's post-anesthetic recovery, we were prepared to be entertained by what Dad was going to be doing. Another blip of horror, soon to dissipate when the drugs left his system. We would have more good stories for the holidays to go with the one of my mother furiously pinching an imaginary something between her fingers and shrieking, "There's *popcorn* in my sheets!"

He began to get better, gradually. He was growing more lucid, albeit with moments of relapse, such as the evening Mom, my sister Mary and I were visiting. He told us he and his nurse were busy writing the obituary for him and my mom. Mom laughingly asked if there was something he knew that she didn't, and he seemed puzzled. He continued to compose the obituary, saying he and Mom had been married in 1984; since we had celebrated their 50th wedding anniversary three years before, Mary and I teased him about wanting a refund on the party we threw for them, and wondered why we didn't get invited to the wedding, since we were all well into adulthood by then. He asked whether the mortuary director was the same man he had known, and Mom told him the mortuary had been sold some time ago, but it didn't matter, because he wouldn't need one.

These are things we should have listened to more carefully. But we didn't believe him, attributing his comments to his confusion, sleeplessness, and the drugs, so we teased him. We told him there were so many people praying for him he could never die, to which he groaned and said, "Oh, please, I hope that's not true!" Another clue.

Ken and I had a grand European/Holy Land cruise planned for the middle of the month, and we were rapidly approaching that date. I was beginning to get nervous, as there were a number of things we had to do to get ready, but I didn't want to return to Oregon until he went home from the hospital. It certainly never occurred to us to cancel the trip, because he was going to be fine, even if it was taking longer than we had anticipated. It was clear he was going to need considerable follow-up after his surgery, including dialysis, since the trauma to his body had a number of effects, but he was improving. The doctors expected him to go home after the weekend, and he convinced me he was going to be fine. I said good-bye to him on Thursday afternoon, telling him I would see him at Christmas, and promised I would call when I got home. We left.

I called on Friday, and he was doing well. I called again on Saturday, and he was more lucid than I had heard him yet. He was buoyant, chatting about going home on Monday, and then he said, "You have a great time in Europe!" I laughed and said, "I'm not leaving for six more days! You have time to tell me that later!" He said, "I know, but no matter what happens, you don't let anything get in the way of this. It's the trip of a lifetime, and you just have a great time." I laughingly told him he was full of shit, and said I loved him and would talk to him tomorrow.

Those were my last words to him. He died in the middle of the night.

One would think I would have been prepared for his death, with all the clues he was dropping, and since he came so close those other times. I was not. The very fact of how close he had come before allowed me to maintain hope and a deep belief in his invincibility. I couldn't lose my father. I couldn't. I still feel the same way. I can't lose him. I pick up the phone to text him during pretty much every 49er game. I hear his voice saying apt things like, "It is what it is," and "You go with what you got," and "When all else fails, punt." I relive the moment he told me, when he came to see us in Oregon, how proud he was of me, and of how I had survived things that would kill an elephant, and done it with aplomb, and he was delighted to call me his daughter. He did not compliment often or easily, and I treasure this one moment. I can't help but wonder if he knew even then this would be our last private conversation, alone in the backyard before everyone else got up, over coffee and Word Search puzzles. Another clue.

The Transfiguration should also have been a clue to the disciples and, since I was "there," to me. The Bible tells us the story of the Transfiguration could only be recounted after Jesus had risen from the dead, another dictum that must have startled his friends since they didn't know rising from the dead was coming. What does he mean, "risen from the dead"? Is that some kind of euphemism for something? (So I imagined them thinking, as I thought in my dream.) Seeing Jesus all lit up, hearing the voice of God, they should have recognized the clue about the extraordinary things they would witness in the very near future. But did they? Were they able to go on living in a state of denial only afforded to those of us with a firm grasp on what we think reality should be? Did they think he was confused? Sleepless?

My dream of the Transfiguration and my father's death both reveal, stunningly and forever, the reality, the possibility of things that otherwise seem so disconnected and unimaginable from our daily existence. I'm still arguing with Jesus over whether keeping the transfiguration secret was the best plan, or whether letting my father go too soon was the best plan. But my father was himself transfigured, and I know he is cloaked in the same light I saw in my dream, and I can rest assured God is "well pleased" with him.

This story has a postscript. Several months after my father died, the 49ers made it into the Superbowl for the first time in many years. I rejoiced, but grieved the loss of sharing my joy with Dad. I was still more upset when I learned my husband, who had recently joined a group of friends who watched Monday Night Football together, would be gone for the whole weekend; this same group, long established, went out to the coast every year and had a crab and football feast. Wives were not invited.

I couldn't believe it. The 49ers in the Superbowl, and my football buddies abandoned me for the event.

I invited a friend over, someone who could be trusted not to want to defile the game with conversation, and we made snacks and donned our 49er gear. I placed a large portrait of Dad in the room, set so he could watch the game and we could maintain our usual running commentary (at least it wasn't Joe Buck announcing).

The half-time show was Beyoncé, scantily-clad, shaking her booty across the stage: not exactly my father's cup of tea. At one point I glanced over at his portrait and said, "Sorry, Dad, I know you hate this, but you're in a better position than I to make it stop." My friend laughed.

A short time later, the power went out. The broadcast was silent; the arena was plunged into darkness. It took a moment for us to realize why the broadcast had stopped, but when we did, we gaped at each other. While the news later said there was an electrical surge shutting off the power to the stadium (though not before the half-time show was over), we know what "really" happened. I like to believe Dad had something to do with it, though I would have preferred he used his newfound powers to let the 49ers win. Still, the contrast of the white light of the Transfiguration and the utter darkness of the Superbowl was nicely played. For real.

10

THE FIFTH LUMINOUS MYSTERY:
THE INSTITUTION OF THE EUCHARIST

*At the Last Supper, Jesus offers the sacrifice
of his body and blood.*

Food

JESUS LOVED HIMSELF A good party, centering most of his teaching around food and drink, and the party where he offered the sacrifice of his body and blood was only the culmination of a lifetime of using food to reach us. The reality of the Last Supper was brought home to me when Ken and I were in Jerusalem, shortly after my father's death. We were standing on the hill looking over the blazing gold city and thinking about the final journey Jesus took that we recognize as the Triduum, the days of Easter that include the Last Supper and the washing of the feet, the night in Gethsemane, the crucifixion, and the culmination of the Resurrection. It's never been clear to me how many of the details of his death Jesus was aware of in advance, but he could anticipate the pain to come. To face such dread by throwing a party seems to me the ultimate in courage. To do so with bread and wine, the two most alive substances we can put into our bodies, is sheer love. Take and eat; take and drink; remember me. Don't remember me because of the death of this cow or fish before you (no one talks about what they had for dinner, so I'm just guessing), or because of the vegetables which wilt depressively as they cook, but remember me in these things that grow and live because of the fruit of your labor and be reminded of life. It is the ultimate offering.

As I stood among the olive trees above Jerusalem, wilting depressively in the heat myself, I ruminated about the way food has formed covenants for me throughout my life. A friend of mine once had a conversation with someone who proudly claimed food was so unimportant to him he could not recall a single meal of his life. We laughed and laughed, and then grew sad over the tragedy of such a life. To not remember?

I write this nearly a year into quarantine from COVID-19. We have been unable to travel in all that time, and the frustration grows and grows, so while Ken and I have learned to re-create a number of our favorite meals from restaurants we cannot visit, we have also taken to each choosing one meal, from all our years of traveling, to remember every day. It has been delightful and challenging, and has opened the floodgates of food memories.

One meal in particular, from childhood, remains a shared drooling memory for all four of us children; Ken just gets to hear about it a lot. We had just slaughtered, plucked, and fried one of our own chickens, as fresh from farm to fork as is possible, long before farm to fork was a movement. Mom had made biscuits, slathered with butter and honey that dripped down our chins relentlessly in defiance of any napkins or fingers. Fresh tomatoes and corn on the cob from our garden were at their peak in flavor. And her apple pie, made from the Gravenstein apples on our property, a true gift from nature and from her, perfected the experience. We had all contributed, taking care of and helping butcher and pluck the chickens, planting and weeding the garden, gathering the apples, so we could partake. I was maybe twelve, but vividly recall the bliss of every bite, and the sense of the work and time involved in preparing such an oblation.

Peaches trigger another childhood memory. I had a newspaper route that had me up very early on Sunday mornings to fold, pack, and deliver the papers before 7:00 a.m. so people could read their papers before church. Those papers were heaviest on Sundays, with all the additional ads, the colored funny pages, the entertainment section, and the expanded sports section. For too much of the year, those hours were a slog, often in the dark and the rain, with me trying to untangle the plastic bags from my canvas carrier to sling them onto porches without damaging anything. In the summer, though, I would get home just as the day was warming up, and before the rest of my family had arisen. I would go down the yard and pick one perfect peach, gently cupping it with both hands to ensure it was the right one, and I would bring it in its coolness to the steps of the back porch. I would let the saliva gather in my mouth, prolonging the moment of pure sweetness, examining the perfect spot to begin, before taking that first bite. It was always cool on the outside, still with a bit of morning dew, but with residual warmth inside from yesterday's heat. Slurping the juice, I couldn't capture it all, so I had to lean far over so what I couldn't save would drop into the dirt rather than on me, and invariably, the ants knew immediately and rushed to share my meal. It was a strange sort of secret communion, but communion it was, so quiet in the morning.

Food was certainly connected to family, marking birthdays, holidays, and other celebrations, and I was perfectly happy noshing my way through my mother's repertoir of meals (with some exceptions: if the reliable response to having goulash is to have all four of your children burst into tears, why would you ever make it again?). We rarely went out, and still more rarely did we entertain, so my induction into the world of "foreign" foods came relatively late.

One of my best friends in third grade was Katy, who was half Mexican and half Portugese. When she invited me for a sleep-over, I was thrilled. Her house was exotic, because it had stairs; no one I knew had two stories in their houses. We sat up too late, listening to John Denver in her room; she had her very own record player, too! In the morning, her mother served us scrambled eggs, never my favorite, but on the table was a bowl of salsa, a food I had never encountered before. I distinctly recall my first taste, and the wonder with which I asked, "What *is* this??" I had only ever had ketchup on my eggs, and hated it. But this! This food from heaven! I have never been the same since, and still prefer a ratio of two-thirds salsa to one-third scrambled eggs.

At home, my mother was never a fan of sharing the kitchen, so we did little cooking growing up, other than licking the beaters when she was baking (that's part of cooking, right?) and doing the dishes. When we moved out, then, we each became very experimental in our cooking; my brother even became a freelance chef. From move to move, boyfriend to boyfriend, roommate to roommate, I learned more and more about food and cooking. Especially when money was tight, the creation of a meal was the most loving thing I could do for others.

And money was tight. Contrary to a popular political narrative equating poverty and shiftlessness, it is possible to work five jobs, simultaneously, and go to school more than full-time, and still find one-self incredibly poor. At one point, for about eight months, I made $435 a month, and my rent was $400. At the same time, I fought off various illnesses and injuries, and attempted to stay ahead of bills incurred while ill. If it had not been for one of my bosses who grew too many tomatoes and zucchini, along with another boss who had a superfluous supply of duck eggs, I would have subsisted solely on Top Ramen. It never occurred to me, however, to consider myself a charity case; I believed in the fallacy that if one worked hard enough, life would resolve itself into something like success. I was simply paying my dues.

It didn't take long to recognize the unsustainability of either my schedule or my finances.

When my car tire developed a slow leak, I despaired. I would have to find the money for a new tire so I could continue racing from job to job and then from class to class, and though I was trying to scrape together some cash, the month—and my pay period—was barely halfway through. The outlook was bleak.

Since most of my friends were, like me, broker than broke, when a friend got married, she asked for no gifts, but for guests to bring food for a potluck reception. Grateful as I was to not have to fork out money for a present, I was at a loss for what I could reasonably bring. I consulted my cupboards, and found there flour, salt, ketchup, two pickles, and some random spices. Not very promising. As I look back now, I can see I very well could have attended without bringing food, and few people would have been the wiser, but my pride would not allow me. So I made some rolls. They were not very good: I had to stint a good bit, but they came out like rolls, more or less. I brought them to the wedding, and had a wonderful time.

At the end of the party, the bride and groom asked us to take home whatever we had brought with us, as they were leaving immediately for their honeymoon. Thrilled at the unexpected boon, I packaged up the thirteen leftover rolls, knowing I would have something to eat for a couple of days, at any rate. Maybe, if I sliced my remaining pickles thinly, the rolls could even be palatable; I didn't see the ketchup as part of the recipe.

Driving home in the heat of the late afternoon, the pavement beneath my car steamed as the tar melted; apparently the rubber of my tire longed to meld with the melted tar, and the pop of the explosion was notable, as was the sizzling of the tire dissolving into the pavement afterwards. I was about two miles from home, wearing a dress and heels. This was long before cell phones existed, but even if they had, I had no real options available to me: I had failed to cultivate mechanic friends who would tow and/or fix my car for free.

I would have burst into tears, but I had an audience: the car broke down in front of a woman with four young children sitting on the sidewalk, begging. Her sign said her husband had disappeared and she had no food for the children, but would accept anything. She looked desolate, more desolate than I, and now I was stalled in front of her so no one could see her and her plight. We gazed at each other. In that moment, I heard all the old Biblical lessons: Whatsoever you do for the least among you, that you do unto me. The widow giving her last two pennies. Even the Good Samaritan, though it didn't quite apply at the time. Those kinds of things. I felt acutely my position in the covenant of food and generosity. I got out of the car, clutching my bag of thirteen rolls, and handed it to her, apologizing for having to leave my car there. She began to cry, immediately opening the bag and handing the rolls to the children, who uncritically devoured them, even without pickles.

As I began the trudge up the hill toward my apartment, past K-Mart, past the bowling alley, the Mexican restaurant, the nail salons, the car stereo shop, the other Mexican restaurant, I was feeling somewhat pleased with my charity. I can't say I was jaunty; my heels clung to the sticky pavement with each step, I was leaving a trail of sweat, and I was developing a fine sunburn. Knowing the Payless Shoe Source was the last business before the hill got steeper near the residential neighborhood, I ducked in for one last blast of air conditioning. Seeing all the shoes I could not hope to afford any time soon, hating the shoes I was wearing for the pain they were inflicting, sourly thinking the shoes would probably explode like the car tire, leaving me to walk the rest of the way on blistering pavement in my panty-hosed feet, the full weight of my situation hit me. I had no idea how I was going to retrieve my car, fix the tire, or eat.

I was pretty miserable when I finally got to my apartment, so miserable that when I saw two boxes blocking my door, my first instinct was irritation that now I had to move someone's stupid boxes before I could even get to the shelter of my home. And then I saw the note, from Chris, the woman I worked with at church, who also ran the St. Vincent De Paul food pantry. "I collect and deliver food for people who don't try as hard as you, who never thank me. I cannot stand by and let one of our own starve." The boxes were filled with food. I collapsed in front of them, ugly-crying as I lifted each item out: peanut butter, pasta and sauce, bread, soups, tuna, canned vegetables. There was enough food to take me through at least the next month. I was saved.

My parents have a similar story. Early on in their marriage, my father worked for a hardware company that was irregular in paying him, and he came home one Friday without his paycheck. There was no food in the house and my parents had no idea how they would get through the week. They tell us of praying to St. Jude, the patron saint of lost causes; a very short time later, a neighbor came to their door; he had trees so laden with fruit he couldn't get rid of it all, and asked if they could come and gather whatever they could use. It was truly salvation. Ever since then, for all my life, we say grace and tack on, "St. Jude, thank you and pray for us." St. Jude, thank you and pray for us, indeed.

St. Jude, in fact, made up part of my Novena when I prayed for a husband: it seemed like the patron saint of lost causes was an obvious choice considering my dating life. So it's logical that when I met Ken, with whom I fell so deeply in love, the connection was solidified between that impossible gift of love and the desire to show such love through food.

It is for him I learned how to make homemade yeast bread, and came to really know how spiritual food can be. As I plunge my hands into the risen dough, warm with life, I understand the connection between bread and life. (Yes, I succumbed to the COVID quarantine fad of creating sourdough starter, which we delightedly used for nearly this whole year until I finally grew tired of the demands from the refrigerator to "Feed Me" all the time. I never imagined I would feel such guilt for throwing it away, but it is palpably alive.)

With such a deep sense of the connection between food and celebration, it was, then, with a real sense of grief that I found out I was scheduled to work my dispatching job on our first Thanksgiving together. Shift work meant we would not share the meal that was such a traditional and meaningful experience for both of us. Loathe to miss out entirely, I arranged for everyone at work to bring in a favorite Thanksgiving dish and we would have our own celebration, since none of us would be able to have dinner with our families. Wednesday night, then, my night off, I got a call from work telling me someone had decided to have the dinner that night instead, since some people would have already eaten with their families on Thursday. It didn't matter that those already-stuffed people were not the people I was targeting; someone had already made the change and their dinner was arriving as we spoke. Furious, I huffed and puffed for a few minutes, and then grabbed my car keys. It was 9:00 p.m. on Wednesday, and I raced to the grocery store.

I bought everything: every single thing necessary for Thanksgiving dinner. I made pumpkin pie from scratch, with fresh whipped cream. (First things first, after all.) I stuffed the turkey with croutons, onions, celery, and walnuts and cranberries and giblets, shoving it all into the oven. I made mashed potatoes, yams, green beans, cranberry sauce, and spiced peaches. The tiny tiny house was suffused with the smells of Thanksgiving.

Ken got home at 3:00 a.m., unsuspecting. When he came through the front door, he saw the table set and candles already lit. "What did you do?" he asked slowly. I told him we were having Thanksgiving one way or the other, dammit, and pulled his chair out for him.

We ate until 5:00 in the morning, laughing at how absurd it was to make such a lot of food for two people, laughing at being able to put together the entire dinner in six hours including doing the shopping, laughing with the joy of gratitude. It was a gift to both of us.

Of course other food stories have already been told: our meals where we pretend to be in a foreign country, the Halloween party, Aunt Margaret's brown bread. Birthdays and holidays were always a huge production. We threw a party for my sister-in-law to try to cheer her after her divorce, including a cake made to look like a ball and chain which she could sever. For Christmas every year, we hosted a five-course wine and food pairing feast for four other couples; the preparation went on for days, the planning for months. The cleanup was dreadful. But it too was a gift, to our friends and to ourselves.

As we have traveled, we continue to collect food stories and experiences. When we were in Cambodia, I kept getting bit by red fire ants; besides the pain of the bites, I found the ants aggravating. When our guide, then, said eating the ants was considered a local delicacy, I demanded to know where I could get some; if they were going to eat me, I was sure going to eat them back. The local guide demurred that it was really not a tourist-y kind of delicacy, but the tour guide laughed and said, "Yeah, they can handle it. I had them chewing betel nuts last night." (Not a favorite for me.) After much negotiation with a tuk tuk driver who spoke not a word of English, and after a couple of phone calls, the guide sent us on our way. We drove through Phnom Penh's central streets and out of town. Then way out of town. Pretty soon there were no more businesses and few houses, but we were still tootling along. After about thirty minutes, we turned past the aqueduct and went through some fields, and then turned again into an orchard. There were no visible buildings and what signs there were remained indecipherable to us, no hint of the English language to be seen. Once in a while the tuk tuk driver turned to us and smiled, nodding happily, but we had no way to ask a question. Smiling back, Ken noted we were either going to be the envy of everyone else on our trip or an object lesson.

At last we passed a driveway. There was a kind of makeshift sign on a tree which made the driver stop, back up, and enter the tree covered path. At the bottom, he pulled into a clearing with a shack to the left and a structure ahead of us, on the water over lotus plants. Made of wooden slats and upright poles, the building consisted of a series of "rooms," each divided with colorful rugs and hammocks strung from the poles, but no walls. Our driver spoke with the proprietor who had apparently been warned about us; there was a lot of gesturing, pointing and laughing, but it felt good-natured, so we were not too awfully worried about being murdered, never to be seen again. A woman came out, nodding and smiling, with a bucket of beer and a tray of fresh vegetables. We motioned for the driver to join us and after some hesitation he did, though we obviously had nothing to say to each other.

After some drowsy time with the beer and the lotus plants, the proprietor came out with a whole chicken, stringy and boiled, on a platter. Next came the bowls of eggplant, cooked and mashed up with the fire ants; our hosts stood by, anxiously awaiting our reaction. Our driver showed us how to take a strip of the chicken and use it to dip up the eggplant mixture, eating it all together. It was delicious, though the toxins made themselves felt by the tingling in our mouths. In the battle between me and the fire ants, I definitely won. And in the larger cultural exchange between those who were sharing so much with us, we were also the winners.

My intent here is not just to walk down my culinary memory lane, but to reflect on the bounty, the hospitality, the love involved in food, both in the giving and the taking. I am amazed at the gifts I have been given, and pleased with the gifts I have been able to give. In terms of a covenant, the sharing is everything. It fortifies us for whatever is to come. The partaking of food reminds us of our own incarnation, quite literally. If we were not to glory in it, why would we be given taste buds?

The miracle of the Eucharist itself serves as a reminder of the importance Jesus placed on hospitality, and on feeding each other. Jesus knew we do better when we are at refection. We open up to each other. We talk, we listen, we laugh, we cry, we eat, we drink, we share, we relate, we host. Host. The Bread of Life, the Eucharist, the embodiment of God. The incarnation requires nourishment. We need to live on both the Word of God and the Bread of Life. Martha does all the work, preparing the food, while Mary sits at the feet of Jesus, listening to him speak; while Mary has chosen the better part, Martha's work is no less important, or there would be no food. Both are necessary.

At the risk of attributing motives to myself that only appear in hindsight, maybe the compulsion I felt to bring something to my friend's wedding all those years ago, even if it were only the widow's mite of bread, created with my own hands, was less about pride and more about knowing the importance of hospitality. And the miracle box of food I received rewarded that awareness.

All relationship is covenant, and it is natural, even biblical, to cement that covenant with food, celebrating the elusive miracle of love and connection. Sadly, miracles do not necessarily come when we order them, but they come in their own time, in God's own time. When it may appear we are alone, with no options, the covenant we have with each other and with God reminds us we are never alone. And when God sends bread, sometimes there is also peanut butter.

11

THE FIRST SORROWFUL MYSTERY:
THE AGONY IN THE GARDEN

Jesus prays all night while those around him fall asleep.

Cancer

MY DOCTOR HAS BEEN with me through some harrowing experiences, and she and I have developed a lovely relationship over the years. She is deeply compassionate, and we talk about her family in China and her daughter in New York, about my children and my job, and then peripherally about my health. I had an appointment with her to discuss symptoms I had been experiencing, symptoms with which I was unfamiliar until Oprah discussed peri-menopause on one of her shows and I had my own "ah ha" moment. The doctor and I had finished talking about my night sweats and insomnia and a craving for red red (please make it bloody, so bloody, requiring carnivorous gnashing of teeth) meat, and she was tap-tapping into her computer to order some tests.

I remembered to ask her if she could just take a peek at what felt like a flattened, tough dried apricot slice at the top of my breast. I, of course, knew it couldn't be cancer because cancer felt like a hard pea and this was clearly a dried apricot. Everyone knew this. The pea is what we all feel for every month during our breast self-exams. I mean, I did the 3-Day Breast Cancer walk, with all that entailed, so I was not a complete ignoramus about breast cancer. I knew this so much that I didn't even think about the C word. I just noticed the texture didn't feel the same as the right side; I would not even have called it a lump, because the word is too closely aligned to the C word. My doctor touched it, her cool, kind fingers probing the edges. She grimaced. She actually grimaced. I told myself I imagined that, and then she said, "Let's just put all the rest of this on hold," still speaking as she deleted all the tests she just ordered, "and make sure this isn't cancer."

She said the word. Out loud. Among those things I surely know, I know the metaphor about words reverberating in your brain, the way they ping around and ricochet and take on new meanings as they bounce off other words lodged in our brains. This did not happen to me. The word just sank, lodging not in the pit of my stomach but somewhere near my knee. I knew this because I had been standing and suddenly I was not.

I did find time to wonder about the implications of saying the word out loud. A euphemism is a kind of talisman against the truth of whatever we don't want to hear. If someone utters a word, for someone else to hear, not just in a void, does that mean the fact behind the word clings to reality more powerfully? It's like saying, "Hey, the traffic is surprisingly good!" and knowing there will now be a huge delay up ahead. Did my doctor just curse me?

On the way home from the appointment, which, unusually, I did not attend with my husband, I called him. I called my mother. I called my best friend. I called my sisters. Everyone told me I was being silly, and it was nothing. Of course, that's the flip side of the talisman: in order to remove its power, our loved ones must invoke its opposite, relying on the hope that all would be well.

After a week of nagging, beseeching, and bargaining with God, I went for my mammogram and ultrasound, scheduled for the same day, "for my convenience," they said. The mammogram came first, so I tucked myself into the too-small blue paper robe and went into the dark radiology room. The technician was very friendly and we chatted about our dogs, even as I knew the pictures of her dogs on the wall were really there to make the brutally industrial room look more cozy. It was not cozy. It was barely humane. We talked about the weather, stormy as usual. She mused that if only men had to get their balls squeezed between cold metal plates, they would quickly invent a less painful and awkward mammogram machine. I decided not to pursue the line of conversation pointing out the rampant sexism in her assumption that women were not capable of inventing said machine, realizing not every moment was appropriate for a women's studies lecture; having one's breast in a contraption designed to squeeze juice from an unripe lemon is not the ideal time.

It turns out the only part of my body which appears to be firm would be my breasts, a distinct disadvantage when having a mammogram, so I needed a second round of pictures; she hadn't squeezed hard enough the first time. I tried to be cheerful, the good cooperative team player, but gasped at the pressure. A few minutes after she left the room to check the images, she called out to me that these would work and we were done. She returned to the room, putting away the lead apron, setting up the machine for the next patient, and studiously avoiding eye contact or chit-chat. I tried hard not to notice. As I gathered my things, I asked her if she had any fun plans for the weekend, desperate for the casual interaction we had been having, but she still didn't look at me, asking instead if I had an appointment with my surgeon that day. I was stunned by the implications both of her refusal to look at me and of her question.

"I don't have a surgeon. That I know of. Should I?"

"Oh," she said vaguely, "some people like to schedule those together."

I understood immediately this was a lie. It was not my first mammogram, and we wait sometimes weeks for a radiologist to look at our images and let us know we are fine until next year. That was the routine. I knew she had blundered, and she thought she covered up for what she had revealed. I chose to ignore the slip. I knew she couldn't tell me what she had seen, and I didn't ask; even more, I didn't want to see revealed on her face any more than she had already revealed.

In returning to my changing room, fumbling with a bra that now felt like both protection and betrayer, I took a moment to text my husband, in the waiting room, "Holy shit. Now I'm scared."

He held my hand in the waiting room, assuring me my English Literature Professor Brain was over-analyzing the subtext of my encounter with the radiology technician. I told him, rather pedantically, that over-analyzing is what I do, and I'm damn good at it. We waited. And waited. At last, a mammoth woman from the Ukraine with a smattering of English came out, holding my file, calling me by first name only to avoid attempting the pronunciation of my last name; though I told myself she had no way of knowing the mammogram results, I waited to see whether she would make eye contact with me. She did not, studying the file in her hands as she led me to another dark industrial room.

I again disrobed, and joked I should have kept the same stylish robe from my mammogram so they didn't have to go through two of them.

She did not smile, speak, or look at me. I lay down on the table, amused that someone clearly thought putting a piece of thin crinkly paper over the hard metal surface would mitigate the cold. Without speaking (I had already figured out her language was pretty limited, so was trying not to hold her silence against her), she swept the cold wand with its cold gel over my once-warm-but-increasingly-colder breast. She pushed and shoved, repositioned, pushed some more, glided, and pushed the wand over my flesh, grunting here and there, all the time staring at the screen in front of her, a screen to which I had no access. And then she breathed, "Oh my God. It's so . . . it's just so . . . Oh my God."

In retrospect, I might have said, "It's so *what*???" or "What the hell is wrong with you?" or "Use a damn adjective, will you??" or "Please shut up," or any number of other things appropriate to the moment. But my mind was wiped clear. I had no words. Part of my brain was busily trying to fill in what the missing adjective might be, while the other part understood the talisman concept and knew putting language to the idea would only extend the curse. She stood up, looming over me, breathing fast, and said she would be right back. I was still incapable of speaking, and I let her leave. Seven years (or minutes, I'm not sure) later, she returned with a man who remained unintroduced, and she resumed pushing the wand over my breast while the two of them stared at the screen.

"You see vat I mean?" she asked him. He only nodded, apparently understanding that her speaking was not really allaying my growing terror. He took the wand in his hand and did what felt like the same thing, but must have been different or he would not have had to take over from her clearly incapable hands. And then they had me dress, and told me I could expect to hear from the radiologist in a few days.

I cried all the way home, Ken trying to reassure me: the whole day was just a series of unfortunate encounters with people who had lost their minds. I kept wishing I were more oblivious to subtext.

At 8:22 on a Friday morning—how often our most significant moments accompany a glance at the clock that imprints the time on our brains forever—I was frantically getting ready for my 8:40 class, trying to slurp one more drop of liquid from the tea bag at the bottom of my cup, sitting in a pool of sunlight unusual for a November in Oregon. I knew the results of my mammogram and ultrasound were due, but expected them in the afternoon, so I was doing my best to put the idea of cancer out of my mind until later, focusing instead on how I was going to teach the existentialist dilemma of Samuel Beckett's *Endgame*, that cheerful post-apocalyptic play about two men exploring their responsibility to each other in the absence of an obvious God.

My phone rang. It never rings. Everyone emails me. I had never received good news when my office phone rang. I had never even received neutral news. My hands got that tight tingling feeling you get when you are suddenly going to have diarrhea. Nevertheless, full of dread, I answered before it rang a second time.

"I am looking for Kathleen Heininge," said a man's voice. The only people who call me Kathleen rather than Kathy, beyond my mother when she is reproves me, are professional people.

"This is she. Me. I." Suddenly my ability to consider grammar was gone, but it felt immensely important, as an English professor, to at least indicate I know there is a correct way to answer, even if I couldn't quite recall what the correct way was at the moment.

"This is Dr . . . ." I have no idea what his name is. Was. Is. "I am your oncologist."

"Um . . . I have an oncologist?" I had already concluded what this meant for me. I didn't know I needed an oncologist.

"Oh, my dear, you will have an oncologist for the rest of your life."

This is how I learned I had breast cancer. Stage three. He said more, which I only know because at the end of the phone call, I only had five minutes until class, and it takes me five minutes to get across campus, so we must have talked for thirteen minutes. A lot ought to be said in thirteen minutes. I was busy calculating how long it would take me to shovel my thoughts into their appropriate piles, so I could ignore that pile of shit that is a cancer diagnosis and pretend I care about the pile that is existentialism. The irony of what I would need to discuss was not lost on me: I felt as if my own endgame had just been pronounced.

I was given the option between a lumpectomy and the likelihood of further treatment, or a complete mastectomy, which didn't exactly remove the likelihood of further treatment. There are, of course, apps for that: once we plug in my age, the stage and type of my cancer, and presumably other factors like how much I like pizza rolls and what books I read, the computer expels a number telling me what my chances are under various treatment options. I argued, to no avail, that since we were entering the holiday season, I ought to be forced to choose between fudge and egg nog (it's unclear why one choice excludes the other), not between which mutilation I would prefer. The numbers, and the doctors, however, insisted on a decision. Because the mastectomy did not assure I could skip chemo, I opted for the lesser of the mutilations, hoping for the best.

My parents, my two sisters, and my best friend came up from California for the event. My family makes a holiday out of surgeries and illnesses, gathering and behaving in the least appropriate manner possible. We pride ourselves on having nearly been thrown out of several reputable hospitals because we get a bit too raucous.

In the very early morning, I donned my four-inch red patent leather pumps and my tiara, and we went off to surgery; if, after all, you can't wear a tiara to cancer surgery, I don't know where you are supposed to wear it. The hospital staff loved it, and I was told my sunny attitude would let me sail through my treatments. Yeah.

They put me in another huge blue paper robe, but this one had a hose in it so you could pump in air, either warm or cold depending on what you required. The look was . . . stunning, and we have a photo of my trip down the hall to use the bathroom, dragging my IV rig along with me, wearing the blue robe to approximate a dirigible, enhanced by the red shoes and the tiara. Later, after giving further explanations I couldn't quite follow, they told me I could not wear the tiara to surgery, so as they replaced it with the paper cap, one of the nurses kindly drew a crown on the front of it, to ensure the doctors knew who they were dealing with.

Then the drugs, and then the waking up, and the grumbling because I was quite comfortable sleeping for as long as I wanted, but they must have needed the bed because they were awfully insistent that I wake up. When I did wake up, I found I had an Elizabethan collar fashioned out of paper, made by my family who apparently had gotten bored waiting for me. They even signed it and had strangers and staff sign it, with helpful notes like, "Try not to lick your wounds" and, "Now you can't reach your balls," just in case I reverted to canine behavior. The doctor, with his game face on as he clearly didn't know what to make of us all, told me the margins were clear and it was a triple negative tumor. Even from my haze I knew that negative, in the context of tumors, was positive, so three of them must be great. I smiled and went back to sleep.

When I woke up for good, the nurse who tucked my warm blanket around me commiserated, "I guess it's turtlenecks for you from now on! You won't want that scar to show!" I did not claw her eyes out, mostly because she was hard to reach around the Elizabethan collar, but I was enraged at her assumption: the proper response to my scar should be shame, as if it were a scarlet A or something, marking me as a victim for all time. I suppose her attitude fit a narrative, however: my mother-in-law was only the first of many who asked me, "Oh, honey, what did you do to yourself to get this?" Others assured me cancer was all part of God's plan for me. The underlying message, for those who are into subtext, tells me I did something wrong and ought to be ashamed.

So it turns out a triple negative isn't all that great a thing. It means the tumor has not made it to the lymph nodes, and therefore has not spread. Yay! It means the tumor has not gotten to the chest wall, and so the margins are clear all around. Yay! It means the tumor is hormone negative, which means it isn't being fed by hormones. Sounds like a yay, but it is the kind of tumor they know very little about, and so assurances are not so assured. Thus we come down to the numbers being spewed by the app. If I left the cancer as it was, with no further treatment, I had a 45% chance of being dead from a recurrence of that or another cancer within ten years. If I pursued further treatment, meaning chemo and radiation, that percentage went to 38%. If I go to a party with a door prize to be won, and only two of us show up, I will not win the door prize. That's the kind of luck I have. So I opted for the further treatment.

I went home. My family stayed for a few more days, which was lovely except for how much it hurt to laugh, and we do like to laugh. Perhaps my favorite memory of that time was watching *Gone with the Wind*, which, astonishingly, my father had never seen. In a moment scripted for the sitcom of my life, just as Scarlet O'Hara shakes her fist at the sky to declaim, "As God is my witness, I'll never be hungry again!" the pizza delivery arrived. The poor guy at the door had no idea why we were all exploding with laughter. Second favorite moment: we played Scrabble, and I got the word "areola," which also sent us over the very precipitous edge. And then everyone went home.

Chemo was scheduled to begin after the New Year, on the first day of spring semester. Amanda was due to give us our first grandchild as a Christmas present, so the holidays were a time of delight and fear. My other Christmas presents were uniformly in-your-face gifts to make us all laugh and cry, and my sisters cut my hair to give me a mullet as we sat on the back porch and drank. Amanda gave me a needlepoint kit with loads of flowers and froofy things surrounding the words, "Fuck cancer," because I would need something to do during the chemo treatments. People gave me things like crossword puzzle books, eyebrow stencils (do people really not know where their eyebrows are? Turns out they don't), hats (so many hats!), hilarious shirts (one said, "Cancer, you picked the wrong broad"), cozy pajamas . . . all things to support my approach of defying cancer.

Our granddaughter was born on January 1, too late for me to be able to meet her before treatment started, and I tried hard to pretend I was fine with waiting until the end of treatments to hold her, but I cried harder over not getting to see her than I had over the diagnosis itself.

My first treatment didn't go all that well. I have terrible veins and it took the nurses three hours to find a cooperative one: the veins would either "jump" or collapse. It's a long time to be poked. At one point a tiny drop of the poison splashed onto one of the nurses, and suddenly there were bells and carts and a very urgent response of personnel rushing to assist her, all as I sat there, ignored, with a needle dangling out of my hand. I finally cleared my throat and said, "Speaking of subtext"—which we hadn't been—"do you want to consider the message you are sending me here? You're putting that shit directly into my veins but get all frantic when it gets on her skin?" Someone said, "Oh, this is dangerous."

No kidding.

After they finally got the needle in and began the process of dripping the bright red-orange poison into my body, I began to have breathing problems, so they injected me with a whole lot of Benadryl, and I went to sleep for the rest of the afternoon. It's not a bad way to get through chemo, though I didn't get much needlepoint done.

The drive home took about an hour and a half. My husband was driving, quietly, as I dozed some more, but when I woke up, glancing over at him, I screamed at the huge snake dangling from the lining of the car roof and about to drop on his head. Never mind that we have a sun roof on our car so there is no lining, and never mind that there was (so he tells me) no snake: I was emphatically screaming. When he recovered from his alarm, having successfully stayed on the road, thank heavens, he encouraged me to go back to sleep. I did, for a short while, but awoke again to see the huge antique fire truck, the one with the bulbous red clown nose on it, about to plow into the passenger side of the car where I was sitting. As you would, I screamed again, perhaps louder than the first time.

Ken gets many kudos for his amazing love and support during my bout with cancer, but his ability to keep the car on the road during my abrupt screaming is nothing short of superhuman. When we told the nurses at the next treatment about this amusing ride home, they quickly made a note to forego Benadryl again; the reaction, they explained, is not normal and is, rather, a sign I am allergic to the stuff.

I missed the first day of classes for the new semester because of the treatments, but made it to the second. My kind and generous colleagues and I had painstakingly arranged my schedule to allow for me to be able to teach throughout the semester and still make my appointments. I was delighted when the drugs I was given me kept the nausea at bay, the thing I most feared from the chemo. (I still regularly pray for whoever invented Zofran.) I had forgotten much of what I was told about possible side effects, focusing on staying ahead of the nausea, because once it started, I was told, it got pretty ugly.

The biggest detail I forgot, but remembered very quickly on my way to a meeting at work, was the bone pain. Because my tumor was very aggressive (I had a clear mammogram in March and a five centimeter tumor by October), I was on an aggressive chemo schedule, which meant I had to inject myself with Neupogen, a drug to stimulate the growth of bone marrow while chemo is encouraging its death. There would be, I now recalled someone mentioning, a war between red and white blood cells taking place inside my bones, and for some people, there could be significant pain, and for others there would be virtually none. Helping me remember these warnings was the moment I was driving along, by myself, blithely smug about how well I was doing this chemo thing, when all at once I felt as if I had been dropped from the roof of a two-story building and landed flat on my back on concrete. I didn't put it together at first, wondering what was happening, whether this was a heart attack or what, and waiting for the pain to subside. Even when you land on concrete, the pain subsides for a moment before it really sets in. No subsidence was happening. The really setting in, however, was going on apace. I pulled over, sure such pain could only be temporary. I couldn't breathe so I couldn't call someone. I waited, ten, twenty, now thirty minutes, parked in front of Taco Bell. When I realized it was not going away, I drove to my meeting, crying, upset I was going to be late; that unreasonably responsible part of my brain had evidently kicked back in so I knew my first obligation was to work and my body would just have to cop on to the plan.

After I finally spoke to the doctor, she said I could either take Tylenol (which felt about as useful as using Scotch tape to attach a severed head) or narcotics which "might" impede my ability to think. Since thinking is generally a large part of teaching, I realized immediately I was not, after all, going to be able to teach that semester, which felt like my biggest failure. As someone who put herself through too many years of school, who finally managed to get a tenure-track dream job, who has been trained not to ask for help, who has worked since she was 11 years old, I could not imagine failing at the duties I was assigned, and just spending months sitting on my ass at home. But the pain meant I could do little else; in addition, with my lowered immune system, I got sick every time I tried to leave the house. My options were limited.

My hair began to clump its way out of my life very quickly. Ken and I took a razor and gave each other mohawks, saying goodbye to the Christmas mullet, figuring, much as with the tiara, we didn't know when else we were going to have such adventurous hair. It was not my best look, but makes for a great photo opportunity. He shaved his head in sympathy. (When I finally got to meet my granddaughter, who at four months was as bald as I was, she looked from me to Ken to her mother, as if wondering what her mother's problem was, with all that voluminous blond hair.)

Cancer became my life for the better part of a year. I had months of chemo, sometimes interrupted by getting sick and needing time off to recover before going in for more poison. I had seven weeks of radiation, which brought its own amusing and horrifying stories. They tattoo you so they can line up the machines correctly each time, so now I can tell people I have three tattoos. I did think for a time I was going to have to get another, because I had an allergic reaction to the bandages around my incision so there were large red blisters around the scar, and I thought I was going to have to tattoo a train on them since they sort of looked like train tracks. But those scars subsided, leaving only the main scar on the left and then, later, the scar on the right where they put the port so they could access my veins more easily.

In the middle of treatment, they found another lump on the other breast, and we began the process (mammogram, ultrasound, biopsy) to determine if it was more cancer, but it turned out not to be. My life became a round of doctor's appointments, napping, and trying to find palatable food. There is very little; my staples were grapes, carrots, and Jelly Bellies. And when Ken tried to make a lovely soup for me, the smell of my usually-beloved garlic was so repellent I had to sit outside in the snow until the odor dissipated.

I had what I called "baby sitters," since Ken was still commuting back and forth between Oregon and California and I couldn't be left alone. I kept spiking fevers, which are dangerous and can lead to sepsis, so would have to drive the hour and a half back to the hospital to get the fever under control. I cut myself badly at one point, and the wound wouldn't stop bleeding, necessitating another ER run. So we had a schedule. My sister Rosie would, as often as possible, fly up from California, pick up Ken's truck from the airport, drive to our house, and care for me for four days, until Ken returned, at which point she would drive back to the airport and hop a plane home, leaving the truck for Ken to come home. When she was unable to do that, we had other friends who would come and stay with me for a night or a few days. I felt helpless, stupid, useless, and burdensome. I loved the people who helped, and hated needing that help so much.

Despite the frustrations (or perhaps because of them), a tremendous grace came from the year. Understanding my own selfishness in desiring so much to help others but being loathe to receive help from others was a huge lesson. Recognizing how loved I am, that people would miss me, that so many wanted to demonstrate their love but knew no other way than to offer help, allowed me to begin to accept that help. When the toilet fell through our bathroom floor, allowing for the discovery of an unknown leak (how blessed), we were embarrassed to be unable to fix it ourselves, having neither the time nor the wherewithal to do so, and finally accepted the help of friends who offered to fix it for us. Learning that my students, forty students in a general education class, had chosen to meet at 8:40 a.m. on the Friday before finals, during my surgery, to pray for me during that hour, continues to be one of the most touching things to have ever happened to me: they could have slept, or studied, or had breakfast, but every single one of them came to class to pray, and I never even heard about it until I returned to school and another student mentioned what a powerful experience it was. To this day I don't know who left the pink "Shh, Hair growing" baseball cap in my mailbox, but I love it. My sister Mary knitted her love and fear into nearly a dozen hats and scarves. Unable to go to church myself, I was deeply grateful when Ken would bring me communion, and we would go through the readings and the songs as if I had really been at Mass; I cried through every service, feeling God had abandoned me, and only later realized how much God had been with me, quietly letting me feel my way, through the whole experience.

And yet. As I look back on all the moments, I feel quite deeply the oppression of a medical machine grown too callous, having lost sight of the human beings behind the diagnoses. There is a reason so much of this narrative is what "they" did or said, that nameless, faceless, looming "they." A technician whose behavior changes so radically when she sees something on an x-ray, or one who cannot help but vocalize her whatever-it-was at the sight of my ultrasound, or the doctor who introduces himself as my oncologist before telling me the results of my tests, or the nurse who assumes she knows how I should react to my scars, or the medical team who reacts so strongly to a drop of medicine falling on the wrong person; these and a dozen other experiences tell me these people, these "theys," have fallen asleep when they should be vigilant, while the agony in the garden takes place over and over again.

The spiritual fruit of the Agony in the Garden is that recurrent theme, the acceptance of God's word. I struggle, again, in my acceptance, stuck on the betrayal Jesus endured as his friends failed to keep watch for him. While he suffered fear, presentiment, agony, his friends, those set out to be his guardians, fell asleep. They just fell asleep. Were they unaware of his agony? Were they just so beaten down with their own trials they could not keep vigilant? For me, as I imagine there must have been for Jesus, grace and frustration exist side by side. My "sunny attitude" and great sense of humor, for which I was continually praised, served only to cover my fearful and resentful heart, far from acceptance, as I could only wish the cup, as I drank from it fully, could pass me by.

12

The Second Sorrowful Mystery: The Scourging at the Pillar

Jesus, on his way to being crucified,
is whipped with leather thongs.

Weight

THE SPIRITUAL FRUIT OF contemplating the scourging of Jesus at the pillar is the mortification of the senses, as we linger over the pain he had to withstand on his way to being crucified. The point of beating Jesus has always been a bit murky to me: was crucifixion not enough? It was not as if he were being tortured in hopes of breaking him into some kind of confession or the revelation of the secret code whereby he could communicate with God; even a recantation of his perceived crimes is obviously not going to occur. Scourging feels so entirely unnecessary, if not that too many people enjoy being cruel to those whom they don't understand.

The very physicality of the scourging has always been one of the most painful descriptions for me to consider as it relates to my life. While it may seem petty and ridiculous to associate a weight problem with being flayed, in my heart I cannot dissociate the two, and the connection goes beyond the obvious fleshiness of the two circumstances. Fat remains among the last acceptable things for people to ridicule and despise; those who have never had a weight problem often believe in their own superiority, as if it is a moral issue. Fat somehow signifies stupidity and cupidity and morbidity and torpidity and all the idities. Surely it's just a matter of will power, people think. It's simple math, I have heard: if you eat fewer calories, you weigh less. So the flaying of my own body is literal in the constant dieting, and figurative in that people feel they have the right to comment on my body, to somehow make it their own business. The comments and the disgusted looks are a constant; they are therefore impossible to avoid internalizing so the comments and disgusted looks also come from myself.

The formative "bubble butt" comment occurred while I was in elementary school; I was stung and hurt by the derision in my friend's voice. My father would regularly pat my rear end and affably tease me about how that thing just keeps growing and growing, or try to appease my tears by saying I have good "child-bearing" hips, despite the clear disadvantage of having smaller breasts than my sisters' or my mother's (they used to refer to us as "the mountains and the molehills"). Well before I was in middle school, I knew my body was wrong.

I was fast, though, and tried to mitigate the shame of how my body looked with how well it could perform. I was chosen for football, softball, dodgeball, tether ball, basketball, volleyball, whatever teams were in the running, because I was pretty good, and I was proud of my athleticism. I became so infuriated when a boy from the grade ahead of me, this guy who thought he was so cool, mocked me for thinking I could run fast; I was clearly too fat for that. So I challenged him to a race after school. Everyone heard. Everyone showed up. It was a big deal. I am sure Billie Jean King probably heard about it and this was what inspired her to engage in her slightly-more-advertised tennis match with . . . whatever his name was. It doesn't matter, 'cuz she won. But that was a couple of years later, after she was inspired by me.

I, however, spent the day at school completely unhinged, because he was the fastest boy in school, and we all knew that. I showed up, elbowing my way through a crowd of people who were vying for the best viewing site, and I still remember the smirk on his face as he looked me up and down, assessing my body in a way soon to become all too familiar for the rest of my life. I should be grateful for the sneer, because it fueled me with adrenaline and fury. The race began. I kicked his ass. Not even close. I was way ahead at the start and he never got near me. First there was a stunned silence, and then wild cheering. After all, who doesn't like the underdog? I promptly threw up (never having had to deal with that much adrenaline before); he promptly turned his back on me and never again spoke to me or made eye contact.

Of course that was not the first moment when I knew the myriad ways a body could be vulnerable. It would not be the last. But it was a significant lesson for me that people who thought they knew what I could do would have another think coming. The race was, however, one of the few times I was able to actively do something about the way someone made assumptions about me.

When, in sixth grade, two girls decided I was a "fat piggy," they proceeded to wait for me every day after school, behind the well in the small woods I had to traverse on my way home, so they could beat me up, or at least harass me. I could run but didn't know how to fight (and would have been in trouble for it had I tried), and it was a torment for the whole year. I often tried pleading a stomach ache to keep me home from school, but that didn't work. I begged my teacher for extra credit work after school, hoping the girls would be bored waiting for me and let me go home in peace, but they were patient little bullies. (This is when my teacher assigned me the task of copying out the dictionary by hand every day, a task I am sure was intended to discourage me from staying after school and bothering him, but which ended up being endlessly fascinating to me. I got up to "F" before the end of the year.) When the bullies were torturing me during one recess, I finally spoke up for myself, telling them to "go to hell!!!" in my strongest little sixth-grade voice, for which, of course, I was excoriated and punished while they skipped away laughing. Yet another lesson.

I went on from there and joined track in high school, throwing the discus and putting the shot, doing the 100-yard dash and the long jump and failing quite formidably at the hurdles. I was good at discus, for about six months holding the girl's record for being the first girl to throw the discus more than 100 feet. I loved the feel of the discus as it rolled off my fingers, straight and true, to sail through the air propelled by my strength and balance. But of course, discus throwers tend not to be on the petite side, so even as the boys would help me work out and lift weights and practice my throw, they teased me for surely not being "prom material." The association between my ability, my body, my appearance, my weight, and my worth was being laid upon my consciousness daily.

Thus began a lifetime of dieting, of exercising, of not dieting, of not exercising. I am the classic yo-yo dieter, and have clothes in my closet ranging ten dress sizes. The only time I have ever successfully been thin—and perceived myself as such—was when I tore the muscles in my jaw and could not open my mouth wide enough to put a spoon in it, could not chew, could barely talk, for nine months, until I could have surgery to fix the problem. I got down to a size ten and was elated. Also miserable, malnourished, and in a lot of pain. But still, I was a size ten, and so proud, up until my boyfriend at the time insisted I should cut my four hours of sleep a night to three, so I could do sit-ups and "get rid of that little pooch you have going on there." Yes, I dumped him shortly thereafter. Sadly, I did not do so right at that moment, because after all, we dieters suspect everyone else is right in their assessment about our bodies, and it takes a while to get the nerve up to defend ourselves.

There is a catalog of stories to go with being large, stories about unbelievable things people say, but I will tell just a couple.

There was the doctor who, when I was 16 and experiencing abdominal pain, asked whether I was pregnant. I told him I didn't have a boyfriend. He urged my father to leave the room and asked the question again, now that my father wasn't there to hear my confession. I joked there was no star in the East that I knew of, and no, I was not pregnant. He said I could be, at my size. He then proceeded to give me a pelvic exam with three fingers, laughing when he burst my hymen, "Oh, I guess you were a virgin." He failed to diagnose the appendicitis that landed me in emergency surgery the next day, instead sending me home with an admonishment to diet, as if my pain were caused by my weight. To be clear, at this point I was a size 12, not exactly a behemoth, but I certainly internalized that I was.)

There was the later doctor who, examining me for another incidence of abdominal pain, chuckled and said, "You would be fine if you just lost weight. You have so much blubber on you, you could be lost in the tundra for a month and you'd be fine." Unsurprisingly, he did not diagnose the ovarian cyst causing my pain.

There was the physical therapist who, in giving me exercises for my dislocated kneecap, assured me he "used to be an elephant too" and proclaimed smugly that losing the weight would make all the difference in getting my knee to heal, as if being catapulted over the front end of a wave runner in Mexico would have had an entirely different result if only I had been thin.

There was the woman working at a women's lingerie store who, when I came in to look for a bra, scanned me up and down, turned to walk away from me, waved her hand dismissively and said, "We don't have anything in your size."

There was the doctor who asked me, "You know you're overweight, right? Have you ever thought of doing something about it?" That time I snapped, feigning shock, "*What*?? I had no idea!!! I have never ever tried a single diet in my life, except Weight Watchers, Nutrisystems, Jenny Craig, South Beach, Keto, Atkinson's, no sugar, no salt, no wheat, no meat, no grain, nothing white, only grapefruit, no fruit, weighing and counting everything that enters my mouth—but only those ones. Are there others I should consider??" (Say that out loud. It takes quite a bit of time, and his increasingly gaping mouth indicated how rare it was to have someone react to him in such a way.)

There was the moment in Costa Rica when, traveling with a group of students, we went zip-lining. The last run took ninety seconds, a pretty long one as zip-lines go, and I was told not to brake or the momentum would not carry me across. Because I was heavier, however, I was put in a different kind of a harness, and as I was pushed out, I was given a little spin. As I flew out over the canopy 6,000 feet above ground (I'm pretty sure that's how far it was, though math has never been my strong suit), the harness began to twist and choke me, and I could not make myself spin the other direction without braking. I gently tugged on the brakes, and came to a full stop, still choking, trying to untwist myself, in the middle of the canyon. And then it began to rain. As I was the last one across, everyone else watched from the other side of the canyon, filming what they thought was hilarious. They loved it when a fairly attractive young man zipped to me from their side of the canyon, scissored his legs around me, and dragged me to safety, huffing all the time, "If you were smaller, you wouldn't have needed this kind of harness."

The obsession with weight leads to horrifying moments, demonstrating how much the oppression of it weighs on my thoughts as much as on my body. One of my first thoughts when I was diagnosed with cancer was, "At least I will lose weight." Nope. Didn't happen. When I had the flu for more than two weeks, I found myself thinking with every round of vomiting, "At least I will lose weight." When I would end up on crutches for the umpteenth time, I would worry, "Now how am I going to lose weight?" When I would go on vacation, I would worry about how to avoid putting on more weight.

I thought, once upon a time, if I only had a man in my life who accepted my body for what it is, I could relax and learn to love my body too, but I was wrong. I do have a man who is accepting of me and finds me attractive, but I can't accept myself in spite of his constant assurances. How do I do so when I can feel the waves of condemnation directed at me from so many others? Even going home for holidays is fraught: either I hear about how fantastic I look, because I have lost weight, or there is utter silence and a bit of grimacing or chiding because I have put it back on.

How much, those around me might ask, is in my imagination? It is impossible to tell. When I recently found pictures of myself as a Junior Miss contestant, lined up with the other young women, I was shocked to find I looked to be nearly the same size as most of the others, when I had despised the picture so much. When in high school and later, I thought I ballooned beside everyone else, when in fact I was maybe two sizes larger than the thinnest of them. I certainly did not imagine the comments I received through my life, but I have to wonder how much my self-image contributed to my increasing size. The feedback loop of that self-image allows me to interpret the glances and grimaces in a way that reinforces what I already hate about myself.

Besides the weight, besides the cancer, my body has let me down in countless ways. I have had twenty-one surgeries, numerous broken bones and torn ligaments and bizarre illnesses. When I was in fourth grade, I developed a strange rash all over my torso, exquisitely itchy, that turned out to be a condition most often seen in elderly bedridden patients. When I was in eighth grade, I got a breast infection nursing mothers get, though I was far from being a nursing mother; it was so painful I could barely endure laying a sheet over my body, never mind wearing clothes. When I was sixteen, I fell down a flight of stairs, resulting in an injury that took doctors more than nine months to figure out; in the meantime, I was told over and over the pain was in my head. I have had mononucleosis three times, though supposedly the norm is only once.

My accidents have often involved me falling down flights of stairs, falling off crutches, or falling off shoes, although car accidents account for many of them as well. I grow random lumps that need removing. I develop strange skin rashes and am not supposed to notice when a diagnosis of "contact dermatitis" tells me exactly nothing except my skin is inflamed. I have had surgery for tempro-mandibular joint syndrome (connected to the torn jaw muscles); I have had surgery for carpal tunnel syndrome; I have dislocated my knee cap three times. I have had excruciating back pain for 30 years. I have had pain in my hands since the chemotherapy.

Waa waa waa. I could go on but this is not meant to be an inventory of complaints; it is meant to explain my ambivalent relationship to my body. While I may be disappointed and disgusted with my body, I also recognize the inescapable fact that it is the vehicle for my life. I can't do much without it, and I still plan to do things. I am grateful when I can walk; I am grateful when I can eat; I am grateful when I can swim or sleep or laugh, and I take none of it for granted.

The problematic part of this mystery for me is that Jesus accepted the scourging, knowing all along it was unjust and unnecessary. A life begun in such hope, with a star shining boldly to proclaim a birth in a manger, an infant beloved and longed for, the actual Messiah prayed for by so many, will end in such pain and violence, beaten with a leather thong with small sharp bones attached to it. When we talk about the incarnation of Christ, we so often focus on the birth, and we rarely think about the implications of his incarnation in terms of his physical torture. We speak of his embodiment as a blessing, because he was able to join with us in our humanity, but dying on a cross is hardly what most of us have to suffer. Even so, his pain is human pain, pain we can all imagine and experience. In what way did he deserve his end? He was a criminal only insofar as his accusers didn't approve of what he stood for, didn't understand him, and didn't accept their own role in condemning him.

The disruption of the physical experience, the ambivalence about living life in a body, is what I take away from the mortification of the senses. While being fat is in no way equivalent to the torture of Jesus, the scourging at the pillar keeps me mindful of the challenge Jesus accepted when he came to us fully human. Being willing to accept a human body, with all its foibles and maladies and pain, with all its glories and triumphs and joys, is no small consideration. We need to be reminded of such acceptance.

13

The Third Sorrowful Mystery:
The Crowning with Thorns

Jesus' tormentors place a crown of thorns on his head.

Curses

FOR SEVERAL YEARS, I worked as a 911 dispatcher for a busy city of 150,000 people, and our dispatch center was responsible for police, fire, and ambulance services, as well as maintaining surveillance of the jail. A full contingent of dispatchers was three: one to monitor the main police channel; one to monitor the back-up channel, run warrants, check maps, and other police support duties; one to answer both emergency and non-emergency phones, monitor fire and ambulance channels, and keep an eye on the jail video feeds. We were shockingly understaffed, especially during any kind of "extraordinary event" (which took place far more often than one might presume), and I often came in to work a ten-hour shift only to find I was being held over for five additional hours, with no notice. Days off were canceled faster than they could be scheduled. Obviously, the inability of the department to plan ahead seriously impeded employees' social life, child care and health. I have yet to forgive them for the Superbowl party I was hosting but was unable to attend. (At least the 49ers weren't playing that year.)

Work breaks were virtually unheard of. We learned to avert our eyes as each of us remained plugged in to our headsets as we went to the bathroom, unable to shut the door completely. We each brought our meals from home, eating them at the consoles, only to find we didn't bring enough for the mandatory holdover hours. The water at the police station was undrinkable, and as a cost-cutting measure, the administration removed our water service, so we had to bring even our water from home.

Dispatchers have plenty of stories, of course. One of my favorites was the woman who called 911 to report she had just been "robbed" by her upstairs neighbor; she had bought cocaine from him only to find it was flaky soap, and wanted him arrested and her money returned. I paused. I said, "You know this is a recorded line, right?" She screamed of course she knew that, but she knew her rights and she demanded the police show up right away and arrest her neighbor. I sighed and assured her the police would indeed come.

Police work swings wildly between boredom, comedy, and horror, and it all begins with the calls that come into dispatch. We had the usual calls from people (usually women but not always) who had managed to get various objects stuck inside them: Coke bottles (they create a vacuum), tool handles, or, most memorably, a round brush. One night a woman reported a suspicious person in a car parked in front of her home who had not moved in some time; when the police arrived, it turned out her neighbor had left a blow-up sex doll in his car. (That particular call was made even funnier by the hitches in the new computer-aided dispatch system we had just installed. It kept leaving random spaces in the text sent from one terminal to the other, and when I put the call out, not having read it in advance, I said over the radio, "The do me light is on," having failed to guess "dome light" is what was meant.)

Conversely, I was on the phone line for the call when a police officer from a neighboring agency was in a fight at the BART station, and the caller said it looked like the cop was losing the fight; I heard the gunshot which killed the officer. I was also working the night one of our own officers, working an overtime job as a nightclub bouncer, was ambushed and shot to death. I took the repeat calls from a ten-year-old child whose parents routinely beat each other up; he called so often, he had favorite dispatchers he asked for by name. I took the call from a woman whose husband was drunk and attacking her; as the officers were on the way, I kept her on the line, gathering information but also trying not to lose contact with her until they arrived. When she told me her name, I froze; both she and her husband, the violent drunk in the background hurling invectives at her, were in my prayer group. I never revealed who I was, but that was the moment I knew this was not the job for me.

Dispatching can be a great job. It pays well, with good benefits. It keeps you on your toes, requiring creativity, focus, and multi-tasking. It requires good listening and the ability to synthesize a story into clear and concise information for those who need only essential details and need them immediately. One of the best features of the job is being able to leave it behind when your shift is over: there is no such thing as working from home. Dispatching also requires excellent typing skills. There is so much typing. When I began, I was able to type 100 words a minute, though I suspect it was better than that by the time I left. Practice is as practice does, you know.

The department where I worked, however, was not ideal. Morale was beyond terrible; no money can make up for being perpetually under-staffed, overworked, unappreciated, stressed out, and miserable. There were a few people who were lovely to work with, but most of them were very cliquish and nasty; there was some inexplicable feud between the department where I worked and the one where my husband worked. Actually, it wasn't that inexplicable, as it stemmed from the divorce of one of our dispatchers from one of their cops, which somehow became extrapolated into the scorn and then banishment of anyone with any ties whatsoever to that other department, but it was certainly juvenile, in-tense, and painful.

I am less aware of what the specific stressors were that led to divi-sion among the police officers, but the situation peaked the night one of the sergeants got supremely drunk and began loading all his guns in his garage, fulminating over the hit list he had composed of those who had wronged him at the department. His son was frantically unloading the guns as quickly as his father could load them, but when one round inevi-tably went off in the frenzy, the police were called. After much ugliness, the sergeant was committed to a rehab center for his drinking problem, but the episode had exposed some unaddressed issues in the department.

The stressors bled over into dispatch as well. Sitting at a keyboard for ten to fifteen hours a day, with few if any breaks, takes a toll. Add the stress of a demanding and consequential job with an unfriendly atmo-sphere, and it's no surprise when carpal tunnel syndrome abounds, a con-dition where nerves in the wrist become inflamed due to repetitive stress. I was about three years into the job when I began to have tingling pains in my hands and found I was losing my grip—such a great metaphor, even when it's literally true. I was finding it increasingly difficult to open jars, lift heavy objects, drive for long periods of time, hold my newborn nephew.

In reporting my symptoms to Human Resources, I became the pariah, suspected of faking my injuries in order to get worker's comp benefits. I was called names and mocked. My doctors gave me specialized braces and medications that were supposed to help, but part of the campaign to prove the falsity of my claims was additional work hours, so the condition continued to grow worse. I remember one conversation with the head of HR, who called me at home to dispute whether I needed surgery. Sarcastically, she asked me what kinds of things I couldn't do with this supposed pain in my hands. I told her I was unable to do laundry, to wield a kitchen knife, even to put on a bra. She scoffed, "That's ridiculous. No one can live like that." I retorted, "Exactly. Which is why I need the surgery."

Shortly thereafter, a van with blacked-out windows began appearing parked in front of our house. It belonged to no one we knew in the neighborhood, but was regularly parked all day. I knew someone was watching to see whether they would catch me in the act of trying to carry in groceries or prune the roses, *in flagrante* strength, I guess. I waved at whoever it was daily, both hands encased in braces.

When the worker's comp doctor finally conceded my condition was egregious, the department took me out of the dispatch center and placed me on "light duty" where my job was to interview and ergonomically retrofit the work stations of all the employees, not just in the police department but in the entire city. Woefully unqualified for such an assignment, I was sent to several schools to learn about the mechanics of repetitive stress syndrome and the equipment available to remedy the situation. Thus I learned that nearly a third of the employees in the city had similar complaints.

I ended up having the surgeries, four of them, on both hands and both arms, to release the nerves that were being aggravated.

Thus the curse began.

After the first surgery, I had a cast on my hand to protect the wound. In cutting the carpal tunnel, the nerve is no longer protected should it, say, receive an impact. Scar tissue, when it develops, offers a bit more protection, but the wrist remains a sensitive spot. I was delighted the day the itchy and smelly cast came off, and anticipated a long, hot bath to soak off the dead skin. Ken went to work, and I basked in the water, nearly dozing, when the phone rang.

When you're married to a cop and he is at work, you don't let the phone go unanswered. Sadly, although by now cell phones existed, we had not yet succumbed to the new world, and our phone was hanging on the wall in the kitchen. I jumped up from the bath, grabbed a towel and scurried out to the kitchen, grabbing the phone.

And then I slipped on the wet floor and fell, hands down.

On the scale of painful experience I have had, this one is high up there. My understanding of the one-to-ten pain level chart got seriously adjusted that day. I was unable to speak, though I could hear Ken frantically asking if I was okay, having heard the thump of my fall. The incision had opened up and was bleeding all over the floor, and I could barely breathe, much less tell him what had happened. The pain went through my wrists, up my arm, expanded in my neck, and exploded in my head. He raced home and took me to the hospital where they stitched the incision back up again, this time without the anesthetic. I can't even remember why they couldn't use one, but they didn't. I was not brave.

When my situation returned to normal, meaning I was back at work dispatching and the city had given me a settlement for my expenses and for pain and suffering, we decided on two things to do with the money. We bought a new-to-me used car, a convertible Sunbird, a cute little thing I adored. It was the first car I ever loved, a car exceeding mere functionality and promising fun. And we bought a cruise for Ken and me, Amanda and Aaron, and both sets of our parents. We were at the sweet spot in time when the kids, at ten and twelve years old, still liked us and all our parents were healthy enough for travel, so we thought this would be perfect. We parked the new car in the garage and went to the Carribean.

The cruise began so well. We even rented a limousine to take us all to the airport, a splurge we enjoyed immensely (and which turns out to be cheaper than trying to get eight people to the airport separately). The kids got their own ship cabin next to ours, and thought heaven hath no delights to exceed being able to order chocolate cake from room service, being able to get hamburgers at any time, and swimming in the pool. The Carribean was largely irrelevant to that.

On the third day, Amanda cut her foot on a loose flange by the ship's pool. She required thirteen stitches and just missed her Achilles tendon, but would need to keep her foot dry for the duration of the cruise. No more pool. No swimming in the Carribean. At twelve years old. She went on shore excursions in a wheelchair. She was a trooper, and we have a memorable photo with both of her grandfathers and her father carrying her out from the beach around Grand Cayman, while I held her foot aloft, so we could dunk her in the water and she could at least say she got to feel the Carribean. It was not quite the cruise we had envisioned.

Less than a week after we returned home, Ken and I were driving in my new car on a Friday afternoon, during rush hour on a notoriously nasty freeway in the Bay Area. He was driving, the top was down, and I was singing at the top of my lungs, blissed out in the sun. Traffic ahead was stopping, and the car to the right of us was apparently having mechanical trouble and was trying to pull over, but the stream of traffic to his right would not let him. The driver of the car behind him was enraged at how slowly he was going, and began honking and gesturing, all the while talking on his cell phone. Furious, he pulled into our lane behind us and accelerated, still gesturing wildly at the slow driver as he passed him, trying to make eye contact, missing the fact that we had now stopped. He rear ended us going fifty miles an hour. Our car flew forward into the car ahead of us and then went air-bound, landing sideways in the other lane. We didn't get hit a second time only because the slow driver was still trying to get over, and he blocked the traffic behind him.

If you've ever been in an accident, you'll know there is a strange moment when you become sort of disconnected from yourself, so you are watching your response as if it has nothing to do with you. Without knowing what I was doing, I put one hand over my eyes and the other on the back of my head, and began rocking and moaning. If I couldn't see it, maybe it hadn't happened. Ken grabbed my leg and said, "Hold on, it's not over," waiting for further impacts, but thankfully it was over. Sort of. I couldn't look. He got out of the car while I remained rocking, and I could hear him talking to someone. Then he got back in the car. "How bad is it? Is my car okay?" I asked.

"Oh, honey. You'll never drive this car again."

The next thing I knew, I could hear a horrible scraping noise as a CHP car began shoving us out of the roadway; the back end of our car gouged the pavement as we were being pushed. When I finally turned to look, I saw the trunk was accordioned into our backseat; had the children been with us on that trip, it is unlikely they would have survived.

I realized my hands were covered in blood. My head had been slammed into the leading edge of the windshield and the muscles in my skull were severed. I also had whiplash. Ken's seat had broken on impact and he was unscathed.

So. The carpal tunnel settlement money was gone.

We got another settlement from the cruise line for their culpability in the injury Amanda sustained, though it certainly did not pay for a replacement cruise. And we got still another settlement from the insurance company for the car.

We took the car money and bought another car, much less exciting but with excellent safety ratings and a hard top. And a big trunk. And a large back seat. Back to functionality, skipping the fun.

We took the cruise settlement money and opted for a resort in Mexico rather than another cruise. If all the kids really wanted to do was eat and swim, a resort was a much cheaper option. Off to Puerto Vallarta with us, then. Swimming pools and nachos and beaches and fun for us!

On the third day of our week-long holiday, we rented wave runners and rode them out into the ocean. Plowing through each other's waves, enjoying the sun, laughing gleefully, chasing each other, we were having a blast. When I hit a particularly large wave and was catapulted over the handlebar of the wave runner, I wasn't especially alarmed, because I really like water, and landing in it wasn't all that painful. As I tried to maneuver my way back up on the wave runner, however, I realized how little upper body strength I had after all those months of not using my arms due to the carpal tunnel syndrome. I kept trying to heave myself up, to no avail. Trying to swing my leg up, I realized something was seriously wrong there as well; my body just was not responding as it should. I had hit my knee on the handlebar as I flew over it, dislocating my knee cap.

As I floated out there for a while, Ken and the kids began to suspect something was wrong, but couldn't really do much to help me. Fortunately, the people who operate the wave runners also realized there was a problem and came out to rescue me. They tried to help me up onto it, but there is strangely little traction to be had in water, so they just told me to hang on to the back and they towed me in, the jets from the propulsion pummeling my stomach for the twenty minutes it took to haul me in like a flopping fish.

It turns out bladders are not fond of being pummeled, really for any length of time, so I was left with a bladder infection and crutches for the rest of the vacation.

Grumblingly, we took the rest of whatever settlement money we had and paid off an especially unpleasant dentist we owed, hoping the curse could be passed along to someone else. There was certainly no luck in the original settlement, nor in the trickle-down settlements thereafter.

The mystery of the crowning of thorns reminds me of these events. The connection to pain is obvious, but I have an abundance of memories to bring me into contact with this story. These events in particular connect me to the pain Jesus endured in that moment. Even the sites of the injuries seem to anticipate the crucifixion: the holes in my wrists, the severed skull muscles, the dislocated kneecap, in such close temporal proximity to each other. For Jesus, the story went far beyond pain: the mockery and humiliation, as his tormenters refused to see him for who he was, must have been salt in his wounds. In the audacity of proclaiming his kingship, Jesus was presumably asking for it. But Jesus did not writhe under the injustice. He was the Son of God, with legions at his command, but he did not tell those around him how much they were going to regret their behavior. He didn't say, "Do you know who my father is?" He endured, not as a Stoic but as a man committed to God's word.

As I pray this mystery, then, the association with my own story goes beyond the pain, and I wonder about the purpose of settlements and litigation. At the same time I believe we were justified in claiming our rights—my carpal tunnel was directly caused by unsafe working conditions; Amanda's foot was cut because of negligent maintenance on the ship; our car was totaled by an inattentive and angry driver—I have always been uncomfortable with that assertion of our rights. Where does personal responsibility enter in?

I am reminded of yet another dislocated kneecap (there were three altogether: Mexico, the basement stairs, and this one). I was coming home from school, getting onto the escalator at the BART station in Berkeley, a dizzyingly steep one. At the top was a small table where a man was selling newspapers. Wrapped up in his jacket and scarf, he had fallen asleep. I saw people stealing the papers, but when a man went to grab the money box, I felt compelled to intervene. I had just taken a step onto the down escalator and I turned to wake the man up. In doing so, being such a graceful and elegant human being, I tripped and drove my knee into the leading edge of the escalator. My shout of pain woke the vendor up, so at least I accomplished that.

Of course I was in public and had to pretend I was fine. Just fine. I limped a bit as I made my way to the train platform and thankfully sank down into a seat. Only then did I notice the trail of blood I was leaving behind me; my black jeans had hidden the wounds initially. Someone came to me, urgently asking whether I needed an ambulance. Of course not, I indignantly declared. Someone else came, a BART representative, to ask what had happened. I explained it was my own stupidity and clumsiness, but they had to shut the escalator down anyway and take a report. I watched two of my trains go on without me while I assured people I was fine.

By the time I got to my home station, I realized my leg was terribly swollen and I could not walk. My car was much too far away. Because I worked as a dispatcher in that same city, I knew the BART dispatchers, so I called them, hoping to capitalize on our relationship to convince them to give me special treatment. I asked them if they could just wheel one of the office chairs down and then wheel me to my car; I would be fine from there, and promised to drive straight to the hospital. They laughed at me. (This laughter happens an awful lot in my life.) I finally agreed they could call an ambulance, but only if the ambulance did not respond with lights and siren. I was not an emergency.

Lights and sirens are so much louder when they arrive in a concrete structure like a BART station, and seem louder still when they announce the level at which I had been betrayed by my friends. So much for avoiding ignominy.

I had dislocated and punctured my kneecap. You might notice, as I now do, that escalators come in a variety of patterns: the one I thwacked into had cogs that fell into what I call an "ABAB" pattern, but some come in an "AABAAB" pattern, like stanzas in a poem. You can tell by the scars they leave.

Almost immediately, I began to hear congratulations. I was going to own BART. In the lawsuit, I could command any amount for the damage inflicted upon me. BART had such deep pockets that of course I was going to be set for life. Even if the Eagles hadn't just come out with their hit song, "Get Over It," which admonishes people for such thinking ("You don't want to work, you want to live like a king, but the big bad world doesn't owe you a thing"), there was still the little detail that none of this was the fault of BART. What could they have done to prevent the accident? Post a sign saying: "Going up the wrong way on an escalator could cause injury"? Duh. How could I sit in front of a judge and jury and pretend I thought they were culpable?

Which brings me back to Jesus and enduring injustice as well as pain. Have we become a society so wrapped up in assuring we are never maligned that we miss the point of Jesus entirely? Is there such a thing as reparation for mockery or physical pain? Is there supposed to be? If we become so concerned with coming out even in some celestial score, do we lose the grace of suffering?

I am really uncomfortable asking these questions, even of myself. It is antithetical to our training to turn the other cheek, to offer up our trials, to wear our own crown of thorns uncomplainingly. I am terrible at it. I am too much imbued with a sense of justice and fairness, and I fight hard to make sure I am never downtrodden. But the lessons of both the story of the cursed money and the story of the crowning of thorns suggest to me I have much work to do in this regard.

14

The Fourth Sorrowful Mystery:
The Carrying of the Cross

Jesus is forced to carry his own cross.

Mononucleosis

WHEN I WAS TWENTY-SEVEN, I was working five jobs, trying to maintain a long-distance relationship, and going to school full-time, just beginning work on my master's degree. I was recovering from having torn the muscles in my jaw (eating a Dorito at a Dan Fogelberg concert; I still can't hear "False Faces" without wincing a bit). Medical professionals were still arguing about whether tempro-mandibular joint syndrom (TMJ) should be treated by dentists or physicians, and the losing party was the patient who had to wait for them to decide. I spent nearly ten months of struggling to find a doctor who would take me seriously, or who would work with a struggling student who had no insurance. One dentist disbelieved in the syndrome so thoroughly he yanked my mouth open further than I could get it, tearing still more muscles in my jaw; it makes an unforgettable rending sound that close to your ear. For all that time, I was unable to open my mouth wide enough to stick a spoon in it. I could only eat what didn't require chewing.

I muddled on, teaching, singing, answering telephones, trying to make myself understood without opening my mouth. My debt continued to grow as the medical expenses piled up. I asked my parents to loan me the money to fix the problem, but they refused, telling me it would be "character building" for me to get out of the situation myself. I suppose it was their way of ensuring I carried my own cross.

When I finally found a dentist who understood the condition, he did an MRI. I sobbed with relief when he saw the results, acknowledging me by saying, "Oh my, you must be in so much pain!" I fell in love with him on the spot. (I sobbed some more when he suddenly died of a brain tumor two years later. I only whimpered, though, when the dentist's chair I was sitting in caught fire while my mouth was propped open for treatment, but that's another story.)

I at last saved and borrowed enough money to have surgery to relieve my condition and to begin feeling human again. The surgery created a new set of problems, having severed a nerve in my lip so ever since I have to keep my lips moisturized at all times lest I lose sensation in them and begin to drool, but that seemed like a fair trade-off as long as there was no pain and I could eat.

Mmm, Doritos.

I wish my wincing over Dan Fogelberg translated, more logically, to hating Doritos, but I still like them. No, I don't learn lessons very easily.

Being unable to eat for a long time is the best weight-loss program I had ever tried, but it left me weak, and susceptible to pretty much any germ circulating. I was beyond run-down, so when I came down with a fever during finals week of fall quarter, I was not surprised, but felt I could surely drag myself through one more week of exams. I was so close to being able to have at least a break from school work, if not from my five jobs.

After the first two exams, however, I realized I had overestimated myself. I phoned my professor to beg off the last final, but she refused, warning me of impending failure in the class if I missed the final. As it was a miserable class to begin with, I decided I would rather do a poor job on the final than retake the class, so I went. I arrived on time to find the classroom locked, and all the students waiting in the hallway. Weak and tremulous, I lay down on the floor to wait, hugging the cold concrete to cool my fever, and my classmates, arrayed around me to protect me from being trampled, grumbled about the tyranny of professors who would force someone to take an exam in such condition. The professor unapologetically showed up thirty minutes late for the final, pretty much the last thing I remember about the experience; I took the test in a yellow world of words that appeared to hover over the page, elusively skating away from my pen like frozen peas on a single chopstick. I left the final and drove myself to the student clinic, where the doctor told me I had the flu and should go home. I did.

Two nights later, I knew things were bad. I was living alone, and my long-distance boyfriend lived too far away to be of help. I had been unable to hold any food down for some time, and I knew my fever was high, although I didn't at that time own a thermometer. I popped some Tylenol and called a friend, and she came with food and a thermometer. When we realized my temperature was 104°, even after the Tylenol, we opted to go to the hospital, despite my lack of insurance.

Not all hospitals are created equal. Having spent a stupid amount of time in them (I was only sixteen when I chattily greeted the x-ray technician with, "So! You're new here?" and she looked at me, alarmed, and said, "Why do you know that?"), I could do a study on the dramatic differences between medical facilities. Some are quite luxurious, with caring and nurturing staff who cater to those who have plush insurance plans or so much money they don't need insurance; these hospitals have spiffy waiting rooms with plentiful upholstered seating, piles of current and neatly displayed magazines, and cafeterias providing hot, delicious and varied food. At the other end of the spectrum are the bare bones hospitals, with surly staff providing the minimum service necessary; what seating one can find is plastic and often broken, and instead of cafeterias they have vending machines, often broken. Some places are rural and homey, serving a wide variety of patients and complaints, and some are highly specialized, serving, for example, burn victims. The one I went to was an urban trauma county hospital, where they specialize in gunshot and domestic violence victims, AIDS patients, and non-English speaking families who don't know any other way to get essential medical services. And uninsured students.

By the time I got to the hospital, I was barely able to sit up on my own, slumping over every time someone tried to prop me up. I was only vaguely aware of most of my surroundings, though the exasperation of the intake nurse was clear to me at the moment I told her I had no insurance. I apologized effusively. I was told to wait my turn. I have no idea how long it was, but the wait seemed endless, even longer than I had had to wait for the professor to come administer the exam. I am sure I dozed—or lost consciousness—but Ann, my friend, stayed with me, trying to keep me from falling over. When they finally called my name, she told me she would wait for me.

Much to my relief, they let me lie down while they worked on me. I was so out of it, I may as well have been anesthetized by then. My temperature was still high, and they decided to do some blood work. I remember the rubber tourniquet on my arm because it seemed to hurt inordinately, and I remember the continued poking while the nurse tried to find one of my very playful (hide-and-seek mostly) veins. But as she released the tourniquet, I vividly recall the sensation of utter coldness as my blood stopped coursing through my body and began to settle downwards, a most peculiar feeling. Up to a point, I felt all my muscles completely relax. Completely. And then I felt myself leave my body, a chilly feeling (both literally and figuratively) of my substance leaving a body no longer useful.

I floated, balloon-like, neither quickly nor slowly, somewhat aimlessly, to the upper corner of the room, where I looked down on the nurse and an EMT working on my body. I could hear the EMT panicking: "Oh my God! We've lost her! There's no pulse! Get a doctor!" I gazed down, watching with great detachment, and noticing everything about the room, most particularly its lack of cleanliness. From my position in the corner of the ceiling, I took special note of the hanging fluorescent lights, which were filthy on top, and I remember thinking, "I thought emergency rooms were supposed to be sterile, but all that dirt, far beyond dust, could just float down onto the bodies below, and that couldn't be good." I remember thinking I was only twenty-seven, and my mother didn't even know I was there, and I couldn't just die like this. I heard the nurse, as she squeezed my hand, saying, "If you can hear me, squeeze back," and I remember thinking, "You stupid bitch, I'm dead! How am I going to squeeze your hand?" and then thinking, "Holy shit, those had better not be the last words I ever think!" and then thinking, "I have *got* to stop swearing!"

Before I knew it, with too many people ministering over my body, I felt myself re-inhabit it. I wasn't exactly sucked back in, but it's not an inapt image. One moment, I was hanging around up in the corner of the room, neither here nor there, and the next, I felt my body begin to chug back to life, like an old truck with a very low battery as it churns and chortles to send fuel back into its lifelines, trying to catch hold of the spark enabling it to run. I was a teensy bit disappointed/alarmed to have seen no bright white lights earnestly bidding me to come. (Maybe it was all the swearing?) And then I was back, sputtering and coughing as if I had nearly drowned.

Three hours later, after giving me a spinal tap to ensure I didn't have spinal meningitis, they sent me home, with no further instructions.

Ann, who had a life, had spent all night with me, and after dropping me off at my apartment, she went home to sleep for an hour or two before she had to go to work. I slept for much of the day, and awoke to find my fever back, curiously unimpressed as it was by my not having spinal meningitis.

I decided I should eat.

The apartment, one of two units at the top of a tri-plex, was very small, perfect for me and my two cats, Carmen Miranda Mugwumps and Edgar Allan Po' Kitty, with just a few steps between the living room and the kitchen, and a few steps further to the end of the hall where my bedroom and the bathroom were. I opted for tomato soup, the meal of choice throughout my childhood whenever anyone in my family was sick. (It usually went with grilled cheese sandwiches and pickles, but such an extravagant meal was entirely too ambitious.) I got up and began to walk to the kitchen, but had to stop on the stairs (three of them) that led up from the sunken living room. I rested there, and then got the rest of the way to the kitchen, where I found I had to sit and rest for a while. Eventually I got up and opened the cupboard where the soup was stored, but was exhausted, and had to rest for a bit. When I felt somewhat restored, I grabbed the can of tomato soup, but that was ridiculously difficult, and I had to rest for about ten minutes. Between having to open the drawer for the can opener, lifting it, getting it set on the can, and twisting the monstrous cogs of the machine to open the can, opening yet another cupboard for the spectacularly heavy pot, setting it on the stove, finding a spoon in the hard-to-open drawer, emptying the can into the pot, adding water, turning the stove on, stirring, opening one more cupboard for a bowl, turning the stove off, emptying the soup into the bowl, and carrying the bowl to the table, I had taken more than two hours, and I was too exhausted to eat. Still, knowing I had to get strength somehow, I managed a few spoonfuls of soup before throwing it all up again. I sobbed myself to sleep at the kitchen table, bewildered by the amount of energy life required.

Later that afternoon, having found my way back to the couch in the living room, I awoke to find a man in my room, standing over me. It was pretty clearly Jesus, but he didn't look like the Jesus I would have expected to see, nothing, in fact, like he appears in myriad photos or even on grilled cheese sandwiches. He smiled gently at me, and I wasn't really as startled as I probably should have been. He told me it was time to go, and I demurred. He reached for my hand but I hesitated to take his, telling him, "I'd rather not go just yet. Can you just take my leg? It hurts, and I can do without it." He chuckled, gently chiding, and said that no, he had to take all of me or none of me, but it was my choice. (I was so relieved to know Jesus has a sense of humor; the thought has sustained me ever since.) I thought about the choice for much longer than one might expect, but decided I'd rather not go just yet, and then he disappeared. It was all quite civilized. I went back to sleep.

I couldn't say how much time passed, but I know I woke up in my bed a long time after that, and remembered I had not fed the cats. I got up to do so, and as I headed down the hallway, I felt as if I were floating again; the next thing I knew, I was waking up on the floor, with my two cats circling me (I prefer to think out of concern for my well-being rather than out of pondering which part of me they should begin eating first), and realized I had fainted. I briefly considered whether this was the time one was supposed to call 911, but calculated the responders would have to break the door of the tri-plex down to get up the stairs to me, and then break down my apartment door, and I couldn't afford to replace two doors, so I opted to slither over to the wall heater, in front of which I fell back asleep for the rest of the night. Happily, the cats did not attempt to eat any part of me, despite their still not having been fed.

In the morning, I called my parents. They lived about seventy-five miles away, and hated driving in the city conditions where I lived, so they rarely visited. No, they never visited. I asked if they could come get me; they were surprised and reluctant, until I told them what had been happening. My father came to get me, first taking me to another doctor. That doctor finally did a full exam, without scowling about my lack of insurance, and determined I had mononucleosis and jaundice; I hadn't noticed the cat-like yellow of my eyes (which helped to explain the yellow tint to everything I saw) or the striking resemblance my urine had to Coca Cola. Less fizzy, but still quite brown. Even without medical training, I was pretty sure that was not optimal. He gave me the choice of going home with my father to try to recover, or to be hospitalized, with no insurance; whatever I decided, I was not allowed to return home to recover alone.

After arranging for my neighbor to feed the cats indefinitely, I spent the entire month of December and much of January at my parents' home, alternating between sleeping and being incredibly spoiled as my mother cooked every single one of my favorite meals in an effort to build my strength up: mastaccioli, spaghetti, minestrone soup, pork chops and apple sauce, and even fudge. I sometimes slept on the back porch, despite the cold, lying in the windbreak but soaking up the tepid December sun. My weakness was astonishing to me. I had been such an Energizer bunny just a short time before.

I was very fuzzy, and there is much I don't remember about that period, but I do remember the breakup over the phone from the boyfriend who was afraid of getting sick too, although he hadn't seen me since the beginning of the fever. In fairness, he had underlying health issues himself that made him legitimately worried about infection. He called to accuse me of cheating on him, though how I was supposed to have had the time or energy for that, even before I got sick, is beyond my comprehension. I said the idea was preposterous. He said he had crabs, and I must have given them to him. I was horrified and outraged. He hurled impossible accusations at me. I could only reply, "You know one of us is lying, right? And I know it's not me. So it's illogical for you to continue accusing me." He slammed the phone down and I never heard from him again.

For six months, as I returned to work and to school, I awoke every day, begging Jesus to return now and get me; I knew if he asked again, I would absolutely go. It was too hard to get through every day with no strength, no energy, no motivation. Recovery was just too slow; the fog was too thick. My debt was still greater than it had been before I got sick, as I now had to recover from not having worked for six weeks. My despair was even greater.

My bones can remember the weariness I felt.

When I consider Jesus carrying the cross, I think about the weight. I think about the defeat. I think about the humiliation, and about the inability to carry it by himself. I think about having to take up the cross and drag it around despite having already been beaten up and scourged and bruised and betrayed and bleeding. I think about him having not eaten since that very complicated last supper, about him getting no sleep in the garden while those around him snoozed, about him having been spit upon, about the blood dripping from the crown of thorns and the scourging, about the wood of the hastily-assembled and probably splintery cross, and about how much he really didn't want to do this thing ahead of him. I know people tried to intervene to lighten his burden, but I wonder if he was even in a position to notice, already having been pushed to his limits.

The spiritual fruit from this mystery is the patient bearing of trials. I am not strong in the patient category, and I keep wishing God would just fail me in that class and let me get on with other lessons, but such is apparently not to be. God has continued to ask me to be patient and to endure trials, but my experience with mono and with nearly dying was, though not the first of those trials, certainly the most dramatic, even more than the cancer. It took nearly a year for me to be able to expend the astonishing amount of energy it takes to get through a day, to be able to add a grilled cheese sandwich and a pickle to that bowl of tomato soup. It took even longer to be able to expend just a little bit more energy to reflect on the experience, to feel myself on the other side of it. Patient bearing of trials is one of the great gifts of the Rosary's mysteries, and of life. It is not natural. It takes nurturing and—well—patience to acquire patience. I'm still working on it.

A postscript: I failed the final exam spectacularly. My essay was no more coherent than I imagined it would be, but the professor, upon hearing from others how very ill I was, decided to pass me in the class after all, thus saving me the misery of retaking the class. So even this experience was not without its bit of grace.

15

THE FIFTH SORROWFUL MYSTERY: THE CRUCIFIXION

Jesus is hung on a cross unto death.

Infidelity

I HAVE ALWAYS BEEN drawn to the audacious. It takes some audacity to exist in this world. It is audacious to pursue a doctoral degree, to claim to be a follower of Christ, to teach and influence young minds, to marry. It is audacious to rest secure in any of these conditions, to claim to be educated, to be Christian, to be a teacher, to have a happy and envied marriage. At times, I find myself resting in that security, and that in itself is audacious.

Jesus was audacious in the work he did through his life, and in the claims he made. For that audacity, he was nailed to a cross. I should have been less surprised when my own audacity nailed me to one.

I felt so deeply certain that God's hand brought Ken and I together, I never questioned life could be any other way, and I never doubted we were the happiest couple I knew. When I moved to Oregon, leaving him in California to finish his career while I began mine, we laughed at those who patly told us such a move would be the end of us; we knew the distance would only bring us closer together, and we smugly told everyone it would be like dating again. For the first year, that was exactly what it was, as we saw each other every two weeks for four days, and then during the holidays. Our delight in each other was renewed. We rediscovered romance time and again, and mourned our time apart from each other.

On the first day of the second year of school, in between classes, my office phone rang, and a woman began to speak to me. She asked me if I were still married to Ken, an odd question indeed to one who assumed she was going to be married until death did us part. She told me she had been having an affair with my husband, and that she was one of three women who had been; she was calling because she was angry he was cheating on her and he needed to get his comeuppance. Without knowing whether we were still together, she thought I should know about his infidelity. She was full of lurid details.

I shook, literally and figuratively, and—as if it were normal to do so—I took notes of all she said, a kind of automatic writing, channeling someone I didn't know existed inside me. She gave me names and dates. He had met all the women, including her, online initially. She spewed her glee, knowing she was hurting him, caring nothing about my reaction. Apparently she thought we would bond over our mutual betrayal. When she told me how hurt she was when she found out about his latest fling, I recovered myself enough to say, my voice shaking, "At least you had the benefit of knowing he was a cheater. I, however, did not know this. I can't see why you're surprised by the discovery." She was shocked at my venom, and at last ended the conversation.

Dazed, I stumbled into my colleague's office. A good friend whose candidacy for sainthood I support, she agreed to take my classes for the rest of the day and I drove home. Ken was in California, during one of his spates of work, but I couldn't wait a moment longer to confront him. I called him on the way home. This was, admittedly, not the best idea. Rage driving, I'm sure, has drunk driving beat for total lack of awareness of surroundings. (Driving while talking on a cell phone was not yet illegal.) The conversation did not go well. The details are too painful and ugly to recount now. He made arrangements to come up so we could talk.

Talk we did. We cried and we talked. We prayed and we talked. Nothing helped. I could not understand what he told me, and I knew he was still lying about some particulars; I no longer trusted him or myself. I couldn't understand how I could have been so wrong for so long—the affairs had taken place over the previous six years, not just the year I had been living in Oregon—and I walked around in a haze. I am sure I thought nothing that millions of other women haven't thought, but it was all new to me: the betrayal, the conviction that our entire relationship was a lie, the disgust with myself for not having seen a single sign, the shame that my happy marriage was over, the sick feeling that never left me, not even while I slept—when I could sleep—and that lurked behind every word spoken between us. For months, when I woke in the morning, the fist of pain would hammer me again, my first conscious awareness. When I taught my classes, it seemed every text was about infidelity and betrayal; my job was to avoid crying while teaching and to avoid splashing my story and my cynicism onto my students to ensure every one of them would shun marriage forever. I could not listen to the radio or watch television, haunted by reminders of other people's pain (do you know how many songs are about betrayal??) or of what I thought were happy memories of our time together. I raged at God, trying to understand how this devastation could be the result of the relationship blessed in Medjugorje. I shake even now, to think of it all.

Above all else, my brain needed to make sense of the situations, but nothing made sense. We saw a counselor, and I begged for explanations. Assurances were pointless: much as Ken promised me he would never again cheat on me, I could never have the faith in his promises I once had, such a short ignorant time ago. If it had happened once, it could certainly happen again. Ken did everything he could, but my heart was entirely closed off, trying to protect what little of it might have been left from the explosion. My head was in control, and my head could not understand any of the things he said to me. His reasons were lame, not even making sense as excuses. I tried to use logic, tried to force him to understand the illogicality of what he said, but he couldn't understand what I needed.

I would lie awake, every night, remembering everything from the past six years, every needling moment and conversation, trying to see what must have been there, trying to keep myself from smothering him with a pillow. In hindsight, the only hint I had ever had was a cell phone bill I had come across once, with a recurring number out of our area code, and when I asked him about it, he said he sometimes let one of the guys on his team at work use his phone. The explanation made no sense to me, as it was his personal phone and he would have given one of the guys his work phone, had that been necessary; and besides, why would the same number appear over and over again? And why didn't his team members have their own phones? But I had never had any reason to distrust him before, and I let it go as just something I didn't understand but didn't need to. Of course, in retrospect I felt like an idiot, but at the time the discrepancy didn't really register for me.

Ken began to come up every weekend rather than every other weekend; he was very accountable for his time, explaining any moment I couldn't reach him on his phone. Being able to reach him, however, didn't help me once I realized that on occasion, I had spoken to him while he had been with one of these women. He went to the counselor with me, but I disbelieved the things he said in counseling. I caught him in several other lies, small things which didn't really add to the larger picture but which also didn't help me trust him. He simply didn't want to keep revealing details and make the entire thing worse, not recognizing the lies were the nails securing me to the cross. One night, having discovered some other detail he had withheld from me, I told him I couldn't accept one more lie, not one, not over the least thing, and if he couldn't understand that, we may as well divorce.

After he returned to California, then, I received an email from him, telling me he had filed for divorce, and any future communication needed to be handled by our attorneys. He had set aside money in an account for me so I could retain one, and then he had gone out of town and would not be available by phone. I tried to call him, but his phone was turned off. I left messages and emails, perhaps not as gracious as they might have been, demanding he contact me to discuss this. I couldn't believe our marriage was ending over email. He never answered.

In despair, unable to reconcile the process with my life as I had known it, I got a lawyer. On the day I was scheduled to go see her, I also made appointments to speak with our counselor and our priest. That morning, I sent another email, telling Ken I was going to these appointments, but that divorce was never what I wanted, and I was only doing this because he left me no choice.

I met with the counselor. He was sad for me, but said I was probably doing the right thing. I met with the priest, who was also sad for me, but said I was probably doing the right thing. Fifteen minutes before I was to meet the attorney, Ken called me. Having received my email, he said he was surprised I didn't want a divorce; he thought, when I said it was over, that's what I wanted. He apparently missed the "if you keep lying" part of the remark. He had not yet filed; the paperwork was still on his kitchen table, unsigned. I kept the attorney appointment anyway, asking for advice; she thought I should get out.

Ken came up to Oregon, and there was more talk. Lots of talk.

Blah blah blah.

I am acutely aware of the triteness of my story. So many people have endured such a situation it is probably harder to find people who have not. Nothing I can say is all that new. It sucked. It hurt. It was torture, every day feeling the spikes of my thoughts piercing my brain and my deadened heart.

The challenge was to open my heart to him again. I won't pretend it was easy or quick. It took years (like, eight), and a lot of therapy, and a particularly effective women's retreat, to bring myself to say I forgave him. Our dog, Grania (who also responded to "Angel Dog"), helped remarkably; I got her shortly after The Shit (as we refer to it) happened, and she is the sweetest animal I've ever known. I could physically feel my heart loosening up in her presence, and love oozing its way into me around the nail holes. Even my muscles, knotted up in furious tension for months, began to ease themselves when she was around.

I don't know precisely the moment when I really decided to stay in the relationship. At one point, I remember saying no man had ever been faithful to me, out of all my relationships, so why would I think it is possible one would? And if no man was ever going to be faithful to me, maybe I should settle for fidelity being absent from my life, and embrace what we did have together. We made a good partnership, after all.

It was a paltry way to commit.

There were moments when our relationship inched forward. My cancer diagnosis came less than a year later. (I have a friend who is researching possible connections between heartbreak and breast cancer, interestingly.) Ken's commitment to me during that time, his devotion and concern, his weeping when I was wheeled into surgery, went a long way toward helping my family forgive him. When he later asked me why his obvious devotion didn't do more for me, I pointed out that leaving me while I had breast cancer would have made him a total jerk; he wouldn't have been able to live with himself if he had done that, and he never again would be known as a nice guy, so he only got partial credit.

The Christmas after I finished cancer treatments was also the first Christmas for our new granddaughter, and we desperately longed to be together. Ken had arranged to fly up to Oregon for a few days before Christmas, and then we would drive back to California together for the holidays. The morning he was to arrive, Snow Armageddon hit Oregon. Normally, where we live, three inches of snow creates hysteria and hoarding (of kale, of all things). We got eighteen inches, unheard of in our town; we have no infrastructure for dealing with that much snow.

Ken called to say his flight had been canceled, and being together for Christmas seemed unlikely. I briefly thought I ought to be a grown-up and be resigned to the disappointment, but the unfairness of such a terrible year smothered me and I could barely breathe through my tears. He said he would do what he could. I scoffed. What could he do against an act of God?

So he packed up the truck. He loaded a sleeping bag, water, tools, chains, food, coffee: anything he thought he might need should he become stuck or stranded, and he headed north. He called me on the road to tell me he was going to try to get to me, and he would keep me posted. Grania and I waited, with scant hope. Okay, she was pretty excited when I told her he might be coming, but she had little understanding of the "might" part of that sentence.

The drive was uneventful until Ken reached Salem, about an hour south of our home, and then he hit a wall of snow. By then dark had long since descended, and the roads were deserted, but no effort had been made to shut them down. No effort had been made to plow them, either, so he made his own way. At 1:00 a.m., snow still coming down, he called to tell me he was coming into town. Grania and I stood out in the driveway; it was as if we were the only beings in the sparkly white world, except for the sound of one lone vehicle far away, slowly making its way toward us. She went out of her mind when she saw him. Maybe I did too.

He told me nothing was going to keep us apart this year, of all years.

When we woke up in the morning, his truck was buried in snow, and it was clear we were not going anywhere. That night we hosted an impromptu party for our neighbors, calling it the "Let's See What Kind of Party We Can Throw if No One Can Get to the Store Party." All our neighbors came and brought whatever they could scrounge up: Swedish meatballs, Christmas cookies, Bagel Bites, whatever. We stuck the kids in front of Christmas movies and we sang Christmas carols in the other room at the piano. We kept the Jägermeister chilled in the snow in the backyard and thought that was hilarious. (California people, remember?) Then we sent everyone home, walking our 82-year-old neighbors across the street so they wouldn't get lost in a snowdrift.

Ken was pretty heroic.

The next morning, the snow had melted somewhat but had turned to ice. He said we should try to get to California anyway, since things were pretty clear south of Salem. So with great trepidation, we loaded the truck with presents, supplies, and Grania, and headed south. It was frightening and slippery and nerve-wracking, but once we were south of Salem, the roads looked okay, until we hit the mountain passes between Oregon and California. As we crossed the last one, now late at night, we were barely able to see ahead of us, and we saw the emergency vehicle following us, closing the road. We were the last ones through, and made it to be with family for Christmas.

I realized he must love me indeed to go through all that just to make sure we were together for the holidays, and it played a role in my deciding to stay in the relationship, but still . . .

After that remarkable women's retreat, I realized how measly my "forgiveness" really was. I had been resting comfortably in my sense of victimhood and righteousness as the wronged woman. I even asked our counselor at one point why Ken should get a pass, and why I shouldn't be allowed to go out and have an affair myself to even the score; he ruefully pointed out, "Because that's not who you are. How would you live with yourself?" which of course reduced me to angry and frustrated sobs. But I began to see how I continued to punish Ken, how I allowed him to give and give without giving much in return. I let him stay, but withheld too much of myself. I no longer did the sweet little things I used to do for him: no love notes in his lunch, no frantic kisses goodbye as we left each other for the day in case this would be the last kiss (the consequences of being married to a cop), no special dinners. I didn't even tuck the collars of his polo shirts down when I folded laundry, to prevent wrinkling. In too many ways, I let our relationship continue while I kept one foot out the door.

The sticking point for me, above all else, was that line we all repeat so often: "Forgive us our trespasses as we forgive those who trespass against us." All those years of saying it, of thinking of the meager little teaspoons of forgiveness I had ever been asked to portion out, I never understood. Forgive the person who stole your parking space? Sure! Forgive the person who made you look foolish? Okay, I guess. Forgive the person who hurt you more deeply than you even knew you could be hurt, who took the most precious element in your life and pulped it? Umm . . . Yeah. No. How do I do that?

God's love. Geez, if the point of sacramental marriage is, as we are told it is, to be exemplars of God's love on earth, of all God's love can do for us, then forgiveness has to be part of that. Maybe even the whole of that. And if I ever hope to be forgiven for all the stuff I've ever done, I have to understand what it is to forgive. I could say it, but I wasn't living it.

Isn't that inability to forgive at the core of sin? Sin is, at *its* core, that which hurts us. God wants the best for us, and if we hurt ourselves, God's own beloved creatures (in the Julian of Norwich sense of creatures as God's creations, not so much the monstrous version), then we sin. If we remain mired in hate and resentment over being trespassed against, we hurt ourselves, and that's sin. If, however, we can learn to forgive, we experience God's love twice over, as we model it and as we receive it. We can begin to understand the astonishing love God has for us, when we are forgiven again and again despite the hurt we cause. If God's forgiveness is as lame and half-hearted as mine was for Ken, we are all in trouble.

I had to try. I had to re-commit to the vow I made. "For better or worse" sounds so cute when we say it in the midst of "better," as if we are talking about that horrible moment when we might both have a cold or, God forbid, the flu at the same time. Did I really mean "for worse"? I said it and asked for the help of my community, family, and God, should we ever have to face "worse." My community and family seemed to think I needed to get out of the marriage, insisting I was strong enough to walk out, but I just couldn't hear God telling me that. So I stayed. And trust me, staying is where strength is required. Walking out is easy.

The fifth sorrowful mystery is the Crucifixion. Infidelity made me feel nailed to the Cross more than at any other time in my life. I felt I had hauled my cross over the rocky path, and put it up, and then someone brutally hung me from it, so I couldn't breathe. I cried out, over and over, "My God, my God, why have you forsaken me?" and longed to hear an actual answer. This is not a rhetorical question, I insisted. I wanted to understand how, after bringing about this relationship, God could allow it to become so degraded and degrading, and then leave me alone in the midst of it, forsaken.

I really thought about the word "forsaken": Jesus cries out, "Why have you forsaken me?" and then the same words are echoed in our marriage vows: "Forsaking all others." How are those connected? Should the association be a warning to us? Jesus says, "It is finished," and I thought that was true for us as well. The spiritual fruit of the Crucifixion is the pardoning of injuries: if, after the immense betrayal Jesus endured, pardoning is the fruit we are to gain, how can I deny that suffering and sacrifice by refusing to pardon?

Telling this story is painful. It also feels dangerous. Ken is the nicest guy I have ever known, and most people feel the same; that changes when people hear this story, and I hate that. But this story is too large a part of who I am, and it is too large a part of our marriage. I also hate hearing people tell me how easy I have it because I am married to the nicest guy in the world, and we have obviously never had any problems because we are so obviously in love with each other. It is possible to be the nicest guy in the world and make enormous mistakes. I hate seeing students believe our marriage is a fairy tale, and they are holding out for such ease in a relationship; I hate watching them walk away from thriving relationships over trifling problems. I hear them, over and over, talk about God's purpose for them, God's one plan, God's one choice for their romantic future; if things aren't going well, then, clearly they misheard God's voice and picked the wrong partner, so they need to leave and find the right one. It's the strangest logic. Consequently, I hesitate to talk about how Ken and I were brought together by God, and about how angry I was with God for such a terrible idea. I fear I am only reinforcing that troubling narrative.

And so I need to tell the story of why I stayed, and of how we have been blessed in that decision and in the work of our mutual forgiveness, truly God's work. We are no longer smug in our marriage or in our happiness. We remind ourselves often of how close we came to blowing it all up, and we know that every success we have now, every trip, every friend, every moment, grows out of The Shit, and while I can never say we are grateful for the manure, we are grateful for having made our way out of the muck, pointing toward our own resurrection.

16

THE FIRST GLORIOUS MYSTERY:
THE RESURRECTION

Jesus has risen from the dead.

Cycles

THE BIRTH OF JESUS would have been little more than a pretty cool event—a good story with a virgin mother, lodestars, and evil kings—without the crucifixion, and the crucifixion in turn would have been little more than the story of yet another recalcitrant political hothead except for the resurrection. Everything ties into everything else so we celebrate the life of Jesus as a cycle, telling the story so its progression and repetition are evident throughout the year. Easter is contained in Christmas and Christmas is contained in Easter. T. S. Eliot says it best when, in his poem "The Journey of the Magi," one of the kings reflects: "were we led all that way for / Birth or Death?" Even the shape of the rosary indicates the cyclical nature of the story of Jesus, everything tied sequentially and then renewing itself.

Resurrection is not, however, quite the same as recycling. While recycling repurposes something which may have lost its use in its original form, the resurrection takes what has died, keeping its elemental nature, and brings it to life.

It is an interesting way to think about the sometimes tyrannical, ever-widening cycles in our own lives. What is resurrected and what recycled? Everything has a rhythm which most of us rarely notice. We live through continual renewal, experiencing death and a kind of resurrection over and over. Each day is broken up, regardless of what kind of schedule we might have: we get up, we eat several times, we go to bed. Other stuff happens in between, with varying levels of regularity. The end of a day is a kind of death, and the next may be the same in its elements, but it is a renewal (unless, of course, it's Groundhog Day). A week has its own patterns, broken up by days of work, days of rest, days of errands, days of chores: shopping, laundry, cooking, cleaning, preparing for the rest of the cycle. There is a reason TGIF is ubiquitous as a concept, and even people who do shift work or have rotating days off still refer to the end of their work week by saying, "This is my Friday," with relief.

A month is a wider cycle: we recognize the transition of a month when we have to pay bills, when we have to change the date as we write it, and when we keep track of other people's birthdays.

The seasons come along as well, marked by changes in wardrobe to suit the changes in weather, by what happens in the yard. Crocuses and daffodils begin the parade of the seasons, and have long been my favorite flowers; I routinely slow the car down as we pass daffodils, oohing and aahing, recognizing their gloriously cheerful bobbing yellow heads as the heralds of the pageant starting over. Next will come the irises and lilacs and hyacinths, and then the azaleas and rhododendrons, and then the roses and lavender, and then the lilies and gladiolas, and the Naked Ladies, and then the hydrangeas, and then all the oranges and yellows of asters and marigolds, and finally the bright red of the poinsettias. Each bloom portends the end of something that stirs us deep inside—regret? joy? nostalgia? allergies?—and the beginning of something else that has yet to stir us.

Those brilliantly colorful and predictable seasons rotate into years. Every New Year's Eve, we gleefully kick out the old year and welcome in the new, never quite cottoning on to the fact that the optimism inherent in such cheer is wholly unwarranted: Who on earth says the New Year is going to be better than the old one? And yet, as we take the Christmas decorations down, we generally do a thorough cleaning so we can begin again, ever hopeful. We take a deep breath and plunge in.

Our bodies are also ruled by cycles: circadian rhythms, the obvious monthly cycle that toys with women, the cycles of illness and health, injury and recovery. Aging (its own strange cycle as well as an alarmingly rapid trajectory towards the end of cycles) is just another aspect of it all, complicating how those cycles affect us.

Even our taste buds have their expected cycles. No one has hot chocolate in August, and it's mighty hard to find pumpkin chai lattes in March. Potato salad has its place in summer, with the corn and tomatoes, while chunky beef stew is best in the autumn. It took our family the longest time to realize we could actually disrupt the cycle and have corned beef any old time, not just on St. Patrick's Day, but we usually have to corn our own beef, since prepackaged corned beef is also hard to find off-season. (I can never figure out whether the grocery stores dictate the timing of our food choices or whether our food choices dictate what is stocked at the grocery store. Why can't I buy a whole turkey to smoke in June?)

We have the political cycle sucking all the air out of the atmosphere: who is in charge, who is running for office, how close we are to an election, how intense the rancor and division get. The process all culminates in either tremendous relief or rampant fear as someone else comes to power with a new (or recycled) set of agendas.

The cycle of the school year, more so than a calendar year, has long been of great significance for my life. Since I was four and my brother went to school, promising to bring home every sliver of information he had garnered during the day spent away from me (in exchange for my telling him every breathless moment of "Captain Kangaroo"), the rhythms of the academic calendar have guided my life and pushed all its other rhythms around.

There is nothing quite like the beginning of a school year, so fresh and bright and full of promise. Anything might happen. The year projects the possibility of new friends, new experiences, new information to be gleaned, new teachers who might make all the difference for us as students. Shoes are new and unscuffed, for the moment. Clothes are a little too big, leaving room to grow into, but new, at least to us. Pencils are long and sharp, with erasers still pristine and pink; the smell of freshly sharpened graphite has always evoked excitement and possibility to me. Notebooks! Oh, my! Why is a brand new notebook, its pages as yet untouched, waiting to be written upon, perfect uncreased edges, so much more alluring, so much less intimidating than a blank computer screen?

As a teacher, I have found all of this eagerness has remained. I still love fresh pencils and notebooks; I still like my clothes a little too big in case I grow even more. I still like to get new shoes for a new school year, and I still find myself sometimes admiring them rather than listening to a dreary faculty meeting where we hear yet again the sky is falling, education is dying, the humanities won't sell, and we need to learn to do more with less (so Buck Up!). But a new school year, even a new semester, means another chance to get it right, to learn from whatever didn't go well last time, to capture the minds and hearts of a new batch of brilliant young people. It is the only job I know where our task continually revitalizes itself while staying fundamentally (elementally) the same. Teaching is anything but drudgery.

Then the middle of the semester hits. Only when Ken pointed it out to me did I notice the pattern of the middle of the semester, when I despair over the Sisyphean project ahead of me. No, "anyways" is not a word and never will be. Yes, you need to cite your sources, and this is how it looks. No, Shakespeare did not create the role of Romeo for Leonardo DiCaprio. Yes, "defiantly" and "definitely" are two different words. No, Dracula and Mina Harker are not in love; you needed to read the book, not watch the movie. Yes, Virginia Woolf is spelled like that, not like the canine. No, you cannot turn your papers all in at the end of the semester in one big unedited push of gormless energy. Yes, I remember when you told me you had to get an A in this class, but you were supposed to do the work. Sigh. I begin to think there is no purpose to my existence, and maybe it's time to join the Peace Corps. Teaching is the dumbest thing in the world to attempt.

Every semester, though, I muddle through to the end. In an effort to continually improve, I always ask students as the semester concludes what the most useful thing was that they learned, and what I should dump. My favorite response, one repeated over and over again, is, "I hate to read, so I dreaded this class, but I ended up loving this class more than any other." I am still more heartened by those who change their major to English. I almost always end the school year feeling elated at what has been achieved, anxious over how much more needs to be done, and downright morose when students I have come to cherish graduate and leave. But I have a summer's worth of time stretching ahead of me to perfect my offerings for students I have yet to meet. It's a delicious feeling.

These are all cycles I more or less recognized at work in my life. There are others, though, which I only came to recognize when I had to step out of life, to discontinue my participation, hitting the pause button on life, generally through no fault or plan of my own.

The first hiatus was when I had mono and jaundice: for the bulk of that six month period, I was largely unable to function. Sleeping was my primary chore, and I excelled at it. Because I had been mired in school and work and got sick at the very end of fall semester, Christmas came to me as a shock; I had slept through several weeks when I was supposed to be doing my Christmas shopping, and now was unprepared. I asked my father to drop me at the mall, planning to whip around and pick up something, anything, to give as gifts. I figured I could get it all done in an hour, and arranged to meet him back at the entrance, thinking I could surely handle that.

I severely overestimated my recovery. I remember walking into the store, unequipped for the torrents of shoppers, overwhelmed by the vigor of the displays and the chipperiness of the music, clueless about what I might buy. I remember grabbing things, somewhat randomly, gathering sweaters and knickknacks in my arms and already realizing I didn't have the strength to carry them. Exhausted, exasperated because I kept dropping things, I succumbed to sitting on the floor, my goods around me, scooting forward as the line progressed toward the cash register. (No one offered to help or checked to see why I was sitting on the floor.) The whole crucible lasted fifteen minutes, and I made my way to the bench outside the mall, where I promptly fell asleep until my father returned. I had gifts, more or less, but felt I had failed at such an elemental duty of life.

I felt the failure so keenly that six months later, when I was significantly better, I threw a Christmas party in June. I found a tree, put up lights, put Handel's Messiah on the record player, and made Christmas goodies, inviting all those who helped me get through my illness. I had to invite the neighbors or they would have thought I was insane. (They may have, anyway.) So even the holidays provide their own expectations in the cycle, and missing them throws everything off.

When I was undergoing cancer treatments, I again dropped out of life. Unable to leave the house because of my lousy immune system, I was fiercely aware of being severed from my cycles. If a woman receives chemotherapy at a certain age, she may go through a sped-up version of menopause, as did I. (Ken says the advantage of going through menopause this way is that, for better or worse, he never had to deal with mood swings; there is pretty much just the one predictable mood operating all the time.) My last period was the day after my lumpectomy, and I was thrilled. Menstruation wasn't doing me any good anyway, always unpredictable and sometimes painful to the point of fainting, so being rid of it was the best part of the whole cancer experience; it was also the *only* thing three different doctors (all male) recommended I get therapy for, mansplaining that having a period was the thing that made a woman really a woman, and losing it often made it difficult for a woman to locate her identity. None of them offered therapy for, say, facing mortality, pain, the stigma of cancer, or any of the other baggage merrily traipsing in with a diagnosis, but hey, we all love to menstruate, am I right, gals?

Unable to work during treatments, I bowed out of the school cycle too. School holidays, spring break, midterm grades, finals: none of it mattered to me.

My only significant cycle then was the routine between infusions, and even that was a murky mess: unable to keep track of my treatment plan, I had to rely on Ken to keep a detailed log of my medications and my reactions to them, as well as my temperature, my appointments, and all the blips in my progress. I was vaguely aware of the seasons passing, but mostly because as it got warmer, I needed fewer blankets while I spread out on the sofa. And Grania, our dog, got muddier, as she hunkered down in the crook of my knees so she could keep watch while I slept. The days, months, and seasons ticked on with me blithely unaware.

I did, however, become acutely aware of missing the liturgical seasons, something I had taken for granted before and had not even really recognized as a cycle. Because of the timing of my treatments, Christmas was the last Mass I was able to attend for many months, so I missed the actual Christmas season. While I was aware of the rhythm of holidays, I was less aware of the way my internal clock was attuned to the interval of Ordinary time between Christmas and Lent, that space to breathe. I missed Lent, Easter, and the entire Easter season. I missed the influence of the liturgical calendar, in its own cycle of resetting our souls, of adjusting our gaze toward God: the anticipation and waiting of Advent (and how lovely is it to wait for something without being afraid it might not show up?), the joy of Christmas, the freshness of Ordinary time (kind of like cleaning up after a big party), the sobriety and self-reflection of Lent, the deep sadness of Holy Week, and the tremendous celebration of Easter that propels us to sing, "Alleluia!" I had no idea, before being unable to actively participate in it, how much the liturgy shaped my own thoughts and attitudes on a day-to-day basis. I mourned the loss, even as I continued to be mad at God for giving me cancer to begin with.

These illnesses, obliterations of cycles, were both bleak times, but I have also experienced the blessing of two sabbaticals, times when those cycles became complicated and uneasy. The first sabbatical was insane: I wrote a book on Virginia Woolf, presented at three conferences, and published four articles. It was not very sabbath-y. My father's death also took place at the beginning of my first sabbatical, and I am grateful I did not have to teach as I grieved. I was exhausted when I returned to teaching, but I love research, so was enthusiastic about all the work I had accomplished. Even as I was not teaching, however, I still lingered in the cycles: I was always cognizant of how much time I had left to finish all my projects before returning to the classroom.

My second sabbatical, though—that was a doozy. I was determined not to overwork myself like I had the last time, as I was at the end of my rope anyway. My scholarly project was simply to catch up on my reading. Because the bulk of my teaching load was contemporary literature, and because I never had time to read other than what I taught, I needed to update my syllabi. The beauty of this plan is that such reading can be done pretty much anywhere in the world.

Thus began the magical year that made us look like we won the lottery. (We did not. We are excellent shoppers, and we were showered with good fortune, friends, and ludicrous opportunities which we could not possibly refuse.)

I began the year with a writer's retreat at the Oregon Coast, with an amazing group of friends. It was inspiring as it shifted my focus away from teaching and towards study and writing. Rain cascading down the windows, whales spouting close to the beach, ideas being bandied about, wine being poured, delectable food being made and consumed: it was the perfect beginning to my time away (and a good place to begin serious work on this book).

I went on a cruise from London to London with my best friend and her daughter, taking advantage of an outrageous sale of both cruises and airfares.

Ken and I went on a wine tour to France with friends who, originally from Burgundy, now run a winery in Oregon. They had arranged a trip for wine club members, twelve of us, and it was one of the most remarkable trips we have ever been on, giving us access to some of the most exclusive wineries and restaurants in France with a group of newly-made and lasting friends.

I went to Ireland with a friend who was going with her boyfriend when he changed his mind about the trip at the last minute (causing her to change her mind about him); she had not yet decided on an itinerary, but thought she would go anyway. I finagled my way into suggesting an itinerary that largely invited us visiting my family, and the next thing we know, the boyfriend gave me his frequent flyer miles so I could go with her for free. It was that kind of year.

We took another cruise with friends from Australia, down the Eastern seaboard to see the fall colors, something I don't get to do when the cycle of the school year controls my life.

Yet another cruise at Christmas took us to Cuba. We went to Mazatlan with our friends who own timeshare there, and took a quick trip to Palm Springs to see my sister.

We ended the year with one last cruise from Venice to Venice, where we got to see the Bay of Poets in Italy where Percy Bysshe Shelley drowned and where Lord Byron hung out, where we got to tour the Greek Islands and pretend I was Clytemnestra welcoming Agamemnon home, and where we got to see the beach where Ulysses washed ashore in *The Odyssey*, only weeks before I was able to incorporate all these experiences into my teaching.

In the middle of all this, Ken's mother died of leukemia; some months later, his father was diagnosed with esophageal cancer and also died. Our fun and games were punctuated by great grief. Sabbatical has been tough on parents.

We took twenty-three trips in fifteen months.

Among them was the pilgrimage to Italy with our priest, Fr. Zani, followed just a few days later by a Tuscan food and wine retreat hosted by friends.

There were eighty-two people on the pilgrimage. That's a lot of people to haul around the crowded, bus-wrecking streets of Italy. Fr. Zani's goal was to lead Mass every day in a different church, and to cover as much territory as possible in ten days. Being young and inexperienced in European travel, he definitely overshot the mark, failing to account for potty-breaks and tiny restaurants for so many people, but we made it work. We went to a Papal address, where we stood about six feet away from Pope Francis as he passed. Fr. Zani got to say Mass in the Vatican, and I actually got to lead some of the singing, which was an overwhelming experience. (I sound really good in those kinds of acoustics!—but I think pretty much everyone does.) We went to Mass in Assisi, in Florence, in Sorrento, in Rome . . . in a bewildering array of amazing churches throughout Italy. The itinerary was dizzying but spectacular, and we were all depleted at the end of our time together.

After leaving that group, we met up with our other friends in Tuscany. We stayed in a 1000-year-old tower at a winery, going on day trips for wineries and sightseeing, and had delectable meals prepared for us in the evenings. We went out for a couple of meals, but those in the tower were most memorable, with superb food and wine and even more superb fellowship and laughter. Jesus would have liked it.

Continuing the blitz of the year's blessings, Ken and I, having finished our duties for dinner preparation, took our wine out to the back patio overlooking a valley in Tuscany. As we sat there, basking in the beauty and watching the clouds rolling in, feeling inspired, I began to sing "How Great Thou Art." As I got to the line, "I hear the rolling thunder," at once a massive peal of thunder clamored over the valley, followed almost immediately by the onset of a tremendous lightning storm. Ken and I looked at each other and he laughed, "Daaaaaaang. I didn't know you could do that!" I told him I didn't either, but now that I had God's ear . . . well, I didn't end up with a million dollars, so there's that.

The year was filled with such moments. My spirit, so worn out from constant work, was being renewed and I was being prepared to re-enter real life, but at every point, the cycles went on around us. We were constantly aware of them, drawing me back to my job.

And then COVID-19 hit, months after my return to work, ending school—and life—as we knew it and certainly ending travel, ending getting dressed, wearing make-up, or hugging people. I am sure everything has been said about it that could be said. Everything shut down. Restaurants were among the first things to go, and schools followed shortly thereafter. Lesson plans had to be adapted at the same time new technology and delivery systems had to be learned. Every aspect of my job had to be reconsidered, restructured, and repeated. There was less teaching than there was bookkeeping, trying to devise new policies, and fighting the computer.

Then they took away church, just in time for Lent and Easter. To have no access to the Eucharist has been much harder than I guessed it would be. At least during cancer, I was able to take communion at home. Ken and I went back to in-person Mass once, for Pentecost, but I was appalled at how poorly people were maintaining social distancing and how few of them kept their masks on. I have a terrible immune system that was still further brutalized—I mean compromised—by cancer; even all these years later, I go home with every germ that winks at me from across a room. I simply cannot take the chance of getting this disease. So I have not been back to church, except via YouTube (very unsatisfying).

Because all of these deprivations weren't enough, apparently, then COVID took away my job. I am—I guess—retired. COVID gave an excuse to the university where I worked to hurry along changes already in the offing: more on-line delivery of classes, fewer humanities being offered, tighter control on the conservatism taught in those classes, and so on; I was interested in none of it. It was a good time to accept the offer of an early retirement, made at the end of the school year.

So now I am at home, still under quarantine. As I write, the vaccines continue to roll out, but I am still weeks away from being eligible; the wait is torture. I have not had a haircut in over a year, other than the childishly crooked bangs I lop off every now and then. The seasons are still succeeding each other, maybe more emphatically than ever without so much human intervention. Animals are encroaching in places they have long avoided. I am gazing out right now at the beauty and destruction of an exceedingly rare three-day ice storm; everything is encased in crystal, but tree branches gave way under the unexpected weight. For reasons I don't quite understand, the robins are having a field day, and the cacophony was so loud this morning I couldn't sleep.

Nearly all the other cycles are meaningless. The days of the week are irrelevant. For a time, football helped us: we knew what we would be doing Monday night, Thursday night, and all day Sunday. But that's only a few months. Ken and I are constantly asking each other, "Wait, is that today?" or, "Wait, did I shower today? Yesterday? Should I do that sometime?" All those shoes I have, from all those new school years, just sit there, longing to be aired out, but slippers are all I need, for the most part. A television schedule, which might have regulated rhythms in our youth, is insignificant when you just record everything on a DVR. (I assume one day that acronym will be as dated as the VCR on which I used to record *All My Children*, but even with that life-changing technology, I needed to know the program was on Monday through Friday from 1-2:00 p.m. on ABC. Now I just speak into my remote, "Record *This Is Us*," and magic elves in the black box figure out the rest.) The holidays, with all their decorative clues, are barely marking time since we don't go anywhere to see the decorations: Christmas was just another day at home, with more phone calls but no human contact. Thanksgiving was more food, but still just another day at home.

I don't know what the future will look like. I don't know how many of the cycles that have regulated my life will return, or whether I have been set free permanently from anything that differentiates the year.

What is clear in thinking about cycles is how enclosed they are. They are never, nor can they be, open-ended or linear. Even when one cycle seems over, such as menstruation or a school schedule, we see it as contained in the whole. The birth, life, death and resurrection of Jesus make up a whole cycle, visible and significant only in its completion, but it is also one of many cycles operating in our lives, while our own lives will only be a complete cycle of many other cycles when we are done and can see the whole work of our lives in their entirety.

While so many of my cycles seem to have ended, at least for now, for the first time in my life I have a regular schedule, creating its own rhythm. We go to bed at much the same hour, with a routine, and I don't have to set the alarm. I close things up and get ready for bed; Ken takes our dog, Roscoe, out for what we call his "Pee Walk," down the road to a grassy open area, and they are often joined by our cat, Earnie, who waits for Roscoe to find a spot and then joins him so they can pee together; it's kind of like the end of James Joyce's *Ulysses*, and Earnie and Roscoe are about as well suited for each other as Leopold Bloom and Stephen Daedalus. When they all troop home, I am in bed, reading, and Ken tells Roscoe, "Go tell Kathy goodnight," and Roscoe happily trots to my side of the bed for our evening ritual of petting and cooing. So maybe new rhythms and cycles for the life that is to be will inevitably assert themselves, performing their own resurrection and renewal.

The fruit of this mystery is faith, and part of that faith is believing even the least likely of scenarios are possible. The very nature of a cycle is restorative, even when we can't see what might be restored. I won't—can't—know how my own story will renew itself, until the end, when my story unites completely with the story of Jesus, perfecting the circle. In the meantime, I rejoice at every new opportunity to celebrate the Resurrection, of Jesus and of life eternal. The daffodils are coming.

17

THE SECOND GLORIOUS MYSTERY:
THE ASCENSION

Jesus is raised to Heaven.

Ambition

A PROFESSOR AT A Christian college, especially a woman, lives in a perpetual state of tension between the messages she receives. On the one hand, she is taught throughout her life to be the servant, to abase herself, to be humble. Teaching is a job of service, both to students and to the universities that take and take and take whatever we are still capable of giving, and a Christian university in particular relies on our having internalized what the Bible has told us: we turn the other cheek; we don't let the left hand know what the right hand is doing; we know it is more blessed to give than to receive, that God loves a cheerful giver, that the last shall be first and the first shall be last, and that our reward will come in Heaven. So we say, joyfully—for the most part—here I am, Lord, despite increased workloads and dwindling salaries.

On the other hand, we are also in a profession which perpetually demands we propel ourselves forward, upward. We have to defend our existence, especially if we are in the humanities, by explaining and demonstrating over and over again why what we do is important and how we are effective at it. We have to publish, which involves further selling of ourselves, and proclaim our success in having done so. We must advertise the good work we are doing, telling our stories about student success and external validation so our budgets won't be cut yet again. Every year, at my institution, faculty is required to write what is called a Faculty Growth Plan, wherein we brag of our successes, bemoan our failures, and lay out a plan for the future, all in the areas of teaching, service, scholarship, and faith. Doing so ensures that knife edge of bravado and humility is always jabbing us, usually in the ribs from behind but sometimes straight through the heart.

Consequently, I have spent considerable time thinking about what it means to ascend. The symbolism of rising, of things looking up, of ascending the ranks, of climbing the ladder, is too well ingrained in us to ever be disrupted adequately, and the mystery of the Ascension is a part of that. Jesus is raised, bodily, to Heaven. He is above us all. He can look down on us. We are the lowly. Up is good; down is bad. Language constantly asserts the binary; we cannot miss it.

So we strive to go up. Ever in the back of our minds, however, is the image of a bunch of upstarts building a tower in Babel, trying to draw nearer to God by raising themselves, and being smacked down pretty hard. We see, as well, the person who presumes to sit near the head of the table; the rebuke is striking, and that person is sent to the bottom of the table, out of favor, humiliated, repulsed.

So what to do? Work to ascend? Remain satisfied where we are, never trying to improve? Pretend to ascend but do it quietly? Place ourselves at the foot, hoping someone will notice our feigned, possibly misplaced humility and raise us? Resolving this conflict seems impossible.

In my own climbing, both literal and figurative, I have sometimes been rewarded and sometimes punished. I have seen the ambivalence about ascending play out over and over in my life.

I grew up in a house at the bottom of a hill, and through most of my childhood, that hill was an obstacle. We would torturously drag our bikes to the top (my brother could ride all the way but I struggled) so we could free-fall our way back down. We had to climb the hill and go down the other side when our mother sent us to the store to amend some shortfall, and then climb back up again on the steeper side with the added burden of whatever we had purchased. The hill was part of my paper route, and I despised it in the cold rain and in the broiling sun; I tried to rearrange my route so I would have gotten rid of most of my papers before hitting the hill, but it wasn't practicable, so I always had to climb it when the bags were at their heaviest, often zig-zagging my way up to lighten the strain.

By the time I became an angsty teenager, I realized it was not such a monumental hill, and I came to covet it. At the very top, there was a small weed-filled knoll with an embankment forming the perfect seat. I could sit there and be partially obscured by the weeping willow tree at the side; someone driving past would be hard put to see me, and I was not easily visible from the surrounding houses. At first, I would bring a book; I remember sitting there reading *Wuthering Heights* for the first time, captivated by Heathcliff and Cathy, the first heroine I'd ever read who had my name, even if she spelled it wrong.

Soon, though, I began to bring along a notebook, and I started to write. It was peaceful; I was alone; I was unmolested; I was inspired. I was sure I was the next great writer, musing carefully over each word as I gazed romantically out over the valley, composing brilliance. I wrote poetry, songs, short stories, plays. (I never brought my diary; there was always the possibility of discovery in such a public place, and though I could tolerate having my literary masterpieces accidentally discovered, I did not feel the same way about my diary, even though my diary was largely filled with lamentations about how my hair didn't work that day or which guy I desperately hoped would notice me.)

My favorite time on the hill, though, was at night, after the sun went down. Then I was truly invisible, and I could look out over the lights of the valley below. It was too dark to write, but I took each light as my inspiration to concoct a story about the people hidden behind the obscuring brightness. I was awestruck at the thought of how many different lives were spread out before me, like a banquet I could never taste.

My curiosity aroused, I began to talk to the people on my paper route. As the only female paper carrier in the county, I was an object of curiosity for them too, as well as pity. They saw me struggling up that hill every day, poor girl that I was. Especially when I was collecting their payments at the end of each month, I was invited in for cookies, cocoa, or lemonade, and a chat. Mrs. Payne, whose one-armed husband ran the presses for the town's newspaper, was especially lovely to me, giving me huge tips, helping fund my first trip ever (a class trip to Washington D. C.), and trying (oh so unsuccessfully) to set me up with her grandson by taking us out to lunch at a place so fancy I had to actually wear gloves. Another customer, a man who once answered the door by thrusting a knife through the aperture, was mortified because he was expecting someone else; he was friendly and apologetic afterwards, though I never accepted his invitations to come in. Mrs. Farrington, recently widowed, told me long and fascinating stories about the neighborhood and all the scandals it had ever harbored; for a woman I never saw outside her home, she had a remarkable grasp on what was going on around her. I was surrounded by stories, and they were there for the asking, and in my mind, such stories were only gifted to me because I dared to climb to the top of the hill and look. Ascending, then, paid off.

Further afield from my home, I quickly learned the way trips nearly always form a sojourn of the soul, and no sojourn of the soul is ever quite complete without a trek up a mountain, some more successful than others.

On my first trip to Ireland, I went to County Mayo, ancestral home of my father's side of the family. It is also the site of Croagh Patrick, the mountain named after St. Patrick, and a site of holy pilgrimage. People climb the path up the mountain, about a three-and-a-half-hour hike, believing blessings will ensue; blessings may very well multiply if you do the trip barefoot or, even better, on your knees (in which case, I'm guessing, the hike will take a lot longer than three-and-a-half hours).

I knew little about any of this when my friend Lisa and I went to Westport, but when I heard about it I knew I should try the climb; I could always use blessings. Lisa, not at all religious, was less interested, so I was left to make the excursion on my own while she wandered off elsewhere. I remember the day was cool, early October, but not raining and not too foggy.

At the start of my clamber up, I had only the vaguest idea of how far I had to go, or how I should prepare. (This is perhaps the ideal way to approach any obstacle; ignorance may not be bliss, but it's not as discouraging as knowledge can be.) Feeling young and intrepid, I began the climb barefoot, navigating the rocky path as best I could, but after about an hour of mincing around trying to avoid jagged rocks, I realized I was going to mutilate my feet for the rest of our trip through Europe, so I donned my boots. I remember very little about the trek, and can't even recall what was at the top, except a large cross. Some people talked boisterously on the way up, wanting to meet new people, while others were deep in solitary prayer. The views were dazzling, if not histrionic, and the air was fresh and clean. The path was—up. And up. So far up.

The problem with any journey up is there is pretty much always, in the absence of slides, funiculars, or helicopters, the inevitable trip down, a trip that crushes knees in its relentlessness. Quads wobble. I remember being elated at the end of the up-ness of the climb because coming down would be so much easier, but on my way down, I longed for the reprieve of using different muscles to climb once more.

Up leads to down: obviously, a pretty mighty metaphor for life as well.

I reunited with Lisa at the end of the day, exhausted but pleased with myself for having achieved what I felt was quite an accomplishment. But when I bragged about having finished the climb, I heard from a number of people how disappointing it must have been to have conceded to wearing shoes, as if God would of course fail to reward me for the sacrifice of the climb unless I had done it barefoot and with maximum pain. Somehow, I had cheated. I was deflated.

Later, when I went to Medjugorje, there was yet another mountain, and climbing it is considered an essential part of the pilgrimage. Going up on a Wednesday or Friday is not recommended because the fasting will make you weak, and when you do go up, you are instructed to bring water, umbrellas, food, good walking shoes—all the gear and tackle and trim conscientious hikers bring. We had not yet decided what day we would be going up, as such significant preparation was daunting.

One morning, another woman and I were wandering around town before breakfast, and came to the base of the trail; we decided just to walk up for a bit, to see how far we might get. We were wandering, mind you, not hiking, so we had absolutely nothing with us, not even jackets. On the way up, we talked and prayed, and I don't actually remember the climb being that onerous (though I am decidedly not a hiker), but suddenly we were at the top. As we stood there, a rain cloud opened up and slammed the mountain top with a deluge of water, soaking the other pilgrims around us, all of whom had umbrellas and hoods on their jackets. Strangely (quite the understatement), neither my friend nor I were touched by a single drop. The area around the two of us was completely dry, although the small space between us was drenched and muddy. We moved our hands into the rain to feel it, but there was nothing, wherever we touched. I cannot pretend to understand it.

Again, however, I felt to some extent I had cheated. We had not planned on going up the hill, having more or less stumbled upon the whole experience, and it was not that difficult of a climb, It felt as if it didn't count if we had not made a big deal about the preparation for it. Despite our "cheating," however, our reward was great. Stupendous, even.

I attacked another kind of mountain when I signed up to do the 3-Day Breast Cancer walk, a sixty-mile walk around the Bay Area that involved camping in communal tents at night. I joined a team and we trained for months, climbing many hills for practice, naming those victims and survivors for whom we were going to be walking. This was many years before I even imagined I would have breast cancer myself, and contributed to my unreasoning anger over my diagnosis: I had already paid my dues, donating, fund raising and walking for breast cancer; plainly, I should not also have to endure it.

Despite all the training, when the day of the walk arrived, I was still filled with trepidation. Sixty miles is more than a casual ramble. I got my armor together: new cushiony socks with pink ribbons on them, good breathable shoes, comfortable non-chafing pants, requisite free t-shirt, water bottles that fit into the pack around my waist, lightweight jacket, cute little pink hat. Our overnight supplies were packed into well-marked duffel bags proclaiming our team names, and we would reunite with them at the camping site. We were off. We slogged through neighborhoods, up hills, down hills, through parks, up hills, up more hills, geez, who knew there were all these hills?

On the second day, around midday, it started to rain. This was no gentle refreshing mist, but was a pounding rain that blinded us, with a good wind whipping our hair around just in case we dared open our eyes long enough to get a glimpse of something in between the lashings of rain. There had been no word about this in the weather forecasts, so no one was prepared. We trudged on, leaning forward to fight the storm, already exhausted by the extra effort. Cushiony socks were soaked, breathable shoes were not waterproof, wet pants absolutely chafed, t-shirts clung, water bottles were redundant, lightweight jacket was comical, and the cute little pink hat got blown over a cliff.

By the time we got to our overnight destination, hours late, in the dark, the fields where we were to have camped were flooded. At the last minute, the organizers had decided to bus us all to the local race track, where there was at least a canopy over the seats, though the fields there were also flooded. The thought, apparently, was that hundreds of us would spend the night sleeping while sitting up in the plastic stadium seats, huddling to stay somewhat dry, despite being thoroughly soaked (as was everything in our duffel bags, which had sat out in the rain for quite some time while buses were organized for us all). Still, dispirited though I was, I thought I could make it through the third day, until upon removing my socks I found my feet were swollen, bright red, blotchy, and bloody from hundreds of tiny blisters. Thus I discovered my allergy to the latex which was helping to keep my new socks so very cushiony.

There was quite a long line of people at the pay phones, and an even longer line of us standing outside, waiting for our loved ones to pick us up to end the misery. I was not the only one who capitulated, but my sense of failure was no less potent for that.

Not all difficult ascensions were unsuccessful, however. On our pilgrimage to Italy, I had another opportunity. The Scala Sancta is a set of twenty-eight marble stairs imported to Rome from Jerusalem; they are the stairs Jesus climbed when he was condemned to death by Pilate. Normally, they are protected by a wood covering, and people climb them on their knees, praying, able to see the stairs through small slats in the wood. For the first time in 300 years, however, they were uncovered, for two months, such a tiny window of time, exposing the very stone upon which Jesus had trod, and we happened to be there for it. I debated whether to try going up; once someone begins the climb, there is no going back, and one is absolutely forbidden to stand. I have bone spurs in both knees, a propensity to dislocated kneecaps, and carry too much weight, so I knew going up would be torture. It was also a very hot day. But I knew I could not miss this opportunity, so I entered.

I thought I knew what to expect, but the pain was surprising, from the very first stair. Each step had a concavity in the middle of it, a kind of trough or rut hollowed out by centuries of knees, so there was no flat or easy surface where I could rest or sort out where my knee cap was supposed to go before letting all the pain-filled weight settle in order to push forward to the next step. In the meantime, there were people ahead, behind, and to the side of me, so I couldn't exactly change direction or stop. Twenty-eight steps doesn't sound like *that* many, so surely I could do this, I thought until every time I looked up I saw the vast expanse between myself and the top. I prayed. Hard. Quickly. Frantically. (It is possible to get a whole Hail Mary done in one breath, given the right motivation. I also do this when I go to the dentist.) I clung to the thought that what Jesus endured was far worse, reminding myself at least I was not going to be crucified when I reached the top of the stairs. But I also had the teensiest thought (okay, it wasn't as teensy as it should have been) that if I made it to the top, God would owe me.

So I prayed big.

No teeny little prayers about temporary situations, like, "Travel mercies for us all," or, "Help me endure that one person on our trip." No vague prayers like, "Please be with my family and friends." No prayers about teaching me to relinquish control (God is probably sick of hearing that one anyway). Nope. I prayed for two things on my heart, two impossible plights, situations I could see no way out of without divine intervention.

I made it to the top, my face beet red, my hands slippery with sweat, my clothing soaked. As I went to stand, I found my legs were useless below my knees, and I collapsed. As Ken and Fr. Zani helped me up, I was jubilant, not just at the success of a difficult task, but at the sense of being close to God; I felt heard.

My knees hurt for several days, but I rested in the satisfaction of having successfully made it to the top, a once-in-a-lifetime chance to do this incredible journey.

Strikingly, both of my very improbable prayers were answered, though absolutely *not* in the way I would have liked, proving God's sense of humor once again. The circumstances of the first prayer are not my story to tell, so I will just say I learned to be far more specific in my prayer requests for the future, but God did indeed intervene. The results of the second prayer demonstrate how a little specificity might indeed be desirable (even though, as I say this, I overtly contravene my prayer on relinquishing control). I prayed for Mary, my sister, that she stop her drinking.

I still cannot decide whether the answer to my prayers is reward for my ascension or punishment. Weeks after our return home from Italy, Mary was pretty well sloshed when she rear-ended a car while she was driving home from Mom's house. She totaled her own car, but fortunately did little damage to the other car and the other driver claimed to have been unhurt. Mary felt some pain, but knew that without medical insurance, she could ill afford a trip in an ambulance or the subsequent medical bills, so she declined treatment. She was, however, arrested for drunk driving and taken to jail, a first for our family.

Upon release, she went back to work at the garden supply shop; for two weeks she did all she could to avoid lifting lawn mowers, weed whackers, and boxes of supplies. We were approaching Sacred Sisters Weekend, the once-a-year weekend when the three of us get together for several days of too much food, wine, laughter, and Cards Against Humanity, where we wear our hideous seersucker housecoats. The sisters are not the sacred part; the weekend is, because once the date is established, we have each vowed that nothing can ever prevent any of us from attending.

Nothing. Mary knew if she went to the doctor, she would have to break that vow, and she was determined to be there.

She was there, but could barely lie down, and could absolutely not laugh. At the end of the weekend, Rosie drove her to the hospital, where doctors were shocked at her condition. She had broken six ribs and her collarbone, and had developed two abscesses, huge lumps, inside her chest. The local hospital was inadequate for such injuries; even Stanford and the University of San Francisco declined her. She was finally sent to UC Davis, about two hours from her home, on a helicopter. (She still wonders at the injustice of forcing a woman who is terrified of flying to go up in a helicopter, while that woman is in excruciating pain, and then charging her a fortune for the privilege.) Twenty days and multiple surgeries later, with gruesome stories in between of daily debridement of her open chest wound, she was released, unable to drive or even sit in the front seat of a vehicle (the over-the-shoulder seat belts would be impossible with her incisions), unable to lift her arms above her shoulders, unable to pick up anything.

But she stopped drinking. Cold turkey. She has also asked me to stop praying for her.

Clearly, ascending is complicated.

The pursuit of an education is perhaps the ultimate sign of acceptable and even desired ascension in our society. We hear over and over how it is the way out of a penurious future, how only through education can we hope to become model citizens. I never associated my efforts to get an education with ambition, per se. Maybe I am quibbling about language, but ambition is an overwhelming longing to get ahead in the world, to be seen as successful according to someone else's ideal (usually connected to making money), while ascension is the actual act of gaining tools to improve one's being, and is not necessarily connected to financial success.

I longed for knowledge to help me understand the world around me in order to make me a better traveler. Such knowledge, as Alexander Pope so wisely put it, is "a dangerous thing," causing me to long for more knowledge to fill out the knowledge I was gaining. The more you know, the more you know you don't know. We climb one peak only to see the array of peaks still before us. When I would find myself so close to a goal, most often a goal set by someone else (I only need how many more credits and then I'll have a degree?), it was just silly not to go on. Step by step, I found myself climbing a mountain I never even knew I was at the foot of.

Part of me wants to say I fell into my doctorate, finding myself accidentally on the path as in Medjugorje, and that part is true. That part of me has the same reaction every time I achieve a major achievement: when I graduated with my BA, my MA, and my PhD, when I publish a book or an article, when I beat yet another illness or injury: if I could do this, then it couldn't be that special. Anyone could do it. The attitude has much less to do with humility than it does with insecurity and feelings of inadequacy.

Another part of me understands that from the moment my knee touched that pitted marble stair of the academy, I was going to be in for a time. With every setback, my parents would ask me why I was so ambitious, and why I couldn't just take a job and stop with all this schooling. I heard mixed messages about my progress continually: people were proud of me, but people were dismayed by how hard I worked for no discernible reason; people were happy for me that I got published, but people were bored to tears by what I wrote; people were impressed by my credentials, but people thought I must be a snob because of them; people bragged I was now a professor, but people were dismayed to find out how little I got paid.

Keeping me pegged on a lowly rung, two moments stand out in particular. When I was finishing my Master's thesis, written on a typewriter (oh, bless you, word processing programs!), I had to edit and retype all seventy-five pages four times in one week. I had only recently come through both carpal tunnel surgeries and typing was still painful, so Ken and my father both helped me. I was pleased, at first, because it was the first time my father had helped me in any way throughout my education, and as he typed, never having read a single one of the texts about which I was writing, he laughed, "I could have said all this in two paragraphs."

I was wounded. I know he was partially kidding, trying to lighten the moment. I know he really didn't know what it was he was typing; while he was an intelligent man, he had barely finished high school, and read very little literature, finding it too pretentious. He had effectively deprecated two years of my work in one mocking sentence, meant to bring me back to earth just as I was completing a huge milestone.

The other telling moment was when he and my mother were visiting us in Oregon, just before he died. I came to the backyard in the morning where he was sitting with his coffee at the patio table. He had decided, before anyone got up, to read my most recent publication, an article in a book of collected essays put out by a very prestigious press. The book had just come in the mail and I hadn't even had a chance to look at it yet, so it had been sitting out. I should have been delighted he was at last showing interest in my work, but as I sat down, my eyes went to the book, freshly printed; he had rested his coffee cup on the page, leaving a dark coffee stain in the middle of my article. I gasped. I don't even break the spines of books, never fold down a page, certainly never use them as coasters, and this was *my* book. It seemed the greatest disrespect. He glanced down and said, "Oh. Oops. I'll buy you another copy."

"It's $95.00," I said, flatly.

"Oh. No, I won't."

And that was that. I got my smackdown.

Such comeuppance (though, in the context of a conversation about ascension, maybe that should be "comedownance") has not been limited to my family, however. I was elated when my first book, *Buffoonery in Irish Drama*, came out. The publisher sent me a box of copies, the bright green of the cover promising to stand out on a bookshelf. I was in the middle of chemo when they arrived, and I set one up on the table in front of me so I could gaze at it rapturously, when I noticed, on the cover, they had spelled it "Buffooery" rather than "Buffoonery." I kept looking at it, certain my drug-induced stupor was to blame, waiting for the letters to arrange themselves properly, but they never did. While there is a certain punnishness to the mistake, I was not striving for humor in the title. Frantically searching my computer for the proofs I had approved, I was relieved to find it was their mistake, not mine, so now I can say my first book went into a second printing right away.

Even more amusing, after having spent nine years writing the Virginia Woolf book, I got my first royalty check of $18.36. (Academic publishing is not exactly remunerative.) When I took the check to the bank, however, it bounced, adding insult to injury. It turned out to be a glitch in the publisher's system, and they made good on it, covering the bounced check charge and throwing in $5.00 extra for my trouble, so I got to say my proceeds doubled in the first year.

Both instances served to undercut any hubris publishing might have bolstered in me.

Still, there were achievements in my ascension. When I retired as a consequence of COVID-19, the dear people with whom I worked threw me a Zoom retirement party. (I look forward to the day when none of us will remember what a Zoom meeting was.) Other department members, friends, students both current and former, and my family came. The chair of my department began the celebration by reading three pages of accolades about me, which even I thought was a bit extreme, but it was gratifying to hear the list of my accomplishments and contributions to my field and to my institution. I obviously knew what I had done, but when I heard it all at once, I felt somewhat vindicated in myself, knowing I had not thrown my life away. But perhaps the greatest vindication was hearing my family asking, "Who *are* you? We had no idea!"

No, of course not. The tension between humility and bragging was always at play with them as well as with the university. I had experienced enough smack-downs to keep me silent about my efforts at ascension, never knowing when to put myself forward and when to shut up.

Ascending comes with expectations. We expect to feel different once we have achieved our goal, but we still have laundry to do, dinner to prepare, and weight to lose. We want to be recognized for our efforts and our successes, but we hesitate to praise ourselves because we are so well trained to at least appear humble. Ascension must be difficult. It must be elusive. Those expectations themselves make us inevitably disappointed when we get to the top. Did we deserve to stand there? Did we really do enough to earn it? Are we winded enough by our efforts? Was it as difficult as we remember it being? Did we do it in the "right" way? Once we are there, we not only must question it, but we see the peaks of all those other mountains before us, so do we buckle down like Sisyphus and get ready for the next ascent, or do we sit resignedly where we are?

For all the mountains Jesus climbed, where he was tempted, where he saw God's light, Jesus knows he must come back down, as he has work to do. Ascending to Heaven is the culmination of all those mountains. He is taken up to disappear among the clouds.

The fruit of this mystery is to be Christian hope. I try. I really try. I try to see the hope in all these forms of ascension, in their successes and in their failures, in what they teach me and in what they withhold from me. I try to recognize the ways Jesus' mountaintop moments can inspire my own ascensions, even as I believe my ultimate ascension will be to Heaven with Jesus, with Mary. But in the meantime, I cannot overcome my ambivalence about shooting for one more climb: I am elated when I reach the top, but am weary when I see still more peaks, and am disheartened when I am rebuked.

❧

18

THE THIRD GLORIOUS MYSTERY:
THE DESCENT OF THE HOLY SPIRIT

*After the Crucifixion of Jesus, the Holy Spirit comes
to the Apostles and to Mary.*

Friends

THE HOLY SPIRIT CHANGES everything. The Holy Spirit comes to Mary at the beginning of Jesus's life, and the Holy Spirit comes after the crucifixion to inspire Jesus' followers to continue his work. If we were thinking in terms of drama, the Holy Spirit functions as both the exposition of the story, setting up the scene for us, and its denouement, the climax of the story when all the strands are brought together and resolution begins. Often, we confuse the idea of a denouement with the end of the story, but it is rarely so; it is only the beginning of the end, sort of like the endgame in chess.

As I contemplate the mystery of the Holy Spirit coming to a roomful of people in a fierce wind, and as I consider that the Holy Spirit is also symbolized by a dove, I find myself thinking of the ways the Holy Spirit has appeared in my life. Certainly I had the rather extreme example of having been slain in the spirit while I was in Medjugorje—the fierce wind part—but I am also aware of when the Holy Spirit has touched me through other people—the dove part. Often these are people for whom I continue to pray, without ever knowing or recalling their names.

I can only begin to number them.

The dentist who responded to my urgent pleas to see me on a Saturday. I was at a conference in St. Paul, Minnesota, in the late autumn, when I was suddenly struck with a monstrous toothache. I went back to my hotel room and, stupidly, put an ice-pack on my cheek, which it turns out is the worst thing one can do; I fell to the floor, stunned by the pain. Going through the phonebook, crying, I could find no one willing to see an out-of-town patient on a Saturday until one woman took pity on me and agreed to meet me. She later told me it was the worst abscessed tooth she had ever seen, and couldn't believe it hadn't bothered me before; maybe it had, but I was too busy trying to sort out a conference paper and my travel and my classes to notice it. The relief was immediate and my gratitude remains eternal.

The woman who pulled over for two young women hiking along the road in Ireland and gave us a lift. She knew we had many miles of nothing much ahead of us, as we were trying to make our way to yet another aunt on the west coast; we had only the vaguest idea of how far it was. She even returned later that night to drive us back to our hostel, saying her own daughter was hitchhiking her way across the United States and she hoped her good deed would beget more good deeds performed to keep her daughter safe. I also hope it did.

The man who pulled over when my car broke down late one Saturday night in a very undesirable location, known for its violent gang activity, who understood my reluctance to get in a car with him. He drove to the nearest gas station to call for a tow truck (oh, you people who have never lived without cell phones have no idea what life was like back then!), and then returned to park about a hundred feet ahead of me, watching to make sure I was safe until the tow truck arrived.

The man who helped me find my way home from work on another late Saturday night. I had only been living in Dublin for a few days and was still a bit fuzzy on where my apartment was in Rathmines; there was a taxi strike, buses had stopped running, and I was walking. In the dark, I got turned around, but knew better than to pull out a map at 3:00 a.m., so I took a chance and asked a likely-looking guy for directions, even as I know Ted Bundy was also a likely-looking guy. He said he was going the same way, but was also blessedly aware I didn't want to walk through Dublin with a strange man at that hour, so he said he would walk a block ahead of me; when he paused under a streetlight, that would be where I should turn right, and I was on the correct road from there.

Sometimes the Holy Spirit shows up through my Guardian Angel, who has surely put in a lot of overtime throughout my life, saving me from absurd situations, like the night in L.A. when several of us were heading to LAX from a conference. It was also a Saturday night, this one the night before the Academy Awards, when our rental car broke down in the fast lane, the entire electrical system going out. We didn't have turn signals, the power steering didn't work, and our lights had gone out. How we got across three lanes of LA freeway without getting killed or caught (thanks Jerry Jeff Walker) is only attributable to mystical forces.

There was the night (wow, I really need to stay home on Saturday nights) my car blew a gasket on another California freeway, and my friend, her young daughter and I waited an hour and a half in the cold rain for a tow truck; when the driver showed up, hooked up the car, and loaded us into the cab of his truck, we realized he was very drunk, but we didn't know how to get out of the situation. Again, how we managed to get home safely proves those Guardian Angels were at work.

These are all fleeting glimpses of the Holy Spirit at work in my life. But the Holy Spirit is not just a capricious bird who flits around and brushes our shoulders here and there; sometimes it is manifest in enduring, lasting relationships.

I was sitting in my English class on the first day of my sophomore year of high school. (Take note: all the best things happen in English classes.) Having lived in the same town all my life, I knew pretty much everyone in the class already, sometimes to dreary effect; there really isn't *that* much gossip accruing over the summer in a town that size, with people I saw all the time at the public swimming pool or the Sidewalk Sales. I was intrigued, then, when the new girl in class sat right next to me.

Our first activity was to cover our textbooks with brown paper. Our teacher, convinced of our ineptitude from the start, was giving us careful instructions on how to put the covers on, when I reached over and wrote on my neighbor's book: "Don't you hate it when someone writes on your brand new book cover?" I can't remember whether at this point we had even exchanged words yet. She gasped, and then laughed. And so a friendship was born.

Michelle later told me how shocked she was that I had violated her pristine book cover, but doing so began a pattern of note-writing we have retained throughout our lives together, though now it's mostly digital. I only remember what I wrote because she still has the book cover.

We found out we had much in common. Both of our fathers were insurance agents. We both loved the Eagles and Elton John. We both worked hard to keep our hair parted in the middle and feathered back like Farrah Fawcett (as if everyone weren't desperately trying to look like that famous poster). She thought I was funny. More importantly, we were both romantically interested in the same boy, which was highly coincidental because he lived in the next town over; I had fallen for him when he was on the free trip to Disneyland I had won, and she was dating him since they were actually from the same school. We were made for each other.

We spent hours and hours on the phone. We wrote notes back and forth; we had notebooks we called THONs (The Hour of Need) we would swap back and forth. I would write her notes (with our top-secret, highly coveted and protected codes for people in case our books were discovered) all through math class, and leave the book under my desk; she would take the same seat in the next class, retrieve the book, and add her comments. We also took to sharing our lockers, so we had access to the notes at all times. We have dozens of these; we just can't always remember the codes anymore.

We had sleepovers, always at her house because of my mother's agoraphobia, where we would listen to our favorite albums: Journey, Heart, ELO, Leo Sayer, the Doobie Brothers. Jackson Browne would come a little later, but would rise to the top of our list quickly. (Much later, we even got to see the Eagles and Jackson Browne in concert together on New Year's Eve in Las Vegas.) One hot day gleams in my mind: we were walking down the road into town with our latest proud discovery, a boom box, listening to Fleetwood Mac, wearing our Ditto jeans and our super-cool 3/4 length sleeve baseball shirts with our names emblazoned diagonally across the front and our matching rainbow suspenders. Music and fashion, that was us. We reveled in our coolness.

Boyfriends were complicated. She was much cuter and thinner than I, and she was an unknown factor in the town, so everyone wanted to get close to her. I can't count the number of guys who told me how nice I was, and could I give them Michelle's phone number? Or could I see if she liked them? And is she dating anyone? She had her pick of guys, and I—well, I got stood up on the night of my Junior Prom, by the same guy I had a crush on when I met her, and who was secretly only ever in love with her.

Her hotness encouraged me to think we had a chance at cheerleader tryouts. To the tune of Stevie Wonder's "Sir Duke," we spent hours perfecting our flirty routine, and I was sure we were going to be picked, a certainty which only revealed my ignorance about the social hierarchy at our school. The predictable people were chosen; we were not. We elevated our sorrows with a trip to the Brach's candy selection at Safeway, and with Slurpees at 7-11.

When her father reconnected with his brother from whom he had been estranged for much of his life (another detail she and I shared in common, as my father and his brother were also not speaking). He showed us the letter he had received, insanely long, filling him in on the details of his brother's life, and Michelle and I were shocked to read such a comprehensive letter containing not a word about high school. High school was so obviously the pinnacle of a life, with all its excruciatingly important and momentous events, and we could not imagine what would mark a life afterwards. No distinction between the years. No formal dances. No plays, concerts, scandals, gossip, exams, friendships. No Friday night football games, with their pageant of highly orchestrated meetings, as contrived as a Victorian promenade. Okay, there may be a wedding and some kids someday, but other than that, what else could there to be discuss about an adult life? Snoozefest.

We were so cute. And ignorant. And hopeful. And shortsighted.

The Holy Spirit held us together, knowing we would need each other throughout our very unpredictable lives. How could we have seen any of it coming?

I was there with her the night she met her future husband. We were at a disco for underage kids, dancing our hearts out to "Saturday Night Fever" and "I Will Survive," when this really good-looking guy asked her to dance. He had beautiful hair—a requisite for us in this Barry Gibb world—and very tight Angel-Flight pants, and one of those silky shirts with a montage of photos all over it. Very John Travolta. He was also one of the nicest people you could ever meet. She was smitten. I watched, waiting for someone to invite me to dance.

They became a couple, and though they tried to keep me in the loop, even letting me tag along with them on our senior trip, inevitably some distance grew between us. She moved to the Bay Area right after high school, at a time when long distance phone charges were astronomical and when my car was too unreliable to drive an hour-and-a-half away, so we were not constantly in touch, but our letters were pretty consistent.

She and the disco guy were married a couple of years later, after much turmoil in between, and I was in the wedding, my bone-colored shoes sinking into the lawn because there had just been an unusual and torrential storm. I was there right after their first child, a boy, was born, and I was there right after their second child, a girl, was born. They moved to Utah to be near his family, and our conversations were often me regaling her with my dating horror stories while she regaled me with the horrors of living in Utah.

Shortly after I met Ken, still in the gooey stages of our relationship, we went to visit her and her family; her marriage was beginning to fray, more noticeably in contrast to us. We went on a cruise together, the four of us in one impossibly dinky cabin; we asked the cabin steward to remove his name card because we didn't have room for it. We could only get dressed one at a time, and the guys had to shower in the gym; we nearly wet ourselves laughing trying to get Spandex pantyhose on for formal night.

We visited back and forth as often as possible, which wasn't nearly often enough, given our financial constraints.

They moved from Utah to Las Vegas. Their marriage was struggling, but they were still together when their daughter revealed her father had been molesting her. She was eleven. The shock was overwhelming, as if the world had just tipped on its axis. How could this man, such a nice guy, do such a reprehensible thing? Everything we thought we could count on, our own insights about those closest to us, was in question. Michelle threw him out.

At the same time, Michelle was suffering from crippling bouts of Crohn's disease, a debilitating bowel condition that kept her from being able to work reliably. As she tried to figure out how to move forward, she uncovered much more information about how sick her husband really was. He regularly molested other children to whom he had access, seduced mothers at the roller skating rink while the kids whirled about, and went through the phone book to solicit women to meet him in parking lots for oral sex (I remain bewildered by his confession: "Admittedly, many of them said no," when I can't figure out who would say "yes"). He stayed out of jail because he was the family's sole means of support, but he was a sex registrant with restraining orders preventing him from going to places where children might be. He could only see his own children with supervision.

Michelle began to see a man she had dated in high school, having met up again at a reunion, but there were too many problems trying to unite two disparate families and two even more disparate styles of parenting; when he bought a house without checking with her and without room for her children, deciding her son could live in the basement if he must live with them at all, she ended it.

Her second marriage, to the father of a boy her daughter was dating, was quick. She liked him a lot, may have been in love with him, but didn't believe she would ever find the kind of love she had for her first husband; plus, she desperately needed the medical insurance. They married in a Las Vegas wedding chapel in a ceremony lasting almost as long as their courtship. Astoundingly, due to a series of unlikely coincidences, they moved to Oregon three days after Ken and I did, and for the first time in twenty-five years, we lived within a few miles of each other.

Eager to get to know her new husband, Ken and I joined them on a cruise, during which her husband's brother died suddenly and unexpectedly, and during which her daughter attempted suicide. They left the cruise. Things got uglier soon after, and their marriage began to fall apart when it became clear NASCAR would always be the priority for him.

In one of those "only in a poorly-written novel" coincidences, the finalized papers for her second divorce came on the same day as the news of her first husband's suicide. He had been discovered violating his court-ordered prohibitions keeping him from children, had lost his job because of the impending court case, and couldn't face the further shame.

All of these events were interlaced with my own health and relationship crises, and throughout, we asked each other, "Wanna switch lives?" The speculation of which of us had it worse was always a useful concept to really consider and we always said, "Nah," but we remained a primary source of support for each other as we rode out storm after storm.

Michelle met another guy from a dating website, and I warned her then that if she married him, I would not be there for her. He made my skin crawl, staking an ownership in her that he had not yet earned. I still remember the day he tried to explain, after he and Michelle had been together for about three weeks, that her relationship with her daughter was complicated, as if I hadn't been there for pretty much all of it, good and bad. I longed for her to remain single long enough to figure out who she was without a man to be her foil.

In the meantime, she again began to talk with the high school boyfriend. The third time's the charm; it seemed like fate. Everyone loved him, he loved her, she was happier than she had ever been, and they married soon after. They moved back to California.

Then the gaslighting began. He would alternate between loving kindness and devotion to alienation, abuse, and infidelity. One moment he would be praising her and cooking for her, taking her to concerts and on trips; the next he would be screaming torrents of abuse. On the way to a houseboating week we were to spend together, he flew into a rage because she used the wrong hotel booking website, screaming at her as she drove down the freeway. Scared, she pulled over; he jumped out of the car, racing to her side as she locked the door. He began furiously kicking the door as he roared at her, putting a dent in his own car.

Ken and I were still heading south to meet them, with our car stuffed full of supplies for the week, when she called us to tell us she was afraid her marriage was over. We didn't know what to do, so we agreed to meet up where we had originally planned to meet, and see what we could figure out; we were trying to calculate how to squeeze her, her two dogs, and her stuff into our car to bring her home with us. When we got to the hotel, it turned out her husband had made a reservation with his own booking website, which, amusingly, put him in the hotel room right next to Michelle's. They talked. They agreed to continue with the week and ultimately with their marriage.

It was a mighty uncomfortable week for all of us. Houseboats are very small, and I do not excel at pretending, even for short periods of time.

Their relationship went on for too long. He was a man desperately in need of counseling, but he was sure counseling was only for crazy people, and there was nothing wrong with him. Michelle agonized over whether to stay; she felt like a failure after all these relationships, and thought people would laugh at her if she couldn't make yet another one work. When she finally did leave, she moved back to the Pacific Northwest, now about an hour from where I live.

Her story is inextricable from mine, a kind of palimpsest over everything that has occurred to me. We have rarely been happy at the same time, our lives more like a seesaw of failed relationships, ailments, troubled children, and crappy jobs, swaying into excited romance, health, delightful children, and fulfilling jobs. She told me once, "You made all the right decisions. I made all the wrong ones," shortly before my decisions began to look like the worst ones I could have made. I told her, "It ain't over 'til it's over, and we don't get to know who made the right decisions until the end." We haven't even reached the denouement yet. Every decision either of us made, as I texted her almost daily for nearly six months, was made with the best information we had at the time. We cannot guess what the people around us will do. We cannot guess what our own bodies will do. We cannot even guess the ways in which we will fail each other as friends, which has happened over the years. But we have a history of love and understanding, a history that allows us a kind of shorthand to give context to every new circumstance, that is irreplaceable.

The history binds us, and the Holy Spirit has blessed us with that shared history.

I was there for her when her mom went through cancer; she was there for me when I did. I was there for her when her father died; she was there for me when mine did. I was there for her when her relationships failed; she was there for me when mine did. I was there for her when she married; she was there for me when I did (though I owe her a couple of weddings).

We have been there for each other while: our children surprise us, not always in wonderful ways; we are financially flush and when we are stone broke; our families make us crazy; there is a sale at Ross. We have been together for many, many excellent concerts, often marveling at how frequently we end up seated next to people who just sit like lumps, never even bobbing their heads, while we go wild with ecstasy over our favorite music. We have held each other's hands when we have gained and lost beloved pets, and we have supported each other when we have dieted and when we have binged. No, it has not been perfect. I have failed her when I have been too busy to be a friend; she has failed me when she slept with the guy who first broke my heart. But none of that can erase the countless times we have laughed until we cried, or, more likely, peed, even when our bladders were young and strong.

It sounds like marriage vows: for better or worse, for richer or poorer, in sickness and in health, to love and to cherish. Through it all, we have been friends. We have laughed a lot; we have cried a lot; we have solved the world's problems over and over, if only someone would listen to us.

The list of things we had in common in high school seems feeble, as if it couldn't last. There are ways in which we have little in common. I pursued an academic career, while she did not. We don't like to read the same things, and we don't always agree on movies or television shows we love. We usually agree on music, though for reasons that remain beyond me, she doesn't like The Indigo Girls. We don't travel the same way: I am intrepid and am endlessly fascinated by everything; she doesn't like to get in the water unless she can see what is brushing past her feet, and prefers that nothing does. She can craft like nobody's business; I enjoy it, but find it tedious after a relatively short time. She is not religious, unable to reconcile a God who would pick who goes to Heaven among those of her friends who are all good people. Who gets to win: the Catholic? The Mormon? The atheist?

We will always be united, however, in the things we were right about even in high school. Then, we were sure with our whole hearts that this world offers few pleasures as exquisite as driving just a little too fast on an open road with the sunroof open and the stereo blasting music we can sing along with at utmost volume, the sun making our skin glow. And the car really needs to be red. And if we could be on our way to go shopping, all the better. And there must be laughter. And food. And good shoes.

She fully agrees with my post-cancer philosophy: If it doesn't sparkle and it doesn't make me laugh, I'm not interested.

People come into our lives, some for a moment, some for the long haul, and each of them touches us in different ways. I wish I could devote a chapter to each of the people I love, all those doves who have helped me in ways large and small, all those who have no idea they have even left an impact, each of whom has been a sign of the Holy Spirit at work. But a friendship that lasts through joys and trials for over forty-five years is also a sign of the Holy Spirit's faithfulness to us, working to guide us. Sometimes, indeed, a sound comes from heaven like the rush of a mighty wind and fills our house, and we are changed forever.

19

The Fourth Glorious Mystery: The Assumption

Mary's body and soul are taken up to Heaven.

Bodies

OH, THE BATTLES THAT have been waged over the female body! It is adulated and praised, it is mocked and spurned, it is abused and raped, it is fetishized. All the woes of the world have been blamed on women, from Eve on. Women are temptresses, luring men to their doom through sin; women are figures of art, representing beauty, subject to the male gaze. Women's bodies are the receptacles of men's lust and rage, and they are the hope of the future because only they can reproduce.

The mystery of the Assumption, then, has always been a deeply problematic one for me, rooted as it is in the fate of a woman's body. Mary is raised, physically, to Heaven. Upon Mary's body a great battle has been waged. She endured pregnancy and birth though she remained a virgin, and she must have endured persecution from a community which would have trouble believing her tale of an angel coming to her. She raised her son at a time of great political turmoil, watching as he set himself up as the enemy of the state. (Did she ever recommend that he back off, fearing for his life? Could it be that part of her submission was to have been resigned to his preordained fate? Did she even know what that fate was going to be?) Grief-stricken, she witnessed his murder on a cross. She lived on after his crucifixion, in Ephesus, in a tiny house, where she helped nurture the Church's beginnings. Finally, she was raised to Heaven, her body now removed from any possible corruption from the world.

I taught Women's Studies for a long time, where we discussed the consequences of bodies, especially female bodies and the expectations loaded upon them. In those classes, I asked students to describe their gendered "coming out" (which is certainly not the same as that bizarre phenomenon called a gender reveal party). I often get puzzled looks, since I purposely employ language connoting homosexuality, but I ask them to consider the moment in their lives when they first realized their gender matters. I go first.

I was eight, and was an entrenched tomboy. My older brother, Jim, was my hero (unless he was siding with his friends and taunting me), and I did all I could to hang out with him. The two of us were most often aligned, leaving my two younger sisters to find their own way in girly things. I was the quarterback when the neighborhood kids played football; I threw baseballs, apples, pumpkins, rocks, dirt clods, basketballs, or pretty much anything just as well as anyone; I raced; I rode bikes, though never quite with the same demonic carelessness Jim did; I helped dig the huge hole in our yard; I climbed trees. I was uninterested in the mechanical things he did, refusing to tinker with bicycles and gadgetry, but I eagerly read Mad Magazine with him, eschewing the *Mother's Little Helper* book my mom, hinting broadly, gave me.

Jim had his circle of friends in the neighborhood, boys who were older than I and some even older than he. That summer, Steve got a new tent for his birthday, and came over to tell us all about it. He was going to have a sleepover in it that very night, and we were invited. We spun out into a bacchanal of planning: there would be hot chocolate with marshmallows, Twinkies, maybe potato chips if we could lure someone's parents to splurge on them. There might even be orange Fanta from the soda machine Chris's dad had in front of their garage. I had been reading Edgar Allan Poe, and was going to bring his *Complete Tales* to read out loud, and Steve would bring his flashlight so he could light up his face from below his chin and be spooky. Jim and I had been playing endless rounds of the card game War, and promised to teach Steve (which, given the game's intricacies, should take about thirty seconds). We had no sleeping bags, but were undaunted; it was summer, and a couple of blankets and a pillow would do.

Plans firmly in place, we broke ranks to go gather the requisite supplies. Bursting into the kitchen to ask Mom for things only she could supply, we never even considered the need to ask permission. Some things were just too obviously fated to be. So when she interrupted, almost casually, to say, "Jim can go. Kathy can't," we were both too stunned to speak at first, gazing at her, stupefied.

"What?" (Really the only appropriate response to so many things.)

"Kathy can't go. She's a girl."

"What does that have to do with anything?"

"Steve is a boy. Boys and girls don't spend the night together."

"I spend the night with Jim every night," I whined, perplexed.

"That's different. He's your brother. You can't go."

It was final, and there was no further attempt to explain it to me. But it was the moment when I knew for sure there were consequences to being a girl, and I didn't like them one bit.

My story opens students up to consider their own lives, and most often, the stories come pouring out, stories when girls realized how unfairly they were being treated compared to boys, stories when boys realized how lucky they were to not be girls. Most often the stories are rooted in the recognition of double standards: different curfews, different freedoms, different chores, different expectations for behavior. What is clear is that each story only opens the floodgates for the memories of subsequent injustices and frustrations, as my story does for me.

When I was twelve, Jim suggested I get a paper route. He had one, and was bringing in money hand over fist (or so it seemed to us). I spoke with his manager, the man who brought the truckload of newspapers to the house every day. He laughed at me. "Girls can't deliver papers," he said, turning away as if the conversation were over.

"Why not?"

"They just don't."

"Because?"

"They're girls."

"I throw better than Jimmy does. I can lift the bag," heaving one over my head to rest on my shoulders.

"But what would people say?"

"They would say, 'Hey, my paper is here.'"

He finally looked at me, surprised by my insistence but probably also surprised by my snippiness. I was maybe staggering a bit under the bag but desperately attempting nonchalance. "You know what? Fine.

We'll try it for a month," and even at that age, I recognized the dismissal in his tone. He knew I would fail, and he would have the chance to say he told me so.

I didn't fail. In fact, I won several prizes (including a free trip to Disneyland won with Jim's help) for the most new subscriptions and for the most customer satisfaction. People were intrigued by a girl delivering papers, and I benefitted from that. But the struggle to prove I was as good as a boy was well on its way.

Lest it seem as if Jim were always my champion, there was also the moment when he got hold of my first bra, a wishful-thinking kind of bra, and ran down the street waving it like a pendant, shouting, "If no one is supposed to see it, why is there a butterfly in the middle of it?" He was always unpredictable that way.

I was eleven when Title IX passed, so sports seemed like the logical arena to pitch a battle about gender inequity. When I got to junior high school, I longed to show off my skills as a quarterback. I was excited to play against a bigger variety of opponent. There was a boy's football team, but because gender had never been relevant to our neighborhood games, I never considered the possibility of my exclusion from this team. When they refused to even let me try out, I was enraged, and gathered every girl I knew to form a girl's football team, sure we would be able to beat the boys. But a football team needs equipment, even if it's only a ball, and needs to be able to use the field, even if it's only when the boys weren't using it. The school refused. After much back-and-forth, they finally agreed to let us have a flag football team, telling us they were worried about having us get tackled or hit in the area of our budding breasts. They actually told me that. It was more infuriating for those of us still in the wishful-thinking bra category, who were skeptical that there would even *be* budding breasts.

Flag football is stupid when you've been playing tackle in the mud. We played for a season, but quickly abandoned it out of boredom.

Basketball? We could have a girl's team, but at that time, girls could only play half-court, for fear we would wear ourselves out. I don't know if they thought exertion would cause us to faint or what, but it's not like we were in the era of girls wearing stays and corsets. Boring.

High school is when I began throwing the discus and putting the shot, and also when I began writing for the school newspaper. My dream was to become the sports editor, and be able to one day cover the Superbowl. That dream died earlier than most of my other dreams, when I couldn't gain access to athletes to interview them; they scurried into the locker room, laughing, knowing I couldn't follow them in.

The same pattern continued into college, where I did actually work as the sports editor for the school paper, but I spent more time assigning stories and editing grammar and headlines than I did reporting. (Covering the Superbowl is not a dream for which I had the stamina or gumption, especially given that only recently have women been used as NFL commentators, and then mostly as eye candy who could discuss injuries and uniform designs, but never strategy or coaching. I was thrilled when I first heard a woman's voice actually announcing the game, but made the mistake of reading the nasty misogynist comments about her later. I am too old and tired to take that kind of abuse.)

Clothing was another battlefield. In high school, I was starting to rebel against the clothing restrictions my siblings and I had always been held to, and where I became conflicted about who I wanted to be: the lady-like daughter my mother wanted and the tomboy I had been. We had always worn dresses and skirts, often homemade, never with heels or pantyhose. I vividly recall how desperately I wanted a sizzler, which everyone was wearing. It was a flaring A-line skirt, very short, with a matching top. My mother made me one, deep purple with a bright white contrasting lapel, buttons up the front and a tie in the back. I loved it, except the skirt was nearly to my knees. Sizzlers were meant to be so short they came with matching panties. I was mortified, torn between being grateful for her having worked to fulfill my wish, and embarrassed by how far it had fallen short from my dream. So every day that I wore it, the moment I reached the end of our driveway, I hiked the skirt to just below my bra, giving myself a relatively short skirt, and marched smugly to school, certain I was styling at last. Never mind the obvious bunches of material that were not as hidden as I imagined.

I realized one day I could buy my own clothes, and would not have to get approval in advance, so I bought myself my first pair of jeans, high-waisted bell bottoms, and felt myself growing in independence.

I even bought a pair of one-inch heeled white sandals at a garage sale (we were not allowed to wear heels—too slutty—or sandals—no protection for our feet). I was in full—and comical—insurgency, and felt it as I walked to school, twisting my body in the oddest angles because I had discovered that if the sun hit me just right, the shadow of my shoes on the pavement made my heels look even higher, allowing for full-on strutting.

While I was unraveling what it meant to have a female body, the darker side of that body was also becoming obvious. I learned early on the ways in which it could draw unwanted attention, as if I had not figured that out when I was five.

The walk to my junior high school was just over two miles. Every morning, along would come a blue van, windows down, cruising slowly down the street, and this guy would lift his hips and flash his penis. Every day. At first, I ran, but could never outrun the van. Soon, girls formed groups for the walk, hoping there was safety in numbers; Laurie, Carla and I could scream much louder than just one of us. Eventually, we just ignored him. He never did anything more than wave his thingy around, and besides, everyone knew about him.

Years later, I was watching television with my mother when an alarmed newscaster warned of a flasher. I rolled my eyes, wondering how such a thing made the news, reminding my mother about the guy in the blue van. She was shocked, demanding to know why this was the first she had ever heard of it. I couldn't believe it was. Again, I thought everyone knew about him. But I started to think about why we may never have reported such a thing. If everyone knew and no one did anything, apparently flashing was normal behavior and we just had to learn how to deal with it, kind of the way we had to learn how to deal with bullies; there was no benefit in telling anyone about him. Otherwise, surely someone would have put a stop to him. Even all these years later, I had rolled my eyes, having heedlessly accepted such behavior as the norm.

I had learned quickly to just try to ignore assaultive behavior. Such was my lot in life as a woman, I assumed. I wonder how many girls and women have similar stories to explain the way such treatment gets normalized for us.

As is true for most women, the #MeToo accounts are nearly endless, reinforcing not just the normalcy of harassment but also its inevitability.

On my first trip to Europe, my friend and I split up for a while: she wanted to go to Austria and I wanted to go to Lourdes, so we agreed to meet up again in several days. I loaded myself and my huge backpack onto the night train and tucked myself into a corner to sleep, so much cheaper than getting a room in a hostel. Early in the morning, the train began to fill with commuters, mostly men in nice business suits on their way to work. Such a man opened my compartment door, waking me up. He smirked and spoke to me in French; while I could speak some French, I was still too befuddled with sleep to remember enough for a conversation. He crossed the compartment to sit next to me, though as I was alone, there were seven other places where he could have sat.

"American?" he asked. I nodded.

"Alone?" he asked. I hesitated. That was a loaded question, I had learned. I had already purchased a fake wedding ring in hopes it would ward off predators and pinchers as we traveled. I waved it at him but he laughed. "He's not there, though, is he?"

Uncomfortable with his leering nearness, I stood up to get my backpack down from the shelf above my seat. As I stretched to reach it, he grabbed my crotch from behind and began to rub and squeeze. Furious and terrified, I grabbed the bag and rounded on him, hitting him across the face with the back of my hand. The velocity of the bag helped my rage, and he flew to the opposite window, hitting it and slumping to the ground. I ran.

Determined to tell someone, I looked for a police officer or someone in authority, but when I found the conductor and he at last understood my complaint, he merely laughed. I was American. I was alone. I was a woman. What did I think was going to happen? My French was inadequate to express my outrage, and I felt defeated by my powerlessness. I disembarked for a connecting train, still shaking.

In the next train, I found a seat in the main car rather than in a compartment, looking for safety in a crowd, and as I sat down, I caught the eye of the man who had attacked me. He looked away, a line of blood still trickling down his temple from where I had hit him. Glancing down, I saw I had a piece of his flesh embedded in the rosette of my ring. Good.

I made it to Lourdes, and was on my way to Germany to meet my friend when the train was delayed coming into Munich, getting in after 10:00 p.m. At the time, Munich had a policy to decrease homelessness on the streets: if one came into the station after 10:00 without a designated place to stay, one spent the night in the locked train station. I had nowhere to stay; I was planning on finding the hostel, but without a booking, I could not prove I could stay there. Resigned, I plopped my stuff down around me, settling on a hard plastic chair.

Almost immediately, an American soldier came up to me, telling me he was also locked in for the night. He said he was worried the train station was not a safe place for a single American girl, and so he offered me his protection. I was relieved to find someone who would look out for me, trusting his military status as a mark of his honor. He said the train cars were open and were much warmer, and would provide sanctuary from all the fragrant homeless people around me. Wary, I followed him into one of the cars, where he promptly tried to attack me, telling me he was lonely and horny for some American ass. Dismayed, I found myself again grabbing my backpack and fleeing a train car, this time with him running behind me, shouting about what a frigid f-ing bitch I was.

I came away from that trip determined to avoid any further traveling on my own, but also appalled that I lived in a world where that would be the only possible conclusion. Why is my body, by virtue of its very elemental femaleness, an open invitation for men? Why is it my responsibility to avoid violation? Why are men not taught to have some responsibility in respecting our boundaries and dignity? The revelations of that trip provided the impetus to begin studying gender theory and feminism.

Proclaiming oneself a feminist, however, protects no one from further attacks. There are too many dates who assumed I would of course put out, who had to be fought off with either tears or laughter. There are too many men who harassed and harangued me in bars or at work or at restaurants or pretty much anywhere. I hate that I have also been saved from these men by, mostly, other men, when my own refusal was not enough to secure my peace. This whole book could easily just be my #MeToo testament.

I thought I was exempt from all this nonsense by now: I am older, I am fat, I am married. Surely I should be safe. Yet it was not very long ago when I experienced a man's outrageously lascivious behavior once again, this time at church, of all places.

I have been in the choir since I moved to Oregon, and one member, unsurprisingly named Dick, has always been creepy. He would often find a way to touch women inappropriately, making it look like an accident. He would make sexist and racist jokes all the time, and if we failed to laugh with him, he would huff off, convinced we lacked a sense of humor. Reminding him he was in church had no effect. He is unpleasant, but I mostly found I could ignore him.

One Sunday, however, all our piano players were out of town, and we were desperate. I play piano, but badly, and hate to do so in public, especially since chemo left my hands nearly incapable of moving smoothly. Nonetheless, I agreed to accompany the choir on this Sunday, since we were out of options. As Mass was about to begin, I was nervously sitting at the piano, with Ken sitting a few feet away and Dick's wife sitting a few feet away in the other direction. Dick came up behind me, putting his hands on my shoulders (which already made me recoil) and whispered,

"I could just reach down and pinch your tits, and then you'd be so mad you'd forget to be nervous."

I wrenched myself away, shaking, sick to my stomach, and went to sit next to Ken for a moment. I told him what had happened. He wanted to know why the guy was still standing, and I pointed out I was in church, in front of everyone, and could hardly hit him the way I wanted to. He said everyone would have understood. I went back to the piano and somehow made it through the Mass.

Our daughter and granddaughter were visiting that weekend. I said nothing to them when I got home, and we began watching football together, but as I sat there, I watched Amanda and Sophia, and I began to cry. I knew in my heart if that disgusting pig had said anything remotely like that to my daughter or my granddaughter, I would have ripped his throat out and fed it to the dogs. So why had I done nothing when it was myself under provocation?

I sent an email to the choir director and to our new pastor outlining what had happened. The response shocked me. The choir director, a woman, defended him, saying we all knew what Dick was like, but he didn't mean anything by it; she said that Christian charity compels me to forgive him. I agreed to forgive him, but said I didn't go to church to feel uneasy, much less befouled, and I would not put myself in that situation again. I didn't know what to expect from our new pastor, but had little hope after the director's response. He, however, came to my side in a conversation I will never forget, and Dick was removed from the choir.

I found myself wondering why, only then, I was finally able to stand up for myself. Why, after all these years of withstanding outrageous violations of my body and my space and my dignity, was this the moment when I fought back? Yes, I hit the guy on the French train, but that was a knee-jerk response of defense, rather than a counterattack. I wanted a man to finally see the consequences of his behavior. I wanted a man to see grabbing a woman is not funny.

Part of my response, of course, was my horror at a country that was okay with electing a man to be President of the United States despite his own grabby behavior. Part of my response was rooted in wanting things to be better for my daughter and her daughter. More than that, however, something had shifted in me after I went on another retreat, in the course of which I uncovered some deep anger over something I had not even suspected before: my mother never wanted a girl.

The realization was so obvious once I saw it. My brother came first (and always has, and always will), and everything she thought she would have in a child was fulfilled in him. A girl—or three—that would come later could be her dolls. She was unprepared for females who would think for themselves, who would want a life different from the one she had, who would writhe against her complacency in a misogynist world. She wanted a doll she could dress up, not the monster who would ruin every pair of saddle shoes she bought me; I wanted cuter shoes, but she only bought me more saddle shoes because they were sturdy and I was so hard on shoes. She wanted a doll she could cuddle, not the wriggling child I was who, she claims, always squirmed out of her arms so I could go off and play. She wanted submissive and obedient girls, but I was not like any of that. She didn't know what to do with me. She still doesn't.

This realization came during a role-playing exercise, and for whatever reason, has given me permission to stand up for myself in ways I never felt comfortable doing before. The tools to fight against sexism were not handed down to me through a matrilineal inheritance, because my mother does not recognize the fight. My only weapon was to be polite, to be self-effacing. Though I found so many ways of resisting, I hated doing so in a way that would make me unliked or unpopular. I was even voted "nicest" in high school, for heaven's sake! I could no more have confronted Dick in front of the church than I could have picked him up and thrown him through the window. According to my training, and against all my instincts, men might be creepy, but they don't mean anything by it.

My mother's ideal of feminine Christian behavior was shaped by a miserable childhood and miserable parents. Her father, a professional musician, was a drunk and an abuser, and left the family when she was eight. After five marriages, he eventually remarried my grandmother thirty-five years later, but in the meantime had caused my mother so much pain that my father finally forbade her to have anything to do with him. While Mom was relieved to be rid of him, she agonized over the biblical mandate to forgive seventy times seven times. Dad urged her to forgive him if she could, but reminded her doing so did not mean opening herself up for more torture. Forgiveness is complicated.

I think she found it a little easier to be rid of him when I was sixteen, after he sent me a cassette tape out of the blue. It melodramatically begins with the sound of organ music swelling as he plays it like some Bella Lugosi intro. He had heard from my grandmother that my greatest wish (I rotated a lot of greatest wishes through my life) was to have a grand

piano, and he was offering to have me come live with him in Albuquer-
que, where he would give me piano lessons and then give me his grand
piano. Having not seen the man since I was five (when we discovered,
to much hilarity, that he wore a toupee, but also discovered he was not
amused when we threw it like a frisbee), I thought this was very exciting.
As the tape wound on, however, he made his stipulation: I must agree
never to see or speak to my mother again. As far as I know, this was the
last communication any of us had with him. I wrote a scathing letter in
response, but only recently found it among my mother's stuff, never having been sent. I still don't know if that was for the best.

Without extended family, Mom didn't have much of a support system, beyond my dad, in raising four rambunctious children. She didn't
drive when we were children, and Dad worked all kinds of odd hours
selling insurance. She has suffered with severe agoraphobia that especially marked our teenage years; she was unable to go anywhere and we
never had anyone over. Even Sunday mornings were a challenge, as she
would often get us and herself dressed for church and then be unable to
leave the house with us.

While Mom spent four years working for the Air Force, she did so at
a time when "conduct unbecoming to an officer" meant something, and
she has spent very little time working outside of the house since she and
my father married. She didn't drive until very late in life, so went virtually nowhere without my father, and she has done very little traveling,
so her opportunities for experiencing harassment were limited. She says
she never faced prejudice as a woman, and although I can point to many
moments from her life where she did, she doesn't recognize the prejudice.
In failing to see it in her own life, she is also largely unaware of misogyny
even when she herself practices it. Her distaste, for example, of female
politicians is colored by her belief that women are supposed to be nice. A
woman who is always nice herself, she believes ambition interferes with
niceness, and so she frowns on ambition.

When I complain about the ways I have been attacked and maligned
because I am female, Mom thinks I am wrong, that I have exaggerated or
outright lied about events and experiences. In fact, my mother doesn't believe most of the stories in this chapter ever happened to me, even those
episodes witnessed by others, insisting such occurrences never happened
to her. She refuses to believe in a world where my experiences could be
commonplace. She asks why she has never heard these stories before,
though I insist she has heard most of them. If, however, she disbelieves

my accounts, why should she trouble to remember them? I learned at a very young age how to avoid her eye-rolling, pursed lips, and sighs, so I simply stopped telling her about things. I have not meant for these stories to be held as deep, dark secrets, but I have withheld them from her for my own protection. She believes I am too thin-skinned, and I hold onto grudges for too long. She is probably right, or I wouldn't be dredging up all these stories from my life, but I also never had the chance to reconcile these events any other way.

When I realized I had to write about the strife between my mother and I, I could hear Virginia Woolf (always) in my ear, warning us that we must kill the Angel in the House before our creativity and honesty can be unleashed. This is the force, all too often represented by the mother, who keeps us repressed and angelic, never objecting, always choosing niceness. I long for the day when the Angel in the House can be killed off before my mother actually dies; maybe then we can find a way to relate to each other. The deep irony is that my efforts to be brutally honest in my writing have led her to disbelieve me more than ever, driving a wedge between us that seems invincible.

The Assumption of Mary, whose physical body is transported to Heaven after all the things that had been done to it, seems as if it could provide a way forward for us. Mary is the emblem for all women. We must aspire to be like her. But when the very fact of a female body (and we have not even touched on the many variations of what that even means) is a site of such contestation, when a body takes on such different meanings, identities, proclivities, expectations, when even two women so closely connected as mother and daughter cannot agree on what it means to be a woman, then what does it even look like to emulate Mary?

My mother must have one kind of response to the Assumption, and I have another. In removing Mary bodily from this earth, is God reinforcing the sense that this world can only ever be a source of corruption, especially for women? Or by elevating her, has God given her the ultimate reward for her faithfulness? I am conflicted. We have no way of telling how Mary felt about her own life, her own body, because that story has been erased in the telling. My mother sees Mary's submission; I imagine her occasional tears. Are these really such irreconcilable images? Is it not possible to both submit to God and to cry over our lot? (Can we not be both nice and ambitious?)

Such are my musings as I pray this Mystery, and indeed the whole Rosary as it focuses on Mary's experiences. The spiritual fruit to be gained here is "To Jesus through Mary," which of course applies to the entire Rosary itself, but getting there is certainly not as simple as it sounds as we exist in our bodies, in this corrupted world.

20

THE FIFTH GLORIOUS MYSTERY:
THE CORONATION

Mary is crowned Queen of Heaven.

Teaching

THE CORONATION OF MARY is the consummation—the perfection and completion—of everything Mary suffered, her reward for her faithfulness and love. The angels rejoiced at her arrival. I picture frolicking and hugging, a party to surpass all parties. I am sure the wine never ran out at that celebration. Her sense of fruition and gratification, even vindication, must have been great indeed.

The closest I can come in my life to such an actualization of my hopes has been my career. While it was never part of my plan—I never even so much as imagined teaching, much less being a college professor—everything I have ever done in my life, every story included here, has led me to the fulfillment of my calling. I took a circuitous path, one which belies the impression of the Ivory Tower where all the elites hang out who have no idea about the purported real world. I know of very few professors who found themselves in their job effortlessly, still fewer who don't acknowledge the sacrifices made both to get and to keep the job, and none who were born into their positions. Every step along that path, though seemingly disconnected and even arbitrary, contributed to my success in teaching literature.

When I graduated from high school, I was determined to be done with education forever. I had a math teacher who should have retired years before, who gave me a C in algebra despite my having received an A on every test and every bit of homework; when I took all my work to the principal to complain, he told me, "He must have his reasons," and let the grade stand. I was infuriated when I had to take the same teacher the following year for geometry. Although math had been my favorite subject, in geometry I never cracked open a book, spent every class writing notes to my best friend, and failed every test; I got a C at the end of the year. He had evidently predetermined what my grade would be based on some elusive set of criteria, and nothing I could do would budge it.

English should have been a delight, but my English teacher was determined to make people hate reading; even at sixteen, I knew I could do better than she did. When we read aloud *The Taming of the Shrew*, I was excited to get to read the part of Kate, but she kept interrupting me to remind me this was an English class, not a drama class, and I should read it more straightforwardly. So much for Shakespeare. She is most remembered by former students for the way she used to mark papers with a red-tipped felt pen, which she invariably tucked behind her ear having forgotten to put the cap back on, so her very-white hair always had a scarlet stain.

Because I had demonstrated some skill, I was assigned to work as a TA for another English teacher, whom I really liked, but who hated his job; he would insult students outrageously, right in front of them, but would do so with language incomprehensible to those students, and while I snickered at his brilliant wordplay, I also learned what a poor approach to teaching such contempt was.

These and other encounters convinced me the whole educational system was corrupt and useless, so I was done. (I had not yet taken any classes that taught me about logical fallacies.) No one else in my family had ever attended college, so my decision was earth-shattering to no one.

After high school, however, when my friend and I embarked on our three-year plan to go to Europe, I knew I needed to know more in order to get the most out of what I assumed was a once-in-a-lifetime opportunity. Community college was free for California residents at the time, so I enrolled at the local Junior College, taking foreign language, history, and art classes to better prepare myself for a European trip. But then I was tempted by music classes, for which I received a scholarship, and journalism classes, for which I received another. And there were English classes, and I had a teacher who encouraged me in ways I had never experienced before. I was loving it. It was so different from high school.

By the time I graduated with my AA, I was mired in a rocky long-term romance. To escape it, I decided to enroll in the state college about an hour and a half away from home, counting on the distance to effect the permanent separation I knew we needed. (Great plan: we continued the long distance relationship and got engaged for a time; he broke off the engagement on my birthday, but we stayed together until Christmas Eve when he failed to meet me at Midnight Mass because he had lost track of time while he was having sex with a woman he had met at a party.)

In the meantime, I fell in love with literature, so much more reliable than men. I was always a reader, but studying and writing about literature helped me understand it in ways I never had through my previous casual reading. I had stupendous teachers: Marcelline Krafchick, the hardest teacher I ever had, gave me good grades but reproved me when she knew I could do better; Jake Fuchs gave me an appreciation for poetry far more advanced than just enjoying Longfellow in the shed, and taught me the value of memorizing poetry; Terence McVeigh, a lapsed Jesuit priest, introduced me to James Joyce and taught me to be a serious scholar. It was also he who, at the end of my undergraduate career, invited me to teach at the university.

Such an opportunity was far beyond my possible imaginings, but lingering in my brain was a conversation I had one night, when several of us were invited for dinner at Marcelline's home. I looked at her house, at her souvenirs from traveling all over the world, at her book collection, and announced, "I want your life. I want to get paid to discuss books, and then get paid to travel around the world to discuss more books. I want your life."

"Then take it," she said, patly.

I was shocked. How could I? How could I even aspire to such heights?

"There is no reason you cannot have what I have. It really is the perfect life."

One of the provosts under whom I later worked used to tell us, "There are no such things as 'throw-away' comments when you are a teacher. You have no idea what students are taking away, what words will change a student's life." He was so right. Marcelline's words changed mine by giving me the courage to dream, to say to myself, "Well, someone has to teach college. Why not me?"

I accepted the invitation to teach.

The trick, however, was that I had to be enrolled in the Master's Degree program, something I had certainly not considered. I had been taking McVeigh's course in Joyce and Chaucer over the summer after I graduated, but sort of cheated my way into it. To have taken it as an Open University course was far more expensive than I could afford, but to do it as part of the Master's program was much cheaper, so I was pretending I was going to continue, though I had every intention of dropping after the one class. But teaching? I couldn't give up the chance, so I remained enrolled in the Master's program, and I began to teach.

And then I learned about the miracle that is teaching.

I was at a state school in the heart of the Bay Area, with a pretty diverse population. I was mostly assigned the developmental writing courses at first, which were also largely ESL (now called "second-language learners"). I learned some powerful lessons in these classes, probably more than my students ever did, lessons that displayed my astonishing ignorance and naivety almost from the beginning.

In my first composition class, I was smug in my theories, some of which were hard won in my own education ("I will *never* do that!") and some of which I had been reading up on. I believed students would write better when they care about their topics (still do, but am much more careful in picking said topics), so I asked them to write about a time when someone close to them was in pain, and how they dealt with that. Expecting essays on things like, "My best friend broke up with her boyfriend," or, "Our dog died and my brother was really upset," I was aghast at the results I got.

The first essay I picked up was by a young man who was babysitting his younger brother. He ran into the house for a quick second to answer the phone, and his brother ran into the street after a ball and was killed by a passing driver who then drove on.

When I stopped crying over that one, I read the next, by a young woman who had escaped the Khmer Rouge in a boat; at nine, she was small enough to be disguised as a young boy, a precautionary measure that paid off when pirates came and raped all the females in the boat, forcing all the men and children to watch; her father was killed in front of her.

I had the young student who, as the eldest of six children, was away at school when her mother, stoned, accidentally set the apartment on fire, killing all five siblings.

One young man came home from school one day to find his father dead on the floor of a drug overdose.

I was entirely unprepared for the gutpunch of these essays, for the challenge of explaining to them why their essays were poorly written while still validating their stories. I had no idea who these people were. I knew nothing about the human beings sitting in my classroom, who had lived lives I could not imagine, while they listened to me pontificate about the proper use of semi-colons. In my cockiness at having been invited to elevate myself to the role of Teacher, I had never even tried to envision who was in those seats, having relegated them to beings who needed what I had to offer. While I thought I had endured some things, these students made me understand the true privilege of my background. I was never the same after that.

By the time I graduated with my MA, I was hooked on teaching, but my position had ended, and it was only one of my five jobs. After working my way through various physical conditions that prevented me from working certain jobs—formaldehyde allergy at the print shop, carpal tunnel at the police department, and so on—I decided to return to school for my doctorate, so I could resume teaching at the college level.

First, though, I had to take the GREs. For those who don't know, the Graduate Records Exam is a special kind of persecution for those with the pluck to believe grad school might be for them. Not only does one have to get up early on a Saturday to spend the day being grilled alive, but one must pay for the privilege. The math exam was comical; I had to again review principals I have learned over and over again only to promptly forget them once the test is over.

The subject exam, on the other hand, is kind of fun, as long as one has prepared, and preparation means a whole ton of reading, which I happen to like doing anyway. The questions are multiple choice, following a passage from some kind of text, and one has to identify the text. This would be a breeze if the passage mentioned someone's name, like Gulliver or Hamlet, something nice and easy. Or if the passage were written in an obvious archaic style, and the choices were a) Virginia Woolf; b) Shakespeare; c) Toni Morrison; d) Alexander Pope. But no. No names were given, and the choices were fairly contemporaneous. The texts chosen were never the famously memorized and ubiquitous things: No "To thine own self be true" (Shakespeare) or "It was the best of times, it was the worst of times" (Dickens) or even, "Last night I dreamt I went to Manderley again" (DuMaurier), but rather, "The world breaks everyone, and afterward, many are strong at the broken places" (Hemingway), or "The longer I live, the more uninformed I feel. Only the young have an explanation for everything" (Allende). You just have to read.

I read a lot. I did well on the exam.

No one warned me, however, of the cruelty of applying for graduate school. My crime of moral turpitude was failing to go to any elite schools as an undergraduate. My little old community college and then state school left me less desirable as a grad school candidate; being somewhat older, married, and tied to a geographic location made me nearly outside the pale. One college sent an especially nasty rejection letter telling me the market was too glutted, I was too old, and I was unemployable, so they declined to accept my application; they went so far as to suggest I give up and pursue something else, though they did congratulate me on my excellent GRE scores. Ugh.

When I was at last accepted, I was elated, despite knowing my new school would entail a six-hour-a-day commute. Moving was not an option; between sharing custody of the kids and Ken's job, we were stuck where we were. I was determined to make it work, somehow.

I have often noted that all the honors in my field come with more work being required of me, and being accepted to grad school is just the beginning of that. Reading over my acceptance packet, including a sheet listing the classes I would be required to take, I began to cry; so much of the language was completely foreign to me. I knew I was in far over my head. In another one of those minor miracles of life, Marcelline happened to call right then. I had not heard from her in years, and she told me she was just wondering how I was doing. I explained my fears to her, and she assured me I would be fine. What she said next seems so obvious, but was exactly what I needed to hear right then, and I have repeated it often to students: "If you already knew what all those things were, you wouldn't have to take a class in them." Boom.

So I went for my initial interview. The chair of the department at the time was a late-middle-aged man who apparently fancied himself a bit of a Lothario, much to my disgust. He was jovial, a "hail well met" kind of guy, but really smarmy. He was pretty much the trope of every puffed up, self-involved, balding, horny English department chair one reads about in novels about college professors. Let's call him Prufrock. He sat me down and one of his first questions was, "Just how married are you?"

This is a question I have been asked many times, and it never fails to astound me. I naively thought there was only one kind of married, and it was for life, but I am evidently in the minority on that one. I told Prufrock I was very happily married, and I didn't understand what he was hinting at (though of course I did). He smirked and told me PhD programs are notoriously difficult on relationships, so my partner (another smirk at the term "partner," because he was far too sophisticated to use the term "husband") and I had better understand from the get-go what our commitment would have to be. I repeated, "We are fine." The interview was pretty much over after that. (Only later did I learn he was sleeping with a number of the female students in the program. I guess I wasn't a viable candidate for that, so there wasn't much more to say.)

A PhD program is both exhilarating and excruciating. It sucks up every moment of time. The extravagance of being able to luxuriate deeply in thought and conversation about ideas, about books that continually stretch one's boundaries, is such a huge grace, a kind of miracle in itself. The counterpoint lies in the need to set all else aside, and the requisite balancing act is tenuous at best. Over the years, when students have come to me wondering whether they should pursue a doctorate, I can only advise them to do so if they take immense joy from studying; if not, if they are at all reluctant, if they prefer to procrastinate in favor of things they find more fun, I warn them away. For the women, the sexism they will face is disheartening and intimidating; for students, especially first generation college students, who lack the contacts or the institutional savvy necessary to succeed—I was at the end of my second year of college before I ever heard the phrase "financial aid"—the bureaucracy is a grind; for anyone who did not come from a prestigious undergraduate school, the biases about ability are virtually impossible to overcome, despite one's successes.

After two years of course work, Prufrock ended up on my exit exam committee; he and another teacher wrote a special Irish studies exam for me and another student. I found out later Prufrock had bet actual money—$50.00—against me, sure the other student would write a better exam, even though Prufrock had never had me in class or seen my work. He was certain, I hear, I had too many factors against me: I was fat (clearly a debilitation that should come first in any academic assessment), middle-aged, married, and came from lesser schools: not really even fuckable (his term, not mine). They graded the exams anonymously, and the chair triumphantly waved one of the exams, saying, "I *told* you! This is the best exam I've ever graded in all my years of teaching!" He was certain he was celebrating the success of my male rival, but the exam he waved was mine. Chagrined, he paid up, and promptly invited me to lunch. I declined.

I finished the program. I had passed all my courses. I had survived taking Irish language courses at one university while I took all my literature and critical theory course work at another. I had passed my oral exams and my exit exams, and written and defended my dissertation. I was a doctor. And I did it two years early, highly motivated by the desire to return to my family life. In fairness to the sleazy chair of the department, out of the fourteen people in my cohort, all six long-term live-in relationships had dissolved by the end of the two years of course work; five of the six marriages had ended; everyone else had been single, but there was a considerable amount of sordid sleeping around going on. Mine was the only relationship that survived, though it certainly took a beating. So he was right: grad school is tough on relationships.

The next step was the job market, another special kind of perdition. There is a strange cycle to academic hiring. Most jobs are posted late in the summer or early in the fall, when the following year's positions and budgets are clear(ish). To apply, one needs to write cover letters addressing both the particular job posting and the institution, and then include one's CV (a kind of resume) and transcripts, as well as a whole bunch of essays: teaching philosophy, research statements, diversity statements, faith statements (to Christian institutions), mission statements, and so on. Keeping the experience from becoming rote, of course, is that no two institutions will ask for the same things in the same format, so applying to jobs can be a full-time job in itself.

The school where I got my doctorate tends to assume everyone is dying for a job at a tier one school (where research is privileged over teaching), and directs us to write cover letters to that end. I did so in the first batch of letters, and got no response. And then I asked myself, if I were an overworked professor who reads for a living all day long, what would I want to read in a cover letter to compel me to want to meet this person? So I rewrote the cover letter, including a smidge of that never-to-be-found, highly-discouraged quality: humor. I got twelve interviews, including six campus visits.

And then I dislocated my kneecap, so was in a brace from hip to ankle, and on hallucinatory pain killers.

The right kind of pain killers can really enhance a committee meeting, I found. At one point, enjoying the pink cloud that comes with the lack of pain, I was watching as the speaker at the head of the table began to levitate. Fortunately, before I expressed my alarm, I covertly looked around the room to see whether anyone else was noticing, and when they weren't, I decided to have someone else drive me home.

As if interviewing is not stressful enough, I had the added suspense of wondering if I would hallucinate my way into making a fool of myself. Had I known I was going to get a job, and had I not been in an incommodious leg brace, I might have relaxed and enjoyed the experience of traveling all over the country. I got to see Kentucky, where there were horses and rolling green fields everywhere. I got to see Kansas, where I had the disorienting feeling that I would be blown away on the obscenely flat prairie. I got to see New Orleans, where I ate my way through the city, saw dead armadillos on the highway with beer cans propped in their tiny arms, and puzzled about drive-through daiquiri shacks.

Even some of the interviews were fun. The process usually spans two or three days, and includes a long list of presentations, sample teaching, interviews with various people, campus tours, informal conversations and meals, and a tour with a realtor. I got to meet some wonderful people.

Some interviews were less fun.

In Kansas, after a long day flying without being able to bend my leg, a student picked me up and drove me directly to a hotel, located way out in the middle of nothing. I assumed someone would be by to take me to dinner, or something, but she chirped, "See you in the morning!" and left me there, though I had not eaten all day, and was nowhere near a restaurant or even a vending machine. Although I could see a faint glow of golden arches far off in the distance, being on crutches did not make me eager to wander down the vacant highway to explore. We were so far out even the local pizza place declined to deliver.

That was still not the worst interview. I have never gotten over the experience in the South of my conversation with the late-middle-aged white chair of the English department at one predominantly African-American college. Speaking of the students at his institution, he referred to them with a term so ugly in its derision that although I had never heard the term before (well, I had heard the "f-ing" part of it), I knew it could only be a racial epithet. I was certain I misheard, as such language bewildered me, especially in such a formal setting. I blinked and said nothing. A few moments later, he repeated the phrase. I told him I would have a problem with that kind of language, and he responded, "Well, obviously you don't say it in front of just anyone. You have to be sure your audience is amenable to it."

"What," I asked, "did I do or say to make you think I would be amenable to it?"

My candidacy was over.

By the time I got to my interview in Oregon, then, the bar was pretty low. One of my future colleagues (it's not really a spoiler alert at this point, is it?) met me at the airport in Portland and drove me to the college, through beautiful towns and woods. I was already smitten. While I had been warned about staying away from personal conversations because even the most casual conversations were fodder for the interview, while I knew never to reveal anything about marriages or children, we promptly found ourselves chatting brightly the whole time, comparing notes about our children who were roughly the same age.

My interview went well, I felt, and I really warmed to all the people who spoke with me. But it was a Quaker college, more Evangelical than Quaker, and I was Catholic; I never expected they would hire me, so I did nothing to fit with what I assumed they wanted. I was perfectly honest in my responses, even when I was sure it was to my detriment.

My interview with the provost, in particular, suggested to me I would not be considered for the job. He asked me pointedly about my Catholicism, wondering what I perceived the key differences were between Protestants and Catholics. I told him the sticking point seemed to be transubstantiation: whether the host was a symbol or was truly the body of Christ. He asked me to explain further. I told him about the time I was the lone cantor in front of the church, singing and playing the guitar at Mass; as Communion went on, I saw an elderly woman fumble and drop the Eucharist, but she was too rattled to stop and pick it up, moving on, agitated. No one else seemed to notice it. I was distracted, watching the white circle on the red carpet, worried lest someone step on it, the Body of Christ. I finally couldn't take it anymore, and stopped the song to go retrieve it, cradling the host while I returned to the mic and finished the song. The provost went very quiet and said, "Oh. You're *very* Catholic." I was pretty sure that also marked the end of my candidacy.

It was not. He decided a sincere faith was more important to students than the name of that faith.

I was offered two jobs: the Oregon one and a full-time gig where I had been working part-time as a post-doc fellow. The decision was a difficult one; Oregon would mean uprooting my whole life, but it would also mean I could teach things I wanted to teach. Teaching at a Christian school seemed like a dream, enabling me to talk about my faith in ways

I had been disallowed in the past, but I worried I would be preaching to the choir, and feared Christian students didn't need my voice as much as some others might. I made lists of the pros and cons, and the two jobs were somewhat equal, even when I included the mundane things like how close my office would be to the parking lot and how pretty the stationery was (which they changed to a completely masculine and phallic design in my first year in the job), or proximity to Powell's Books, the best bookstore I've ever seen. At the same time, my best friend, it turned out, through a bizarre series of events, was also considering a move to Oregon, and we would live near each other for the first time in many years.

In the end, we asked the Magic 8-Ball.

While my mother fears we are dabbling in Satanic forces, we don't quite use the Magic 8-Ball that way. We ask it questions when we think we don't really know what we want to do, and then we pay attention not to the answer as much as to our gut response to the answer. If we say, "Should we go out to dinner tonight?" and the answer is "Definitely no," and our response is, "Let's go with best two out of three," we know we actually do have an opinion, and we go with that. When we asked the Magic 8-Ball whether I should take the job in Oregon, and it said, "My sources say Yes," I was relieved and glad; I knew I had an opinion but had not yet given myself permission to have that opinion, knowing how much it would uproot our lives.

So I took the job.

I worked there for sixteen years. My department had the best colleagues anyone could ever ask for, and our department meetings were always uproarious as well as constructive. I know far too many people in departments full of back-stabbing and gossiping and rancor; this was never one of those places. I felt at peace going to work there, actually looking forward to my job. I had never been able to say that before, even at jobs where I liked my co-workers, and these co-workers have become great friends as well as co-conspirators.

I loved my students. I loved watching them grow both intellectually and spiritually, and I loved getting to be part of their journey. I have been constantly amazed by their hearts, by their desire to make the world a better place, by their faith and hope and charity. I have also been astonished by their youth and their ignorance and their ability to make terrible, terrible choices, but without such qualities, they would not need teachers or mentors, so I consider those things job security.

I had come home. I had finally reached the place I was meant to be, and all the elements in my life cohered. To quote my own statement of my teaching philosophy:

Working as a printer taught me much about textual analysis and led me to pursue a comparison of the Gabler and Random House editions of James Joyce's *Ulysses* while I was working on my Master's degree; the insights gleaned from such a project have been invaluable in teaching students to think about writing as a process rather than a product.

Working as a liturgical music director and teacher taught me about cognitive differences; when I encountered music students who were unable to perceive the correlation between notes "rising and falling" on a staff and notes "rising and falling" in tone, I realized not all students could respond to the same supposedly common perceptions. Teaching music also gave me new tools to help students recognize the rhythm in all language, not just in poetry.

Working as Director of Music and Liturgy also gave me the opportunity to coordinate multi-cultural and multi-lingual (Spanish, Tagalog, and English) choirs and events. The lessons I learned there have been invaluable for my own awareness of cultural investments in language and in learning, as well as my interest in the way power operates within cultural development.

Working as a 911 dispatcher taught me the importance of clarity and brevity in communication in all walks of life, and I use my experiences there to teach students to get to the point, as well as to consider all perspectives in a story. I also learned, as a dispatcher in an urban city, how the tensions between formal language and cultural language manifest themselves in the real world.

Of the foreign languages I have studied, including Spanish, French, German, Old English, and Italian, Irish has been most useful not only because all language learning enables us to understand our own language better, but also because that particular language has some fascinating links between culture and linguistics, leading me to a greater understanding of some of the issues faced by students trying to learn English as their second language.

My experience with health issues have made me more sensitive to the dilemmas many students have to face as they learn to prioritize their lives: their desires, their commitments, their obligations, and their limitations. I never wanted to be the teacher who told a sick student she would fail the class if she didn't show up for the final, and then show up thirty minutes late myself.

Most of these examples have impacted the academic part of my job, only lightly touching on the relational aspects of it, though relationships are the true reason any of us teach. The rightness of my career was brought home to me on the day I was meeting with yet another student in my office. This was a young woman whom I had summoned because, as I was handing her paper back, I noticed the pattern of cuts across the top of her thigh. As she sat in my office, thoroughly covered up now, I realized I hadn't really prepared a delicate way to introduce the topic, and I blurted, "So. You're a cutter."

She burst into tears. When she could speak, she said, "I wondered how far I would have to go before anyone noticed."

After a two-hour conversation (which thankfully forced me to miss a faculty Senate meeting), I learned she was an alcoholic (students sign a lifestyle agreement forbidding them to drink, so this was a huge admission), a drug addict, and an anorexic. She had tried to seek help for her anorexia when her periods stopped, but the campus counselor took one look at her and said, "You aren't even that thin." (I wish I could make this stuff up.) Her father wanted her to be a business major but she wanted to be an English major. She had been writing a novel, more than 200 pages of it, when her father stole into her bedroom while she was asleep one night and deleted it. She knew her cutting was a prelude to suicide, but had nowhere to turn. She was having a hard time disassociating her father's brutality with her image of a paternalistic God, so prayer was harder and harder all the time.

We scheduled an appointment with a counselor—not the campus one—as she sat in my office, and then I gave her a rosary, with my explanation of what it did for me. I told her she might want to give it try. Crying again, she said, "I wish you were my mom."

Only then, despite years of similar conversations, did the penny drop: when I heard the voice in Medjugorje tell me, "You aren't going to be a nun. Your mission in life is marry, and to teach your children to pray," this is what was meant. Amanda and Aaron have been steadily resistant to any talk of religion or God, and I thought I had failed through all these years. But I had far more children than just two, and I have indeed been teaching them to pray. What greater sense of fulfillment can there be? It is my own personal coronation, and I can only hope the heavens have rejoiced in it as well, and that, when I come to the end of my life, I will hear God say, "Well done, good and faithful servant."